LETTERS FROM EGYPT

Florence Nightingale was twenty-nine when she visited Egypt in the winter of 1849–50 with her friends, Charles and Selina Bracebridge. A journey to the fabled land of the Arabian Nights was an adventure at that time and Florence wrote long, picturesque letters to her family describing her visit and her views on the country, its history and its people. These letters were edited and privately printed by her sister, Parthenope, in 1854 and were greatly admired by those who read them, but they have never before been published. For this first, illustrated edition, the original collection has been edited and introduced by Anthony Sattin.

Attractive, intelligent and extremely well-read, Miss Nightingale was one of the earliest women to record such a journey and she researched her subject well. Her letters are a fascinating account of life in a country whose greatest asset, its past, had only recently been discovered. They are also a valuable record of a way of life which has since vanished, as waves of tourists and the building of the Aswan Dam have changed the country for ever. And they are an extraordinary insight into the character of a woman who within five years was to become a legend, who at this time, despite her elegant appearance, was suffering inner torments because of a call from God to which she felt unable to respond.

The brilliant landscapes and unimaginable colours of Egypt also drew artists from all over Europe in the mid-nineteenth century. *Letters from Egypt* is illustrated throughout with the glorious paintings and lithographs of David Roberts, Theodore Frere, Edward Lear and others, conveying something of the romance in store for the traveller to the land of the pharaohs.

The Temple of Edfou by David Roberts (Private Collection)

LETTERS FROM EGYPT

A JOURNEY ON THE NILE

1849-1850

FLORENCE NIGHTINGALE

SELECTED AND INTRODUCED BY ANTHONY SATTIN

BARRIE & JENKINS
LONDON

This edition first published in Great Britain in 1987 by
Barrie & Jenkins Ltd
289 Westbourne Grove, London W11 2QA

British Library Cataloguing in Publication Data
Nightingale, Florence
    Letters from Egypt: a journey on the
    Nile 1849–50.
    1. Nightingale, Florence 2. Nurse
    administrators—Great Britain—Biography

    I. Title
    610.73'092'4   RT37.N5

    ISBN 0–7126–2005–2

Cover picture. *The Mountains and Plain of Dendera by
Edward William Cooke (Mathaf Gallery)*

Typeset in Berkeley by Bookworm Typesetting
Colour separation by Aragorn Reproduction, London
Printed in Spain by Graficas Estella, Navarra

CONTENTS

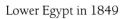

Lower Egypt in 1849

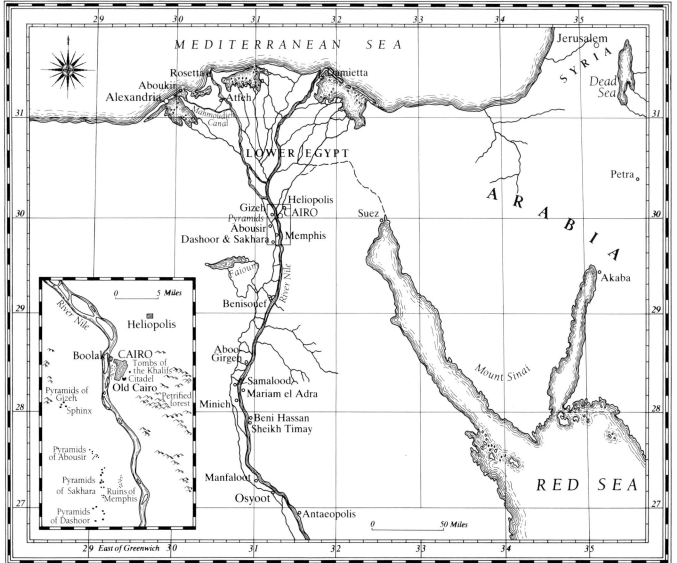

MEDITERRANEAN SEA
Jerusalem
SYRIA
Dead Sea
Rosetta
Aboukir
Alexandria
Atfeh
Damietta
Mahmoudieh Canal
LOWER EGYPT
Petra
ARABIA
Heliopolis
Gizeh
CAIRO
Pyramids
Abousir
Dashoor & Sakhara
Memphis
Suez
Faioum
River Nile
Benisouef
Akaba
Aboo Girgeh
Samalood
Mariam el Adra
Minieh
Mount Sinai
Beni Hassan
Sheikh Timay
Manfaloot
Osyoot
Antaeopolis
RED SEA
0 50 Miles
29 East of Greenwich 30 31 32 33 34 35
0 5 Miles
River Nile
Heliopolis
Boolak
CAIRO
Tombs of the Khalifs
Citadel
Old Cairo
Pyramids of Gizeh
Sphinx
Petrified forest
Pyramids of Abousir
Pyramids of Sakhara
Ruins of Memphis
Pyramids of Dashoor

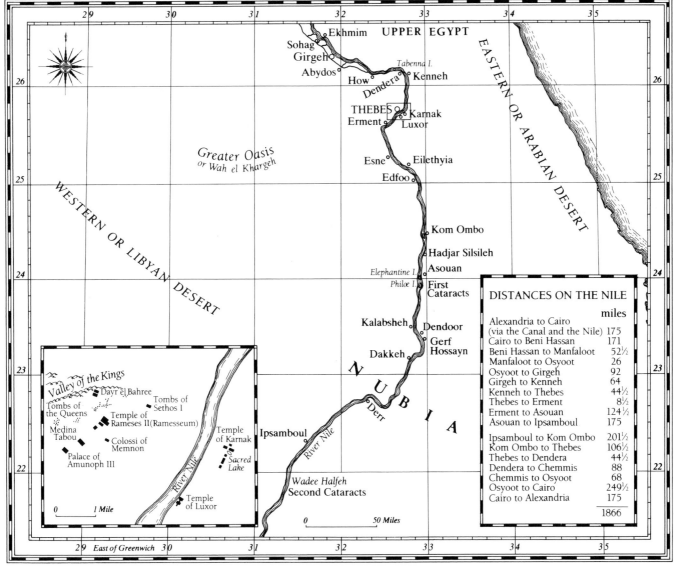

Upper Egypt and Nubia in 1849

Ekhmim · UPPER EGYPT
Sohag
Girgeh
Abydos · Tabenna I.
How · Dendera · Kenneh
THEBES · Karnak
Erment · Luxor

EASTERN OR ARABIAN DESERT

Greater Oasis
or Wah el Khargeh

Esne · Eilethyia
Edfoo

WESTERN OR LIBYAN DESERT

Kom Ombo
Hadjar Silsileh
Elephantine I. · Asouan
Philœ I. · First Cataracts

Kalabsheh · Dendoor
Gerf Hossayn
Dakkeh

NUBIA

Derr

Ipsamboul · River Nile

Wadee Halfeh
Second Cataracts

0 — 50 Miles

Inset (Thebes area)

Valley of the Kings
Dayr el Bahree
Tombs of the Queens · Tombs of Sethos I
Temple of Rameses II (Ramesseum)
Medina Tabou · Colossi of Memnon
Palace of Amunoph III
Temple of Karnak
Sacred Lake
River Nile
Temple of Luxor

0 — 1 Mile

DISTANCES ON THE NILE

	miles
Alexandria to Cairo (via the Canal and the Nile)	175
Cairo to Beni Hassan	171
Beni Hassan to Manfaloot	52½
Manfaloot to Osyoot	26
Osyoot to Girgeh	92
Girgeh to Kenneh	64
Kenneh to Thebes	44½
Thebes to Erment	8½
Erment to Asouan	124½
Asouan to Ipsamboul	175
Ipsamboul to Kom Ombo	201½
Kom Ombo to Thebes	106½
Thebes to Dendera	44½
Dendera to Chemmis	88
Chemmis to Osyoot	68
Osyoot to Cairo	249½
Cairo to Alexandria	175
	1866

East of Greenwich

EDITOR'S NOTE

Florence Nightingale was a prodigious letter-writer and the extent of this collection, a record of her five-month journey in Egypt, is by no means unusual. The letters from Egypt were originally compiled and edited by Florence's elder sister, Parthenope, to whom some of the letters were addressed. They were circulated in 1854, the year in which Florence went to the Crimea.

In preparing this new edition of the letters I have included all the letters from the original edition, but I have edited some of the longer passages where Florence discusses philosophical and theosophical issues. A portentous "meditation" entitled *Vision of Temples*, which was inserted at the end of the final letter, has also been omitted.

The influence of Florence's previous travels abroad, to France and Italy, are evident in the foreign words and phrases which occur in the letters – as they did, presumably, in her speech – and which have been set in italics. The majority of the italicised words and passages, however, were set that way in the original edition, to which I have also added the name of the dahabieh they sailed in and of works of art to which she referred.

Less than thirty years had passed since Champollion had established the principles for reading hieroglyphs and the spelling of place names and of the names of ancient gods and pharaohs had yet to be standardised. There were also variations in the spelling of Turkish, Coptic and Egyptian words, and Florence herself often used several spellings for the same words during the course of her stay. In one of her letters she explained that she spells "whenever I can remember it, in accordance with British prejudices", although she then excused the "pleasing variety in my orthography". Wherever she provided a choice, I have adopted the version which most closely resembles our current usage (with the possible exception of Ipsamboul). I have also used this rule with other spelling variations – so "Moslem" is dropped and only "Muslim" used. Her spelling of the names of the ancient gods and pharaohs was also variable and I have corrected these to her common spelling, but have made no attempt to correct her assertions and assumptions about the ancient Egyptians. In the appendix I have listed the gods and pharaohs mentioned in the text, along with their more common spellings and their accepted functions and dates. There are also notes on many of the people whom Florence met or referred to on her journey, along with whatever information was available on their lives. Similarly, I have listed the books on Egyptology that it seems likely, from references in the text, she had read.

To illustrate this edition I have collected paintings and sketches from the period in which Florence travelled or which are close in spirit to the Egypt she described. Many of the oil paintings were supplied by the Mathaf Gallery. The views of Egypt from sketches by David Roberts, which were made into lithographs by Carl Haag and published as *The Holy Land, Egypt and Nubia* (1842-49 and subsequent editions) and to which Florence refers in her letters, were supplied by the Weinreb Architectural Gallery. The views of Thebes and Abu Simbel in the introduction were painted by Selina Bracebridge and supplied by the Birmingham Art Gallery.

I owe a debt of thanks for their help and advice to Sir Ralph Verney, to Dr Richard Palmer of the Wellcome Institute, to the British Library and London Library for their services and to Dr Miriam Stead of the British Museum for checking my notes. For the illustrations, in addition to the many people who have advised on or lent pictures (listed in the acknowledgements), special thanks are due to Mr Brian MacDermot of the Mathaf Gallery and to Miss Priscilla Wrightson of the Weinreb Architectural Gallery.

ANTHONY SATTIN,
LONDON 1987

The Mid-day Meal, Cairo by John Frederick Lewis (Owen Edgar)

INTRODUCTION

*"One wonders that people come back from Egypt
and live lives as they did before."*

Florence Nightingale was twenty-nine when she visited Egypt. She was attractive, intelligent and extremely well-read, and came from a wealthy family. She had already toured France, Switzerland and Italy with her family and with their friends, the Bracebridges, journeys which had been extremely instructive and through which she made a number of important friendships. Among those in Paris, for instance, Mary Clarke remained her confidante for the rest of her life; interestingly, Mary Clarke's husband, Julius Mohl, was a noted Oriental scholar.

In 1849 the Bracebridges announced that they were going to journey up the Nile and invited Florence to accompany them. What could be finer than an extensive tour of Egyptian sites, many of which were being excavated? What could be more romantic than a cruise up the Nile from the land of the Arabian Nights to sites of ancient Egypt? Society may have viewed this trip as a final adventure

for Florence before she entered into a suitably brilliant marriage. And yet, leaving Folkestone for Egypt, she wrote forlornly to her family: "I hope I shall come back to be more of a comfort to you than I have been".

✳ ✳ ✳

Florence's mother, Frances Nightingale, had far-reaching social ambitions. The Nightingales had done the fashionable thing and gone abroad soon after their marriage to explore post-Napoleonic Europe. Parthenope, their first child, was born in Naples in 1819 and given the Greek name for the city. Florence was born in the Tuscan capital the following year. When the family returned to England, they stayed in London during the season and in the country for the rest of the year. They counted a number of well-connected and titled people among their circle of friends.

Mrs. Nightingale also had ambitions for her daughters. They had grown up to be attractive, accomplished young ladies and the success of their stay in Paris in 1839 had reinforced her high hopes. But in the case of Florence, events were not to turn out as Mrs. Nightingale had anticipated. In a private note Florence recorded that, "On February 7th, 1837, God spoke to me and called me to His service".

The problem for Florence was that the nature of the "service" to which she had been called was not made clear to her. Over the next ten years, however, a cause to which she could devote herself appeared, as she progressed from looking after relatives and friends during their illnesses, to caring for the sick and needy in the villages around the family's country residences. At this point, her parents objected. Nursing was not among the occupational options for a young lady in society and in no way did hospitals or nursing homes correspond to our understanding of the words. Nurses were notorious for drunkenness and promiscuity, and the medical profession was in a primitive state.

Florence's father's suggestion that, if she must do something, his daughter could take up teaching would have seemed more than reasonable to him. But it was not enough for Florence, struggling to find a way of making a useful life for herself without offending her parents. She dealt the final blow to her family's peace of mind when, in the summer of 1849, she rejected the very eligible Richard Monckton Milnes' offer of marriage. His was not the first offer she had turned down, nor was it the last — she believed there was more to life than the apparently inevitable subservance of marriage. But the cost to her health of this search for another way of life was great and the Bracebridges' offer of a lengthy tour abroad was most welcome.

Charles and Selina Bracebridge (who both accompanied Florence to the Crimea in 1854) were a wealthy, childless couple whom Florence had met in Paris through Mary Clarke. They were noted travellers and ardent Hellenists — Mr. Bracebridge had even fought with the Greeks in their revolt against Turkish rule — and the Nightingales gave Selina the nickname of Σ, the Greek letter *sigma*. After their journey on the Nile, the Bracebridges intended to travel to Athens, where they owned property, before returning to London.

Interest in Egypt had been stimulated by Napoleon's campaign of 1798. To accompany his army, Napoleon had brought an equally impressive array of scholars, under Baron Dominique Vivant Denon. They systematically described and sketched all the known sites in Egypt and their work was collected and published as the monumental *Description de l'Egypte* (1809), one of the founding works of Egyptology, the study of Egyptian antiquities. But hot on Napoleon's heels came the British navy under Horatio Nelson, who destroyed the French fleet at Aboukir Bay and earned himself the title of Viscount Nelson of the Nile. The site of Aboukir became a must for travellers in Egypt — especially for the British — and Florence described her visit in her first letter home. Nothing focusses the public's attention quite so well as a successful military engagement and Egypt soon became a powerful influence on the British imagination and a popular place to visit. This interest was developed by the work of the large number of soldiers, writers, artists and travellers who floated up the Nile in the early nineteenth century. Florence read a great number of their accounts and spent time in the Consular Library in Cairo before starting up river; in her letters home she referred to the works of many scholars and travellers, some of whom she met while she was out there. She befriended Selima Harris, for instance, whose adopted father, Anthony Harris, "discovered some names of the Shepherd Kings in the tombs about the Pyramids, which may lead to something", while Florence was there. From each of the ancient sites she visited, her letters give a sense of how much remained a mystery, of how young the study of Egypt's antiquities was.

For a traveller to appreciate a visit to the Nile sites in the era before guided tours and package holidays, a fair amount of background reading was necessary. Sir John Gardner Wilkinson, whose *Modern Egypt and Thebes* (first published in 1843 and republished several times, finally as *Murray's Handbook of Egypt*) Florence quoted in her letters, suggested taking an essential library of about thirty volumes for a trip up the Nile. Florence arrived extremely well prepared for Egypt, having consulted with the Prussian ambassador to London, Baron Bunsen, who was an Arabic scholar and whose five-volume *Egypt's Place in Universal History* was published in English between 1848 and 1859. Parthenope recorded that "Flo had taken tea with the Bunsens to receive the *dernier mot* on Egyptology" and that she·was going to Egypt "laden with learned books". In addition, Florence even borrowed books on the way, from the "mad Count" Benczik, for instance, from whom she hid in Cairo to avoid returning them then.

Florence and the Bracebridges were similarly well-supplied with physical comforts for their journey. Wilkinson's list of equipment for a dahabieh tour ran to several pages, amongst which was the curious Levinge, which Florence referred to with such gratitude.

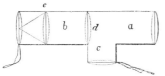

I cannot do better than recommend a contrivance of Mr. Levinge's, which he imagined during his travels in the East, and which is equally adapted to

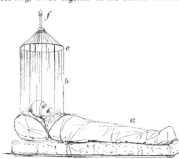

a boat, a house, or a tent. It consists of a pair of sheets (*a*), about six feet long, sowed together at the bottom and the two sides, except where the piece (*c*) is attached to them, and by which you get in. To the upper end (*d*) is added a thin piece of muslin, serving as a mosquito net (*b*), which is drawn tight at the end by a tape or string, serving to suspend it to a nail (*f*). A short way from the end (at *e*) are fastened loops, through which a cane is threaded to form a circle for distending the net. This cane is in three pieces, about three feet long, fitting into each other by sockets. After getting in by the opening of *c*, you draw the tape tight to close its mouth, and tuck it in under the mattrass, and you are secure from intruders, whether sleeping at night, or sitting under it by day. Over the part *a*, the blankets, or coverlid, are put.

(From Wilkinson's *Modern Egypt and Thebes*)

Florence mentioned sleeping in her Levinge both in Cairo and on the dahabieh.

Although touring in Egypt had become less hazardous than when Napoleon's scholars set out, a journey on the Nile in 1850 was still regarded as a romantic adventure. Gustave Flaubert and Maxime du Camp arrived in Alexandria at almost the same time as Florence, and Flaubert, two years her junior, was thoroughly miserable from the outset at leaving his mother for so long and at travelling so far afield. Florence reported that some of the Egyptians she met had never seen a white woman before. Egypt was the first step beyond Europe, the first taste of Arabia and the East — it was, as Florence noted immediately, the land of the Arabian Nights. The P&O was twelve years old when she set out for Egypt and steam travel was still in its infancy. The effects of the dynamic acceleration of travel, to which the British owed so much of the peculiar spread of their empire in the nineteenth century, were only just beginning to be visible. By the time Amelia Edwards went up the Nile, twenty-five years later, travel had changed considerably and Thomas Cook & Son were already running package tours from London to steamers on the Nile. So Florence, floating (at times) gently up river, at the whim of the winds, expressed her disgust at the thought of any means of transport beyond ass and dahabieh: "I am writing in the greatest possible haste for a steamer (!) which has just brought Mr. Murray, and is going on to Cairo. I would never go in a steamer on the Nile, if I were never to see the Nile without it." It was all right to steam as far as Cairo, but travelling by dahabieh was *the* way of seeing Upper Egypt and Nubia. However, as well as being the most picturesque and leisurely mode of transport, it was also the most expensive. Florence and the Bracebridges paid £30 a month for their boat — enough by Florence's calculations to excavate a considerable amount of Thebes. The boat they hired for this sum was, she claimed, the finest on the river and had "never carried Europeans before, being built for his [a Bey's] hareem"; naturally this added to its attraction for them and appealed to their adventurous and exotic natures. Later on in the journey she again remarked that it was the finest on the river: at Asyut (which she spelt Osyoot) the Vice Governor was so impressed with the dahabieh that he sent his carpenters to take its measurements, which they did, not with a rule, but with their hands. Further south, at the cataracts above Asouan (Aswan), she wrote that the dahabieh was the largest to have been pulled up that far and the first to shoot the rapids.

However large and well-appointed the dahabieh, travelling up the Nile in a boat which would have to be rowed or towed if the wind dropped was very slow-going and Florence's journey, which took more than three months, was relatively quick; in her letters she complained at the haste in which they travelled, but the wind was behind them and would carry them quickly up river. There would be time, while floating back down, to see the sights. Along the seven hundred and fifty miles from Cairo to Ipsamboul (Abu Simbel), the temples and villages were often few and far-between and there was nothing to look at but the river bank. Sometimes it was flat and rolled on into the desert with its shimmering horizon; in other places it was high-banked, leading up to the mountains. Florence was struck by the landscape but, however spectacular the play of light upon sand and rock, she would have spent a great deal of time in her cabin, resting, reading and writing letters home.

In several letters she reported that she and the Bracebridges had avoided "society", either at Shepheard's Hotel in Cairo, anchored off Thebes or descending the Cataracts. They dined with the Consul, Mr. Murray, visited Dr. Abbott to see his papyrus (some of which Florence was able to read by the time she left Cairo) and paid a call on an English artist and his wife at Philœ (Philæ); but otherwise they dreaded meeting other travellers who would take up their time with niceties. Florence found Egypt too inspiring

to allow that to happen. Describing the intrusions of the Count — or the Professor — at Thebes, she wrote, "It is very hard to be all day by the death-bed of the greatest of your race, and come home and talk about quails or London."

As a result of the increasing number of scholars, collectors and tourists travelling in Egypt, souvenirs — the spoils of travel — were becoming hard to find. By 1850, important collections of Egyptian antiquities had been formed and sold to private collectors and museums, mostly abroad. (The Egyptian Museum in Cairo was not founded until 1863.) Florence had hoped to find precious objects lying about in the tombs and, to a certain extent, she did, although a letter she wrote after she had left Egypt expressed her disappointment at what she sent home: "As for the Egyptian rubbish, you may do just what you like with it, keep it, or give it away. There is nothing that reminds me of what I have seen, nothing that savours of my Karnak, except the bronze dog, the brick seals which sealed the tombs at Thebes, and the four little seals in the light box — two of which are of Rameses . . . you must not give away what is in the great Nubian basket, because some of that rubbish is Trout's. The Darfur bracelets are for you — I got them at Philœ. Louisa must have a pair of the little figures found in the tombs, but I shall make her a little collection out of the rubbish, when I come home. The thing you will take for a stool, and which is a pillow, was a present from the "Beys" of the Cataracts. I must keep that for "sentiment". The photographs and lithographs are beautifully like (all of Cairo) and are, of course, for you. I have some little scarabs I did not send home (for fear of being lost) for you . . . You don't know how difficult it is to get anything at Cairo — for I know you will think, and very truly, what I have sent home very shabby." And then, rather wistfully, she ended, "As for the Egyptian things, unless you carry away Memnon's head, like Belzoni, I don't know that there is anything to be had."

The Mosque of El Mourestan, Cairo by Carl Werner (Mathaf Gallery)

In 1849, when Florence arrived in Egypt, the country was again suffering from political instability. The relatively settled years of Mehemet Ali were over. Nominally part of the Turkish empire, Egypt had been governed by the autocratic Viceroy since the British had defeated Napoleon's expedition and opposed the re-establishment of Mameluke rule. Mehemet Ali was a soldier of Albanian descent who was the most likely leader for the Egyptians and his successful, if unscrupulous, disposal of his Mameluke adversaries secured for him the backing of the British, who wished to guarantee a safe passage through Egypt to the Red Sea and India. Mehemet Ali's later successful campaign against the Turks led to his family being granted the right to hereditary rule over Egypt. When Mehemet Ali abdicated in 1848, with his mind failing, he was succeeded by his son Ibrahim. He, however, died within four months of his accession and power passed to his nephew, Abbas, a grandson of Mehemet Ali. He was Viceroy when Florence arrived in Egypt and in several letters she expressed her disgust at the cruel and avaricious way he exercised his power — she was unimpressed with many aspects of Egyptian politics which, in her view, consisted of an unhealthy mix of bastinado and hareem intrigue. She pointed to Said, another son of Mehemet Ali and heir to the throne, as a man of greater compassion and integrity, and she visited his wife on her last day in Egypt. Subsequent events showed that she was accurate in her opinion, for Abbas was murdered by his own slaves in 1854 and Said, who ruled for nine years, proved to be a strong and enlightened leader.

*   *   *

Wherever she went in Egypt, Florence was accompanied either by the Bracebridges, by an Egyptian attendant — her Efreet or demon, as she calls him, who warded off the villagers along the Nile — or by her maid, Trout, who is only mentioned once in the letters, at Beni Hassan on her "first real Egyptian day", but who is likely to have gone with her everywhere she went. Coming out of the tombs at Beni Hassan, Florence recalled in her letter, there "was T. sitting

The Great Temple at Abu Simbel by Selina Bracebridge

at the door of a tomb (for she went with us), crocheting a pattern in small of a new polka, with her back leaning against the hieroglyphs". Between them, they would have ensured that Florence was well chaperoned.

Egypt was one of the Bible lands and Florence was a devout Christian. In many places in her letters she stopped to consider what Christ would have made of the modern Egyptians; some of them appeared to her to be beyond redemption. At other times she was intrigued by their customs, excited by their different behaviour and impressed by their devotion to Islam. She was won over by the splendour of the landscape, the river and the desert, but was appalled by the dirt and dust, and by the flies and mosquitoes which thrived in the warm climate. She was enthralled by the remains of ancient Egypt, announcing that on their return to London, she and the Bracebridges would take rooms in Great Russell Street for six months to study the antiquities in the British Museum, but was horrified by the way the ruins were treated by the modern Egyptians, many of whom expressed contempt for the interest of foreigners in their past. Florence was in sympathy with the interest, though. "Without the past," she confessed to her family, "I conceive Egypt to be utterly uninhabitable." But these contrasts didn't only exist within Florence — it is part of Egypt's eternal attraction that the past and present, the sacred and profane, the generous and cruel cohabit so successfully. "I never before saw any of my fellow creatures degraded (thieves, bad men, women and children), but I longed to have intercourse with them, to stay with them, and make plans for them; but here," she wrote of the huts around the temples at Thebes, "one gathered one's clothes around one, and felt as if one had trodden in a nest of reptiles." But at the same time she understood some of the fascination and horror they showed at the sight of her, a white Christian woman. Whenever she stopped to visit a temple or ruin, she was accompanied by the local Egyptians, who went along to look at her. She enjoyed Abu Simbel all the more for the absence of her audience. At the sacred mosques in Cairo, her presence upset the worshippers so much that they rushed at her in protest, forcing her attendant to beat them back with his whip. Her letter recorded her remorse at the incident.

Whatever she felt about the inhabitants of the country, Florence was forcefully struck by the "Arabian Nights" scenes she witnessed, especially in Cairo, where much of the city had survived intact from medieval times. "I would so gladly do something to show you what a land you have sent me to," she wrote home, "what recollections you have secured for me." In her letters, in her "real and individual impressions", she tried to give them something back.

But the journey in Egypt was intended as more than merely an interesting diversion. She hoped that in the warmer climate she would recover her health and that, in the tranquility of the dahabieh, she would resolve the dilemma of her call from God and her duty to her family. Although no mention of this appears in her letters, entries in her diary suggest her true state of mind. In a letter from Thebes she described the "exquisite little temple of Koorneh . . . Upon the steps of that colonnade I have sat for hours, moving with the shadow of the columns, as it turned with the sun, and looking out upon that matchless view under the different lights . . . This temple," she declared later, "is the only place in Thebes I really cared for." In her diary, however, she recorded a more startling occurrence: "Long morning by myself at old Kourna. Sat on the steps of the portico, moving with the shadow of the sun, and looking at the (to me) priceless view. God spoke to me again." When they were nearing Cairo she wrote that, "God called me again", and a week later: "God called me in the morning, and asked me would I do good for him alone without reputation?" On March 9th, while her letter described her visit to the hareem of Mustafa's (the cook's) "womans", her diary records that, "During half an hour I had in the cabin myself . . . settled the question with God."

In her biography of Florence Nightingale, Cecil Woodham Smith has made much of this aspect of her torment and suggests that it was her struggle with her voices which brought her to the edge of a breakdown. Sir Edward Cook, writing his authoritative biography in 1913, made little of this side of her dilemma, concentrating instead on

The Pyramids of Gizeh by Edward Lear (Christie's, London)

her struggle with her family and propriety. This may be because Woodham Smith had access to papers which were not available in 1913. Either way, Florence was extremely disturbed during her journey on the Nile, but seemed to find a new determination between her visit to the hareem of Mustafa's "womans" and that of Said Pasha's wife at Alexandria. On the steamer from Cairo to Alexandria, she could not help noticing the difference in attitude between

A view of Thebes by Selina Bracebridge

the society woman and "a chastened white Nun", who shared the cabin. It was as if she was seeing parts of herself in the people around her. On her last day in Egypt she visited the hospital of the Sisters of St. Vincent de Paul and the Pasha's hareem. "If heaven and hell exist on this earth," she wrote to her family, "it is in the two worlds I saw on that one morning . . ." On her journey back to England, Florence stopped at the Institution of Deaconesses at Kaiserwerth in

Germany, where she stayed for two weeks studying nursing practices. There, at last, she discovered that it was possible to run a "decent" hospital. In August 1850 she returned home; in 1851 she published a report of her findings at Kaiserwerth; and in 1853 fighting broke out in the Crimea. The rest is history and legend.

Florence Nightingale's letters from Egypt are interesting on several counts. As a guide to the more important ancient, medieval and modern sites along the Nile, as far as Abu Simbel, her descriptions are sensitive and authoritative. As a view of early nineteenth century travel in Egypt (Florence preceded Lucy Duff Gordon and Amelia Edwards up the Nile), they form an amusing and valuable record, especially as many of the sites in Nubia have since been moved or destroyed by the building of the High Dam and as travel by steamer (which Florence so thoroughly dismissed) is now viewed as the height of romantic touring. *Letters from Egypt* is Florence's only publication not concerned with nursing. The letters reveal her as an energetic and sympathetic young woman with her life before her — but in places it is difficult not to read more into her observations, as when she described the hardships of the nun with whom she travelled to Alexandria. "So suffer those who pioneer a new road," she realised, "so fall those who throw their bodies in the breach; but they bridge the way for others to tread upon them." It is easy, knowing what was to become of her so soon after her return to England, to smile at her prophetic observation: "One wonders that people come back from Egypt and live lives as they did before."

AT ALEXANDRIA

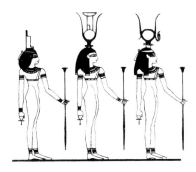

November 19th, 1849.

YES, MY DEAR PEOPLE, I have set my first footfall in the East, and oh! that I could tell you the new world of old poetry, of Bible images, of light, and life, and beauty which that word opens. My first day in the East, and it has been one of the most striking, I am sure, — one I can never forget through Eternity.

I am writing by candlelight, on Monday morning, because I had not a moment yesterday, the day we landed; and one is quite surprised to find darkness at all in this land of warmth, and light, and life. We had a splendid run of ninety hours from Malta, and should have had less, but that we were obliged to put off our steam, in order not to arrive at those dangerous old Syrtes till daylight. Isis welcomed us to her country with the most delicate and silvery of crescents, and at half-past four we went on deck, on the purest and mildest of starlight nights, watching Venus rising so large, that the captain mistook her for the Pharos, and brought the vessel to a stand. Then came up the rose-coloured clouds of dawn, like Guido's *Aurora:* he must have seen an Eastern sunrise, for the colours of his Hours are

exactly those of the early dawn here, and not the least those of an Italian sunrise. It looks not lurid and thick, as very brilliant colours in an English sky sometimes do, but so transparent and pure, that one really believes one's self looking into a heaven beyond, and feels a little shy of penetrating into the mysteries of God's throne.

Alexandria

The Pharos and masts of Alexandria, and Pompey's pillar, and a long low line of coast now appeared against the crimson clouds, and from his own Morgenland, his own East, the sun sprang up as he ought to do. I cannot describe the initiation into old poetry he gives you on his first rising in the East. He does not come up slowly and solemnly, and rather sadly, as he does in the chill dawn in England, while one is feeling a sinking, and a trembling, and a shivering from having been up in the cold to see him; but he leaps from the horizon into the sky, whips his fiery steeds, shouts for joy, and brings in brilliant day immediately; it is his "glad" course here, and the flood he pours forth is "living" light. One never understood the word "living" before. It is as if each ray was a messenger, alive. The northern sunlight is like lamplight. I shall never forget my first sight of him.

Now we crowded on all our steam, and came gallantly into the old port, only stopping to pick up an Arab pilot, and perpetually throwing the lead, which showed us to be in only four fathom water. The crescent and the star was floating idly on the morning breeze; but a crowd of Arabs, the busiest and the noisiest people in the world, came immediately on board, frantically gesticulating, kicking, and dancing, — an intermediate race, they appeared to me, between the monkey and the man, the ugliest, most slavish countenances.

You cannot conceive, besides, the impatience to get on shore after eight nights on shipboard, in a crowded steamboat, with an atmosphere of, I really believe, 120° in our cabin, the men drinking punch from morning till night, the women giggling and clacking.

Before nine we had landed, and were on our way to the Frank Square, in the omnibus, for it was already too hot to walk. Before ten, Mr. Gilbert had called upon us in our inn-yard, and he has already placed a janissary at our disposition (who does everything for us), and given us everything we could want.

The first thing after we had saved our baggage from the hurrying Indians, was to ask our janissary, Alee, who walks before us, and is the most gentle, yet most dignified being I ever saw (I am quite afraid to speak to him), to show us the way to the baths. After a longish walk we came to a gateway, and through an avenue of date-palms, bananas, and petunias, trellised overhead, to a long, low building with Pompeian baths, in red, and green, and blue squares, and with low archways (against the heat), leading from one to

— A soldier —

the other. Egyptians sitting about at their dinner of fruits. They gave us a tangle of palm-tendrils to wash ourselves with, with a lump of beautiful Egyptian soap in the middle of the nest: all European appliances are vile compared to those palm-tendrils.

We came into an enormous square hall lined with marble, then through marble passages into another octagonal vaulted court, lined, floor and roof, with marble, except where the roof was pierced with holes to let in spots and trails of brilliant sunlight. At the four corners were smaller halls, of immense height, with marble basins in each, the floors slippery with water, — the whole like an Arabian Night's description. And when we came out again into that enchanted garden, it was still like an Arabian night. I thought we were in the Chatsworth conservatory and should come out into the chill air, from all that radiant vegetation, and find it was a dream. But we did not. And when we returned, luncheon was spread at the *table-d'hôte*; bananas, and dates, and oranges, and citrons, — such a beautiful table I never saw, — and the stately Egyptian to serve us; women we did not see.

Then we went to church, — a little, quiet, solemn, English church, — and afterwards, Mr. Winder, the clergyman, took us to the garden of the Armenians. Those Armenians have always something so poetic and mysterious about them. Fancy a church in the middle of alleys and tangles of palms, loaded with bunches of golden fruit, stretching every way into a forest, so that you lose the enclosure; daturas, bignonias, oleanders, cactuses, and bananas making the underwood; a great well in the midst, upon the edge of which sat the most beautiful group of Egyptian and Smyrniot women, and the radiant sunset behind.

Of course there are drawbacks to all this light and beauty; the mosquitoes are at this moment (six o'clock in the morning) so bad, that I am surrounded by the dead bodies of those slain in single combat. The heavy dew drove

us home last night before sunset. But what is that to pay for the joy of the East?

I wish I could describe the groups in the Armenian garden — a little triangle of children at the gate, eating their dinner out of a porringer of beans, not gobbling or messing, as European children do, but like little gods, with infant dignity slowly and majestically dipping their sop in the dish, and conversing. One, a magnificent, broad-shouldered boy of four, resting his little paw upon his knee, with one single loose shirt on, looking up at us undisturbed, with an attitude like an Apollo at rest; another, a little coquette of three, with her hand and wrist loaded with bracelets and rings, — but not a vulgar coquette, — she had the airs of a Juno; and the third, a thing of eighteen months, with its leg stuck straight out, and quite as stately as the other two. We did so wish for P. to draw it. Then the group on the well, three Egyptian ladies, in their black silk mantles, which shroud them entirely, except the blue or white pendant in front, which hangs from their foreheads, only letting their eyes be seen. A tall, graceful Nubian behind, entirely robed and shrouded in white, who is not so particular about her black face, which looks so well in that white *Westall* drapery; and two Smyrniots, with their hair dressed *à la Grecque*, large bunches of flowers in it, and Guercino colours of blue, and red, and brown, made, with a yellow woman, the most Oriental group. The Egyptian costume (of the high-born lady), the enormous black mantle, is not graceful; but here you see all costumes, from the Ethiopian to the Waldense. We saw a funeral procession, too, holloaing like forçats. So ended my first day in the East, — a true Sunday of rest and joy.

The sun has now risen as pure and bright as yesterday, and I am sitting on my divan, with a stone floor, and the window wide open, the donkeys, and Arabs, and those hideous camels, setting up the most frightful noise.

This place is full of Roman Catholic Sisters and Lazarists,

Greek church, Armenian church, Muslim Moulas, Protestant Waldenses—Alexandria the Cosmopolite. There is nothing to say about its architecture.

The state of things here is horrible. Every man is a conscript for the army, and mothers put out their children's right eye, cut off their forefingers, or lamed them, to save them from conscription, till Mehemet Ali, who was too clever for them, had a one-eyed regiment, who carry the musket on the left shoulder. The number of one-eyed men you see is frightful.

My time has been spent much to my satisfaction, as I travelled from Paris to Auxerre with two sisters of St. Vincent de Paul, who gave me an introduction to the sisters here; and I have spent a great deal of time with them in their beautiful schools and Misericorde. There are only nineteen of them, but they seem to do the work of ninety. They bleed, dress wounds, and dispense medicines; the Arabs come to them by hundreds for advice. Today I saw there a little orphan girl of nine years, who had found, some months ago, a deserted baby in the streets, and had adopted it! The baby is now ill, and the little foster-mother brings it daily to the convent for medicine: the sisters said the care and love she showed for it was marvellous. They gave her a para a week for it, and the neighbours added dates or rice, — and so the little creatures live. In this climate life is supported on so little, and for clothing a rag suffices. The sisters give a fearful account of the debasement and ignorance of the women; they have no religion, and are mere beasts they say.

There is not much to see here, nothing but the perpetual feeling of being in the East, the eastern colouring, and eastern atmosphere. On the day of the Presentation of the Virgin all the children of the St. Vincent sisters go to a children's mass and sing — so pretty it was — all costumes, the Levantine, the Smyrniot, the Maltese, the Egyptian, people of all nations and tongues uniting in the worship of one God. Many of the mothers were there too.

AT ALEXANDRIA

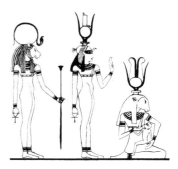

November 24th.

Yesterday we took our first donkey ride to the catacombs; but donkey riding in Egypt is a very different thing from donkey riding elsewhere. The donkey is very small, and you are very large (the Egyptian is a very tall race), and you sit upon his tail; and as he holds his head very high, you look like a balance to his head. After mounting, a feat which is effected by curling your right leg round your saddle bow (the saddles are men's), you set off full gallop, running over everything in your way; and the merry little thing runs and runs and runs like a velocipede. There is nothing in Alexandria but the Frank Square, which is larger than any square in London, and the huts of the Alexandrians, which look more like a vast settlement of white ants than anything else. The hut is always but one room, about eight or nine feet square (the walls prolonged in front to make a sort of alcove), about six feet high, made of plastered white mud, with or without windows, which are furnished with shutters; no chimney; nothing inside but one pot, and sometimes a box. They seldom adjoin; but a space is left between each. The first effect is that of a vast collection of ovens. You can hardly believe they are human dwellings. Some, I should think, were altogether but a cube of five feet.

We went to the catacombs, which, after those of Rome, are rather a farce; to Pompey's Pillar, through a great dismal cemetery: I thought we were coming to the end of the

Pompey's Pillar

world. The earth was strewed, not planted, with little white round mounds of mud, a stone stuck in it, and a dry aloe in the middle, — not one bit of green; often the grave only a heap of stones, — the best, two white slabs. A single figure stood, clasping her hands, her black robe over her head, in the middle of all this desolation. There being no enclosure, but the tombs stretching every way, makes it so striking; and Pompey throws his immeasurable shadow across the plain.

One day we drove to the site of the battle of Aboukir, a dreary plain of white sand covered with white stones; a scanty fringe of palm trees in the distance; the broken wall of Nicopolis, built by Augustus; in the foreground, a road, many inches deep in sand, through which we waded: it looked like the shroud of an empire's body, the ghastly tale of a kingdom's whitening bones. I went down to the sea shore, not being able to bear the abomination of desolation, and walked along the beach, where the breakers were rolling and tossing in; and the sun was setting exactly behind the Pharos of Alexandria, in all the triumphal march of an Eastern sunset, with the green transparent caves of the sea beyond, not like the funeral pomp of that white winding sheet behind, but like a patriot hero going home, full of light and love.

On our way home we saw our first Egyptian monument, the colossal head and bust of a queen, as Isis (the rest of the body, at some distance), in granite, lying in a marsh, half covered with water; a companion Ptolemy, also broken, as Osiris, lying near, the features very beautiful, but blackened with the water; bulrushes growing about.

A running footman always precedes you here, running before the horses, and clacking his whip. What on earth is the use of the poor wretch I cannot divine; the horses could fray their way of themselves. But he looks like an evil spirit, always accompanying you, prompting you, appearing and disappearing, but always there.

I and the gnats have so many ways of outwitting each other. Σ and Mr. B. look as if they had had the small-pox; but I, who would sleep in an Indian rubber tub with a tallow candle in my mouth if it were suggested, shut my windows before sundown; and I hear those who *are* in, furling their wings and uttering little infernal cries of triumph. Then I set my door open, and put a light in the passage, and they think I'm there, and follow; but I'm not,—don't tell them. Then, when night comes, I take out a large sheet of paper and begin to write, and they believe I'm not thinking of sleep. But I leave off in the middle of a word, run with all my might at the Levinge, where I insert myself by so small a hole that you would say a camel *could* get through the eye of a needle; and then I clap my hands, and sing a little ode in honour of Mercury, the god of theft, because I have stolen myself from the hands of the gnats. Meanwhile I hear their whistle of rage and disappointment, and I see their proboscises coming through the curtains, as if they would fly away with the whole concern. I won't deny that some do get in by ways unknown to me,—they have either subterranean passages or latch-keys.

We have a roof to our house; a real Eastern roof, with little houses upon it, and a beautiful view of the sea, which has been so high since we came, that we cannot be thankful enough for our beautiful passage.

I was so very anxious to see the inside of a mosque, to see where my fellow-creatures worshipped, that Mr. Gilbert good-naturedly compassed it, although he said it was an unprecedented act in Alexandria, where they are fanatical Mahometans. I am very glad to have done it, though I never felt so uncomfortable in all my life. We had to put on the Egyptian dress: first, an immense blue silk sheet (the head comes through a hole in the middle); then a white stripe of muslin which comes over your nose like a horse's nose-bag, and is fastened by a stiff passementerie band, which passes between your eyes and over and behind your head like a halter; then a white veil; and lastly, the black silk balloon, which is pinned on the top of your head, has two loops at the two ends, through which you put your wrists, in order to keep the whole together. You only breathe through your eyes: half an hour more, and a brain fever would have been the consequence.

With strict injunctions not to show our hands, we set forth in this gear with the Consul's janissary, who had been denuded of his robes of office that he might not be known. The Consul followed at a little distance, but would not let Mr. Bracebridge speak to us in the streets, and hovered round the mosque all the while we were there, for fear of a disturbance. Up the steep stairs we went, past the great stone pool of Bethesda, where all the Muslims were kneeling round, washing their arms and faces for prayer, for it was just midday; past a school, where the boys were learning the Koran (see-sawing backwards and forwards the whole time), into the mosque. You know pretty well what a mosque is,— arcades, floors lined with matting; a niche towards Mecca, towards which the worshippers turn their faces; a pulpit beautifully carved in network, archway at the bottom of the pulpit, straight stairs to the top; a gallery out of sight, where women are allowed, but only on the evenings of the feasts, and only old women. The mosque was full; the people crowded round us, laughing and pointing. I felt so degraded, knowing what they took us for, what they felt towards us. I felt like the hypocrite in Dante's hell, with the leaden cap on — it was a hell to me. I began to be uncertain whether I *was* a Christian woman, and have never been so thankful for being so as since that moment. That quarter of an hour seemed to reveal to one what it is to be a woman in these countries, where Christ has not been to raise us. God save them, for it is a hopeless life. I was so glad when it was over. Still the mosque struck me with a pleasant feeling; Σ was struck with its irreverence. Some were at their prayers; but one was making baskets, another was telling Arabian Night stories to a whole group of listeners, sitting round him — others were asleep. I am much more struck with the irreverence of a London church.

It is so pleasant to see a place where any man may go for a moment's quiet, and there is none to find fault with him, nor make him afraid. Here the homeless finds a home, the

An Arab School by Frederick Goodall (Mathaf Gallery)

weary repose, the busy leisure, — if I could have said where any *woman* may go for an hour's rest, to me the feeling would have been perfect, — perfect at least compared with the streets of London and Edinburgh, where there is not a spot on earth a poor woman may call her own to find repose in. The mosque leaves the more religious impression of the two, it is the better place of worship, — not than St. Peter's, perhaps, but better than St. Paul's. We mounted the minaret; the muezzin was just there, calling to prayers in a loud monotonous recitative. The abstraction of a Mahometan at his prayers is quite inconceivable; on board boat, in a storm, it is just the same; the hour comes, the Mahometan falls on his knees, and for five minutes the world is nothing to him; death may come, but it cannot interrupt him; even gain may come, but it will not disturb him. Christians say this here, and laugh at it; but you cannot laugh.

The Mahometan religion takes man on the side of his passions; it gratifies all these; it offers him enjoyment as his reward. The Christian religion takes him on the side of penitence and self-denial. This seems the fundamental difference: otherwise there is much good in the Mahometan religion. Charity is unbounded; and it is not the charity of patronage, but the charity of fellowship. If any man says to another "Inshallah", In the name of God, he may sit down at his table and partake of anything that he has, and no man will refuse. The beggar will do this with the greatest dignity. There is no greediness, no rapacity. Nothing of any value is ever stolen from you; there is no need to shut the door: they will take a trifle, but nothing else. Still, what chance is there for a nation whose religion is enjoyment?

Then, the woman. In the large hareem there are 200 or 300 wives, and four or five children. But the woman is not a wife nor a mother: she cannot sit down in the presence of her son, her husband is her master, and her only occupation that of beautifying herself and surpassing the others in his eyes. She becomes his real wife only at his caprice, by a paper given to her, which paper bears that for a certain sum, a few piastres, he may send her away. Then she is satisfied to believe that she will stay at the gate of Paradise, — she, the woman, who has more to suffer here than the man, both in heart, and in spirit, and in body. Their sole occupation in the hareem is politics, and all politics are conducted by *their* intrigues. Every man goes to them with presents.

But from Artim Bey down to the lowest Cadi, everything is conducted by money. The Cadi (the magistrate) pays the Government for his place, the defendant pays the Cadi for his justice, the Mufti (the lawyer) pays the Government for his, and is paid again. English officials are always offered presents; and to make a Cadi understand that in England magistrates are *paid by Government* to administer justice, would be not a difficulty, but an impossibility. As to property, everybody knows that to appear to have any is to secure being taxed and robbed by Government; and an Arab will endure any amount of bastinadoing rather than confess to having anything. The man who is decently dressed in his tent, will come into the city like a beggar. If he is suspected of having property, he is bastinadoed. The Arab would be the most thriving man in the world under any government but this. He will be beaten almost to death, as they constantly are, rather than give up.

But the Bedouin is a much finer man. He drinks neither coffee nor spirits, he never smokes, milk is his only drink. Attempt to beat him, and he will resent it to the last man of your family. (The Arab here would not even run away.) Call the Bedouin a fellah, and he would say, "You had better not say that again."

AT CAIRO

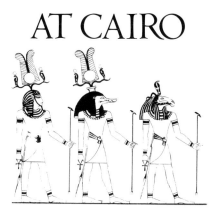

November 27th.

MY DEAREST PEOPLE,
Here we are, our second step in the East. We left Alexandria on the 25th, at seven o'clock A.M. Were towed up the Mahmoudieh Canal by a little steam-tug to Atfeh, which we reached at five P.M. The canal perfectly uninteresting; the day gloomy. I was not very well, so I stayed below from Alexandria to Cairo. At Atfeh, as we were seventy people on board a boat built for twenty-five, Mrs. B. and I plunged out, without a plank, upon the bank, and ran across the neck of land which still separated us from the river, to secure places in the *Marchioness of Breadalbane,* which was waiting to take us to Cairo. Then first I saw the solemn Nile, flowing gloomily; a ray just shining out of the cloudy horizon from the setting sun upon him. He was still very high; the current rapid. The solemnity is not produced by sluggishness, but by the dark colour of the water, the enormous unvarying character of the flat plain, a fringe of date trees here and there, nothing else. By six o'clock P.M. we were off, the moon shining, and the stars all out. Atfeh, heavens! what a place! If you can imagine a parcel of mud cones, about five feet high, thatched with straw, instead of tapering to a point,

a few round holes in them for windows, one cone a little larger than the rest, most of them grovelling up the bank, and built in holes — that is Atfeh, and the large anthill is the Governor's house.

On board our steamer, where there is no sleeping place, but a ladies' cabin, where you sit round all night, nine to the square yard, we have hardly any English, no Indians, for luckily it is not the transit week. Our condition is not

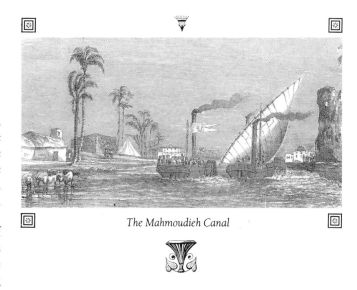

The Mahmoudieh Canal

improved physically, for the boat is equally full of children, screaming all night, and the children are much fuller of vermin; but mentally it is, for the screams are Egyptian, Greek, Italian, and Turkish screams; and the fleas, &c are Circassian, Chinese, and Coptic fleas.

Mr. B. comes down into the cabin, and immediately from off the floor a Turkish woman rose in her wrath, adjusted her black silk veil, and with her three slaves, who

Arab Wedding by Narcisse Berchere (Mathaf Gallery)

all put on theirs which were white, sailed out of the cabin like a Juno in her majestic indignation, and actually went for the night on board the baggage steamer which followed us. She was the prettiest woman I ever saw, more like a sylph than a Juno, except on that occasion, and sat in her close jacket and trousers, with a sash round her waist, when with us. The women who *stood* the onset, were a bride from the island of Lemnos, a fat ugly woman, who had been married at eleven, and was being brought up by two duennas, rather nice old hags in turbans, to Cairo to her husband. The bride was magnificently dressed, and would have been handsome if she had not looked such an animal and so old. Her duennas always sat on either side of her, like tame elephants, and let her speak to none. She was covered with diamonds and pearls, had one jacket on of blue velvet trimmed with fur over another of yellow silk, &c. Most of the women crouched on the floor all night, and talked the whole time. They were amazingly puzzled by us, and I was asked some fifty times if I were married. This redoubled the difficulty; I could not conceive why one said to me so often, "But you *did* go to the opera at Alexandria," and would believe no denial. What we could be going to do in Upper Egypt was another difficulty; and that we should not travel by a caravan. At last we heard them settling in Greek that we were the singing people of the opera at Alexandria; but what could we be going to sing at Dongola for? Another woman was explaining her views on marriage. English, she said, married late, and fifteen *was* late. She never would marry her daughter later than ten or twelve; and when you *began* to think of it, the man ought not to be more than seven. (By the by, we saw a marriage at Alexandria; one horse bore the wedded couple, of six and seven, the lady riding behind her bridegroom, and preceded by men playing single stick.)

At two o'clock the moon set, and the stars shone out. At six the bright and morning star Venus rose; presently the pyramids appeared, three, against the sky, but I could not muster a single sensation. Before ten we were anchored at Boulak; and before eleven, with our baggage on camels, ourselves with the Efreet running before us, the kourbash cracking in his hand (it is impossible to conceive anything so graceful as an Arab's run), we had driven up the great alley of acacias from Boulak to Cairo to the Ezbekeeyeh and the Hôtel de l'Europe.

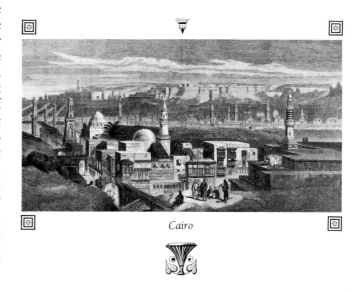

Cairo

I would not have missed that night for the world; it was the most amusing time I ever passed, and the most picturesque.

31

AT CAIRO

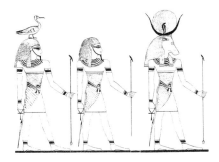

November 29th.

MY DEAREST PEOPLE,

No one ever talks about the beauty of Cairo, ever gives you the least idea of this surpassing city. I thought it was a place to buy stores at and pass through on one's way to India, instead of its being the rose of cities, the garden of the desert, the pearl of Moorish architecture, the fairest, really the fairest, place of earth below. It reminds me always of Sirius; I can't tell why, except that Sirius has the silveriest light in heaven above, and Cairo has the same radiant look on earth below: and I shall never look at Sirius in future years without thinking of her. Oh, could I but describe those Moorish streets, in red and white stripes of marble; the latticed balconies, with little octagonal shrines, also latticed, sticking out of them, for the ladies to look straight down through; the innumerable mosques and minarets; the arcades in the insides of houses you peep into, the first stories meeting almost overhead, and yet the air with nothing but fragrance on it, in these narrowest of narrow wynds! But there are no words to describe an Arabian city, no European words at least: for that *one* day yesterday you would have thought it worth while to make a voyage three

times as long, and ten times as disagreeable, as the one we made, and go back again content, and well content.

After threading these streets for miles, we came out upon the square where stands the magnificent mosque of Sultan Hassan, and above it the citadel, up which we wound,

The Citadel of Cairo

passing the palaces of Ibrahim Pacha, Nezleh Hanum, the widow of the Defterdar, till we came to the mosque built by Mehemet Ali, and not yet finished, though in it lie his bones. It is of splendid size, but tawdrily ornamented, and looks better now with the scaffolding supporting those lofty domes, than ever it will do when decorated like Drury Lane. The obnoxious female is still admitted. Mehemet Ali's tomb is covered with shawls and carpets. I have heard people express the wish that he had lived to see his mosque finished, so much do people's ideas get corrupted here: and within a stone's throw of his splendid tomb is the court where the Mamelukes died; he counted them at break of day, and when the sun set where were they? He sleeps now close to the murdered chiefs; and people can forget that murder, and laud Mehemet Ali!

From the terrace of the mosque is what I should imagine the finest view in the whole world. Cairo, which is immense, lies at the feet, a forest of minarets and domes and towers. The Nile flows his solemn course beyond, the waters being still out (it is now high Nile), and the three Pyramids stand sharp against the sky. Here Osiris and his worshippers lived; here Abraham and Moses walked; here Aristotle came; here, later, Mahomet learnt the best of his religion and studied Christianity; here, perhaps, our Saviour's mother brought her little son to open his eyes to the light. They are all gone from the body; but the Nile flows and the Pyramids stand there still.

We rode down again into the city, swarming with life, for the Arab is the busiest person in the world: you cannot imagine how you will get through the streets; you expect to run over every child, and to be run over by every camel, who, gigantic animals! loom round every sharp corner just as you are coming to it, and are the tallest creatures I ever saw: there does not appear standing room for a fly. You address your ass in the tenderest terms, and in the purest Arabic; you adjure him by all the names of friendship to stop: but he understands no Arabic except his driver's, and on he goes, full trot, while you are making hairbreadth 'scapes at every corner, yet receiving hardly a knock. Out of this city of noise and bustle and confusion you pass through the gate, and come, oh change! oh wondrous change! from the city of the living into the city of the dead. I never saw anything so wonderful as this: as far as the eye can reach you see nothing but tombs, and from these streets of tombs,

where you walk, and walk, and walk, till you fancy Amina, the Ghoul, sitting on one particular tomb (you see her making her repast), there is nothing to be seen beyond but the desert, nothing but the sky and the lifeless earth: it is the union with another world — the "land beyond". And here I

Entrance to the Citadel of Cairo

must recant all that I have said against the worship of the body, the fanatical care of the dead, as I have always thought it. I do see the use of taking care of the lifeless body; of exhibiting it, if you will, making it conspicuous. If it were not for this material mode of making another world visible, we should forget it; to our sensuous natures it is necessary to make the unseen seen, the spiritual perceptible to the senses: the more notorious and conspicuous the dead are made, the better, i.e. without becoming injurious to their still living *fellow*-creatures (you know the plague never appeared till we began to bury).

I certainly never saw anything so striking as this passage from the garden of cities, the buzz of nations, to the city of tombs and the desert. You have read descriptions of the desert till you fancy you had imagined it exactly; ride out into it, and you find that nothing had given or could give you the least idea of it. A curse, a curse, is the only feeling which still moves in your mind; every other feeling is dead, every other idea extinguished, but this which goes wandering up and down your vacant brain, till even the tombs are a relief from it. The desert you *fancy* a great plain, in which there is always something soothing, with a golden sky and opal horizon. You *see* an earth tumbled up and down; not as if Providence had made it so, but as if it had been created otherwise, and clouds of sand, the whirlwind, and the curse had passed over it and unmade it, and tossed and gashed and scathed it, till they had made it what you see. Œdipus scorched with the lightning, rayless and sightless, is what it reminds me of; and we first saw it with the sun "veiling his burning brow", and the sunset dull and glazed, and the moon, not silvery, but dead and white, and a range of black hills beyond, and everything in unison with it. It is not the desolation: there may be the *solitude* of desolation; but this is the *abomination* of desolation. No! no one ever conveys an idea of what the desert is; and no more shall I, nor have I. A curse! a curse! is all you cry: and you think of that great city, that fair city, where scarcely any man knows "what he was put into the world for" (there are a *few* people in Europe who know); you think of the Pharaohs and their mighty power; of Alexander and his; and later of Mehemet Ali and his, how he arose and reigned, and thought that he would be called the Civiliser of the East, a greater name than the conquerors of the East, and now, not six months dead, and scarcely a trace of his institutions remains—because none of

these tried to find out what man was put into the world for, — and the words "the vanity of human greatness" press into my mind with a force a sermon never gave them; mind, not the vanity of *divine* greatness. St. Vincent de Paul's sisters still walk unharmed by all, and blessed even by Mahometans, through the city. Moses' influence is still felt, even in Wellow churchyard; the infant which sat in its mother's arms 1849 years ago, perhaps at that very Heliopolis we are now near, has revolutionised the world. Divine greatness always endures; but what is *human* greatness, when you look at this desolation of the finest country in the world? There were twenty millions of Egyptians; there are now not two.

Well, we rode on into the desert, occasionally meeting a mounted Arab or string of camels coming from Suez, till we reached the tombs of the Caliphs. Imagine yourself in a wilderness of (someone said) 400 mosques, — for every tomb is a mosque, falling to decay, but beautiful in their ruin; every one with a dome sculptured all over with vines or foliage, and round the base of the dome an Arabic inscription on a blue ground. Countless in variety, perfect in beauty, these Moorish monuments (I believe they are Circassian and belong to the Mameluke Sultans of the Circassian dynasty) strike one as the most unearthly records of "earth gone to the earth" one had ever seen. One can hardly believe one's self in broad daylight! Out of these falling ruins come crawling houseless wanderers, like ghouls or lepers, who have there taken up their abode — their unhired and unpaid-for dwelling; and a miserable little garden of one palm and a rose-tree, in the middle of one of the mosques, was almost affecting, as the last clinging of one of these unnatural and degraded creatures to nature and beauty, which he showed in his watering of the one rose-tree and his training the palm. Just then came, like the wind, across the desert (the Arabs really run like the wind), an armed Arab, a police officer, who seized a miserable boy,

Tombs of the Khalifs by Alexius Geyer (Mathaf Gallery)

threw him down, and dragged him away. The boy's white turban came undone, and streamed upon the wind; the bastinado stick appeared: the Secretary (our friend) tried to interfere, but could do nothing. It made one quite sick, as all the details of government do in this horrid country.

Bab-el-Nusr, or Gate of Victory, and the Mosque of El Hakim

Our priceless cicerone dragged me up through a hole in the wall some feet from the ground into some of the tombs: a square court, with arched cloisters around, two minarets at the two corners, and two domes at the other two; under the domes the tombs, along the cloisters, cells, probably for the priests, now for the wild savages, the court open to the sky, — this was the distribution of the largest. The tomb had the turban at one end; an inscription, of which Allah

was alone decipherable, at the other. In a few years all will be gone; but the blue phylacteries of tiles round the domes are as fresh as ever — a dome to every tomb. Oh, wonderful! and the names even of these Sultans are forgotten! We rode home through the desert by the gate of Bab-el-Nusr — the gate of victory; then through the streets of Cairo in the dusk, repeating the wonderful experiment of riding over every man, and being ridden over by every camel, yet without hurting or being hurt. Oh, those curious figures, those wild unearthly figures (in the dusk), of Arab women in their great black shrouds, twining their wild arms about, till they look like everything but a human being!

We have taken our dahabieh; and tomorrow the Bey, whose property it is, and who has behaved very "handsome", comes to smoke the pipe of peace with us, after his mosque, and drink coffee, in order to conclude the bargain. It being Friday, his Sunday, I have not yet seen the boat, which is to be called the *Parthenope,* the name being executed in Greek letters in white tape on a blue pennant. It has never carried Europeans, being built for his hareem; we give him 30 pounds a month. It has two sleeping cabins and a sitting one. We shall not be off before Monday, however; still we trust it will not be low Nile before we reach the first cataract. It is much the best boat they have seen, and is to be our home for the next three months.

Monday we were tired, and contented ourselves with sauntering about the Consul-General's garden, dining with him, making faces at his hippopotamus of five months old. Mr. Murray's kindness to us has been beyond everything. He has put a room, where I am now writing (which is fifty feet long), and his garden at our disposition, lent us an

Arabic library to take with us, begun our collection of Egyptian antiquities, given us shells from the Red Sea, &c. He evidently does the Consul with a conscience; has learnt Turkish, Arabic, and Persian, the first for diplomatic, the second for common, the third for literary business, and has just given me a most philosophic lesson in Arabic.

The Hôtel de l'Europe, where we are, is on the Ezbekeeyeh, the finest promenade in — Europe, I was going to say. We crossed it this morning to call on Mrs. Lieder (Lieder, unfortunately, is ill), then through streets to which the wynds of Edinburgh are Bond Streets, opening upon other streets, of which the first are to the second as the Bond Streets are to the first, but all fragrant with sweet Oriental smells; no dirt or carrion, nothing but fine white sand. This sand is the nuisance of Cairo, everything is covered with it, clothes, paper, hands, table: if one leaves the window open for a moment, it becomes a cloud; it is hopeless to keep one's self clean. Latticed balconies looked down upon us; here was only walking room, and up a narrow winding stair we went into Lieder's house. They have an invaluable head of Cleopatra, evidently a portrait, not beautiful, — she squints, — but very sweet; another, of Berenice.

In the afternoon our faithful cicerone, Mr. Legros, took us out on those war-horses, the donkeys, to the ferry, and we were ferried over to the island of Roda, Ibrahim Pacha's garden, in the Nile. It is not much of a garden, except that the bamboo grows gloriously; but the palm-tree and banana are not half so luxuriant as at Alexandria. But he brought us, just at setting sun, to the other side of the island; and there on the three Pyramids, and the lateen sails, and the solemn Nile was shed the orange light. It was a dull evening, we have seen none but such since we have been at Cairo; and if there is not a great change, I shall think the fuss people make about the glare quite inconceivable. We never go out, of course, without a veil and an ugly; but that is

as much because of the Mahometan's horror of us, as for our eyes.

But the evening was in harmony with the view. It would sound very ugly if I were to describe it; the brown Nile, which takes the lights so well, the brown houses, and the

The Ferry to Gizeh

brown desert, and the orange lights, in such perfect keeping—all such rich shades of brown: the whole is beautiful. The blue and arrowy rivers of Europe would not do here. The Nile would not be the solemn god if he were any other. It is beautiful, beautiful, though one can hardly tell why. I am afraid, though, Cairo will be very different at low Nile when we return. Home we rode again by moonlight; and you have no idea what an Eastern moonlight

An Evening Drink by Charles Theodore Frere (Mathaf Gallery)

is: it is exactly like snow, and the shadows look as if there the snow has been swept up; it is too peculiar, too colourless, to be beautiful.

I have been copying plans of Egyptian temples at the Consular Library (Mr. Murray's). Sometimes we go and sit on sofas in his garden, and a little Greek slave brings us pure coffee in little silver filigree cups, which he carries with one hand at the top and the other at bottom, that his may not touch ours, and a low bow: the Consul claps his hands, and in it comes.

We have had a delightful week at Cairo. I wish we were going to stay longer. It is the riding in the streets, above all, which is so delightful, of which one never wearies; the latticed windows meeting overhead, the pearls of Moorish architecture at every corner, the looking up to the blue sky and golden sunlight from the wells of streets and in the bazaars, the streets entirely roofed in; and as you stand bargaining for a pair of yellow slippers, you see the corner of a street with the spring of an arch covered with Moorish network, and the sunlight pouring through the square holes left in the roof which shuts in the street, or you look into a courtyard, if you want a carpet, and see the men tailoring upon inlaid tables, with the richest fret-work all over the walls.

In riding home by moonlight, the Turk sitting cross-legged smoking under a low vaulted arch, there is not a corner which is not a picture; and no picture can give an idea of the colouring. But you don't enjoy all this for nothing. A Christian female dog has two titles of dishonour here, and she cannot stir out without her ass, her running ass-driver, and at least one gentleman or a dragoman. *A la longue* this dependence becomes tiresome beyond what a European can conceive. It is not that one minds being spat at (which I have been) for a religion which one loves, but one is so afraid of the gentlemen of one's party noticing any insult, as an Englishman's complaint would bring a

bastinado upon the poor wretch, which has often ended in death. Abbas Pacha is so furiously Mahometan that he has just dismissed all Christians from his service, all that he could do without, besides 900 Coptic scribes, who are fallen into the lowest poverty thereby.

Yesterday we went to our own little church in the Copt quarter. Kruse preached a very good sermon, and gave us the Sacrament. One's feelings towards the Anglican Church are very different when she is hiding in corners, struggling with the devil, and still adhering to her own beloved ritual, to when she is stretched out in fatness, with the millstone of the richest hierarchy in the world about her neck, and the lust of the world tempting people to make her a profession and not a vocation. I feel a very warm attachment to her here, though I suspect the good she is doing, with her translations of the prayer book into Arabic, is next to nothing.

You cannot conceive the painfulness of the impression made upon one by the population here. It really seems to matter so little whether an Abbas or an Ibrahim reigns, a swine or a jackal — the only difference being that Mehemet Ali would as soon order a murder as eat his breakfast — it did not spoil his appetite, — while Ibrahim very much preferred it — it increased his zest for the meal; and Abbas, being of weaker stuff, does not order a man to death, but to be bastinadoed, upon which death ensues. One can take so little interest in politics, when it seems to matter so little. The sooner people are put out of their pain the better. One goes riding out, and one really feels inclined to believe that this *is* the kingdom of the devil, and to shudder under this glorious sun, for "this is his hour and the power of darkness". I cannot describe it. In Italy one felt they were children, and their dawn was coming; here one feels as if they were demons; and their sun was set. One rides out to see the sunset, but between you and the sun you see, crouching in a ditch, lumps of low huts, not even *pretending* to keep out the weather; the bulrushes which grow in the swamps round them droop over them, and try to do for them what the industry of man will not. The best have, instead of a round hole in the clay for a window, a pot without a bottom let into the hole; there is hardly any attempt at thatch, and out of these come crawling creatures, half-clothed, even in this country, where it is a shame for a woman to show her face. They do not strike one as half-formed beings, who will grow up and grow more complete, but as evil degraded creatures. I have never seen misery before but I felt, Oh, how I should like to live here! what would I give to take this field! but here one turns away one's face, and "passes by on the other side", thanking God that here one is not to stay. I don't think one could live here. And over all hangs the glorious golden and purple vault of heaven, and "all, save the spirit of man, is divine".

In Cairo itself, exquisite as is the architecture, everything is undone: either it has been begun and never finished, or it is falling to decay; but you never see anything complete, though the Pacha does not mind what money he spends.

Abbas Pacha goes up the river today, Pruner (Mr. Mohl's friend) with him; his only pleasure is to dismiss Christians from his service.

We have dined three times with Mr. Murray: one day he had a Bey and his wife to meet us,—Europeans, of course, by birth. She enormously dressed in jacket and trousers of white and gold tissue, and in her turban a splendid diamond crescent, as big as two of the moon, and two Brobdignag diamond stars,—so much pomp and ugliness I never saw. She sat smoking after dinner, like a child sucking its bottle, in the most masterly manner: and they gave us all pipes (oh, if you had seen us!) ten feet long, with beautiful petticoats on, the end resting in little trays on the ground, and Arabic coffee out of filigree cups. The female Bey, Mr. Murray, and I talked Italian, but she took very little part. The male Bey, who piques himself on his English, and practises a sentence in the morning to Mr. Legros, the Secretary, *débita* after this manner a long practised phrase, "Miss, I have the honneur to present to you a gentleman who fizzles a great sympathie for your beauté".

We have not yet seen a hareem, for all the Pachas are in disgrace, and everybody is in disgrace, and obliged to shut up their hareems. Madame Rosetti, Consulessa Generale de Toscana, whose acquaintance I made on that memorable night, was to have taken us to see her friend Nezleh Hanum, the eldest daughter of Mehemet Ali; but she is under arrest. Some intrigue or other.

Yesterday Dr. Abbott showed us his antiquities; he has adopted the Turkish dress and married an Armenian wife. I hate a collection, but I suppose this is quite priceless. Cheops' ring, Menes I's necklace, &c. Only one thing I should very much like to have understood,— a funeral papyrus, but it has never been read. An Egyptian novel apparently begins with a man's death, and accordingly he dies, as you see by the vignettes, and there are the sacrifices for his burial. Then he is standing before Osiris, who sits with his whip in his hand, and the dog Cerberus opposite him, and Truth writing down his deeds (with an ostrich feather which is her emblem), and the forty assessors or judges, all ranged on a shelf above him, each with a different beast's head; another God is holding the scales, and his good deeds look very light. Then come different stages of Purgatory, which he is enduring; different Hercules labours, of killing this or that beast, which he is to perform. In the last vignette you see him face to face with Osiris, but whether to be condemned or justified I could not make out. But I never saw anything more interesting than this supernatural novel, this romance beyond the tombs—I wish people would write novels so.

We are glad enough we did not take our dahabieh at Alexandria, for yesterday arrived people who had been twelve days on the road; I mean, on the river. While we have had our lovely week at Cairo, she is worthy of all Eastern metaphors — a bride adorned for the marriage; so sunny, yet so retiring, so gay, and yet not glaring.

And the donkeys! one rides along in such ease and luxury on one's ass, like a Caliph, if it were not for that

The Nile, looking towards the Pyramids of Dashoor and Sakhara

creature running by the side; but you have a splendid man in front, a sais or groom, with a noble presence, who runs like a river, so grandly yet so gracefully, and he girds up his garments like a man in the Bible, and runs without moving his arms, carrying things, too, in his bosom.

Oh, if one could either forget, or believe, that the people here were one's fellow creatures, what a country this would be!

FROM THE *PARTHENOPE*

December 4th.

MY DEAREST PEOPLE,
We are really off in our dahabieh; they say it is the best boat on the river. The sitting cabin is quite a pretty little room, painted with green panels, and a divan all round it; the B.'s are in the second cabin, then comes a passage with large closets; the third is mine. The Levinge mosquito net is put up, and is a capital invention; as to being chokey, the cabin of a dahabieh at night runs no risk of being too warm. With regard to beasts, you must renounce all expeditions, all intercourse with your fellow creatures, if you have set it down as a first principle to keep free from them; it is impossible. The men are rowing to the sound of that indescribable roar or recitative they make.

Mr. Legros, our faithful old friend, put us on board last night. He is quite our Colyar II, and I thought that dynasty was extinct. He ordered our dahabieh away from Boulak, where the Arabs and the fleas are dreadful, to the island of Roda, where he took us a twilight walk; the moon rising behind the trees on the Nile bank, and shining through them and the tall bulrushes, on the lonely waters, was the most striking thing I have seen. We started from Cairo upon six donkeys, which carried ourselves and our mattresses, amid the furious din of the Arabs, whose noise and confusion is inconceivable (while the stately Turk never says an unnecessary word), and had a beautiful sunset ride through the alleys of tall bulrushes, out of which you can see

The Pyramids of Gizeh

nothing but the sky, down to Ibrahim Pacha's new palace, by the river side, where Mr. L. had moored our boat to be out of the way. The Pyramids loomed large in the twilight — the frog sang — and the deep quiet of those solemn waters was so soothing. I gathered a nosegay of roses on the island of Roda (Moses' island) to take with us — the last rose of Egypt. Now we are floating up so gently, so smoothly, that you can hardly perceive the motion.

FLOATING UP THE NILE

December 9th.

We shall have been on board a week tomorrow, and are now thoroughly settled in our house: all our gimlets up, our divans out, our Turkish slippers (mezd) provided, and everything on its own hook, as befits such close quarters. Now, if you ask how I like the dahabieh life, I must say I am no dahabieh bird, no divan incumbent. I do long to be wandering about the desert by myself, poking my own nose into all the villages and running hither and thither, and making acquaintances *où bon me semble*. I long to be riding on my ass across the plain, I rejoice when the wind is foul, and I can get ashore. They call me "the wild ass of the wilderness, snuffing up the wind," because I am so fond of getting away. I dearly love our dahabieh as my home, but if it is to stay in it the whole day, as we are fain to do when the wind is fair, that is not in my way at all. However, I must tell you what walks I have had. This morning I went ashore with one of the crew at sunrise; it was cold, as cold as an English morning in October, and there was even a touch of hoar frost. But when I got under the shelter of the palm trees it was warmer. We went inland to a village, the situation of

A Village by the Nile by H.D.S. Corrodi (Christie's, London)

which was marked to us by its fringe of palms. Whenever you see these, you are sure of finding houses. We met a woman leading out her flock to water at a pool left by the inundation of the Nile, her black goats and white sheep. A little further on, we came to a brick-field, mud bricks laid out to bake in the sun, and full of chopped straw to make them adhere. It made one think of Rebekah and the Hebrews' task, at every turn. Then we walked round the village. But no European can have the least idea of the misery of an African village; if he has not seen it, no description brings it home. I saw a door about three feet high, of a mud hut, and peeping in, saw in the darkness nothing but a white-horned sheep, and a white hen. But something else was moving, and presently crawled out four human beings, three women and a child; they made a miserable pretence of veiling their faces before my Efreet. The only reason why they had not their camel with them was because he could not get in; next door was a maize enclosure, which differed from the first only by being cleaner, and having no roof, I looked over, and saw him. My Efreet is so careful of me that he won't let anybody come near me. If they do, he utters some dreadful form of words, which I don't understand, and they instantly fall back.

All the houses in the village were exactly like this, the mud walls very thick, nearly three feet. There appeared to me to be only one den inside, but I did not go in because I had promised not. Some little things were setting out to fetch water from the Nile, each with his amphora on the head, each with a rag which scarcely descended over the body, but shrouded the head (the Arab always covers his head). The dogs, who are like foxes, descended from the roofs at sight of me and my Efreet, but, awed by a similar charm, fell back.

The village, which seemed a considerable place, with a governor and a governor's house, possessed a khan. I peeped in. Strings of camels lay round the walls — a few

inner cells behind them, roofless and floorless, showed tokens of travellers. But I was afraid of a commotion: so veiled my face and passed on. A tray covered with the Turkish thimblefuls of coffee (which we also drink) was coming out — the only refinement the Arab possesses. In every village you see a coffee-house; generally a roofless cabin built of maize stalks, with mud benches round the inside, but always the thimblefuls of coffee, made, not like ours, but pounded, boiled for a moment, and poured off directly and drunk black. You cannot drink our coffee in this climate with impunity; it is too heating. We walked round the village, the huts all tumbled together up and down, as animals build their nests, without regularity or plan. The pigeons seemed better lodged: they had round mud cones provided for them, taller than the houses, stuck full of pots at the top for them to build in, and sticks for them to perch on. There was not much curiosity about me, though they (the Arabs, not the pigeons) could never have seen a European woman before; but they looked on with the same interest which the dogs did, — no more. By the time I came back and overtook the dahabieh, which had been tracked meanwhile for some distance (there was little wind, and that was south), the sun was high, but it was still too cold to breakfast on deck, as we have done once.

After breakfast we all five went ashore together for the first time. Paolo and Mr. B. took their guns to shoot us our dinner and soon killed seven quails. We meanwhile wandered about in a desert place, or sat under what shelter we could find beneath a tuft of grass (the grasses grow as high as reeds), for the sun had by this time risen with a burning heat. A troop of mounted police, fine looking fellows, rode past us, turbaned and trousered, with guns and pistols; the police which Mehemet Ali instituted — ruffian-like Arnaouts — but they have effectually cleared the country and secured the safety of Europeans. No pains are taken to investigate who is the offender; when an offence occurs, the whole village suffers to save the trouble of inquiring who's who. Five years ago, a dahabieh was ordered to meet the governor of India, and was coming down the river. Some Arabs went on board and committed a murder and theft. The village was burnt to the ground, and not one living soul spared, not even the child in its mother's arms. If you miss a pin now, the whole village is made responsible for it, and the whole village bastinadoed. When we stop at night, the village is answerable for us, and men relieve each other on guard the whole night, round our boat. We came on board again and read the English service.

Last night I went ashore at sunset with Paolo. We killed nothing but a little owl. While he was doing this, I found quite an European lane, only it lay between palm trees, with nice tufts of grass and hard walking, and camels and buffaloes were winding their way home to their rest with an old man, who told us he was of "the first times", Arabic for very old. It was my first walk under palm trees; for the groves are at great distances from one another sometimes, and you cannot go ashore where you please. The sun was just setting behind them. But there are no words to describe an African sunset. A pillar of fire ascended from where the sun, so sorry to go, had first slowly disappeared, like that which guided Moses in the Desert — yet not of fire either, it was most like a precious stone, transparent, and yet deep. All the colours of Africa are those of precious stones, the colours of the Revelations, while those of Europe are like flowers. The Nile was of molten gold; and over against the west was a long line of purest blue, extending all along the east, sapphire blue, and over it a band of the most delicate rose-colour; and the whole sky was "so cloudless, clear, and purely beautiful that God alone was to be seen in heaven". The whole Nile is so unnatural, if one may use the expression, so unlike nature — the descriptions of the gardens in the Arabian Nights, with the precious stones, seem no longer here fantastic or exaggerated — it is the description of the country. Flowers or gardens, it is true, there are none — trees there are still less, except the palm; but the Arabian Nights give quite the character of the scenery. At sunset this evening we had a real specimen of the desert: long, low, level lines on every side; one solitary palm seemed the last remnant of vegetation; one solitary Sheikh's tomb, the grave of the last man. The breeze died away, as if it was too weary and worn-out to blow on these ends of the earth. The only sound was the distant bay of jackals, who did not approach, because there were no bodies here for them to eat, and remained where there still *were dead*. All nature seemed worn-out and dying; and the Nile flowed lazily along, like Cocytus. It was the outer desolation: and the sun went down, as if he too had not even strength to colour the clouds.

Two mornings this week the Nile has been covered with a truly English fog; so thick that no one could go ashore. After breakfast yesterday, however, we went, and were spoken to by an Armenian in English. He turned out to be the governor of the villages round. I had a great deal of talk with him, and he invited me to go to his village, and he would show all the houses of the Arabs, &c. I longed to go, but the wind was just springing up, and Mr. B. did not like to lose it, which was a pity, as we might never find another governor among these Turks willing to patronise us.

Our crew are a most courteous and quiet set; they are just like children. Whenever they are not tracking, they sit in a circle, with two water-jars, which they strike like tambourines, singing a sort of recitative, or rather shouting it, for hours together, and laughing immoderately. Hunt the slipper is an intellectual entertainment in comparison. The Reis is a dignified old man, and sits apart. On the poop, atop of the cabins, stands the black steersman, who never moves day or night. They cook their mess of the thinnest broth and bread in the little boat, and eat it there. No one is ever allowed to enter our cabin; Paolo washes us out *every* day.

The Ferry by Charles Theodore Frere (Mathaf Gallery)

Mustafa with his cookery, is at the prow, and a little Mustafet, his son, we have taken in for charity. I am not allowed to walk the deck for fear of bringing in fleas from the crew's territory.

On Friday night Mr. B. and I went ashore at sunset, and walked to a village inland with a minaret, the only one we have seen since we left old Cairo. He shot a crow, nothing else. We took an Efreet with us. I was so delighted to get ashore that I could have run all over the maize fields. The maize is already three feet high, though so lately put into the ground

On the 7th we made Benisouef; 77 miles from Cairo in three days. It is a large town, which means a large misery, and we all went on shore to buy some pots and pans and a pipe for the Reis who had broken his. But I cannot describe it. The glorious golden sun poured down through holes in the wretched mud bazaar (in crannies on each side of which the merchants live), and the sunlight looked like a precious stone in a pewter setting. People too miserable even to drive the flies from their faces, and therefore covered with them, lay about. The usual khan was the only variety to the mud cages, which consist of four mud walls for the camels, with little compartments, also in mud, all round inside for the men! The perpetual contrast between the jewels of silver and jewels of gold which the moon and the sun are scattering all around them, the precious stones which deck the heavens above and the hill below at night, nature dressed out not as a bride in flowers and gauzy veils, but as an oriental queen in gorgeous jewellery and wrought gold, with the sordid mud and clay of human nature and human life, is perpetually before one's imagination.

At this moment our crew have kindled a great fire by night on land, and are jumping through it like devils. child-devils.

It is rather tiresome always to have an Efreet with one on land, which I am never allowed to go without, and to be dogged by him everywhere, but it is a most courteous Efreet, and almost too afraid of my coming to harm. It will not let me even climb the dyke without helping me.

All my work since I came on board has been making the pennant (the flag and name of every boat are obliged to be registered at Cairo), blue bunting with swallow tails, a Latin red cross upon it, and ΠΑΡΘΕΝΟΠΗ in white tape. It was hoisted this morning at the yardarm, and looks beautiful. It has taken all my tape and a vast amount of stitches, but it will be the finest pennant on the river, and my petticoats will joyfully acknowledge the tribute to sisterly affection, — for sisterly affection in tape in Lower Egypt, let me observe, is worth having. The Union Jack flies at the stern, Mr. B.'s colours half-way up the rigging, all made by ourselves. For two days we had no wind, and tracked or rowed or pushed all day. On the third day the north wind rose and we stood away for Benisouef.

The last view of old Cairo was most beautiful, the island of Roda terminated by the Nilometer, a headland running far into the river with a minaret at the utmost end of a long avenue of caroubas. In front there was a little group on the bank, of ladies shovelling up dirt with their hands — then the father came and caressed his child — then the ladies fell out, and one assisted her conversation with gesticulatory motions — then they appeased themselves and fell to, with the same fingers, upon the doura mess which by this time was ready under the carouba, and which they all dipped into with their hands.

For two days we did not lose sight of Cairo, but her glorious citadel, spectral in colour, still towered over everything. I cannot describe the unnatural colouring, a bright line of yellow green bordering the Nile, barley or lupins, the hard brown of the desert behind, a white ghastly Cairo in the background, dabs of Prussian-blue-and-gamboge trees stuck about. It looked as if a child had painted it, and did not know how, and had made it unlike nature.

We clung to dear old Cairo however in the distance. We passed groups of ugly pyramids, the two at Gizeh still kept their pertinacious points up, on the horizon, then came a group of three, those of Abousir, rough and shabby,— then another group of three, those of Sakhara, one, the largest, in steps, having been stripped of its filling-up stones — then the two at Dashoor, scarcely smaller they are than the great Gizeh fellows, stood out like overgrown extinguishers. I could not get up a single feeling about these objects from first to last. There is nothing beautiful about them, nothing picturesque — the ruinous ones of Abousir and Sakhara look like exaggerated beehives — the others, like stray tents. There can be no enthusiasm about any of their recollections or associations — *pazienza*!

We have made a little sail twice in the night, but not much. Sirius shines like a little moon along the water. The moon is now too late for us to see her rise, but we see her in the night shining through the dahabieh windows.

The Nile, when he makes a reach, looks like a great sea, he is so wide — and when the wind freshens, you see a fleet of little cangias coming out, like water-lilies, upon the river (you don't know from where), or like fairy boats, a fleet of Efreets coming up the Nile, doubling a cape, cutting in among each other. There are islands and headlands and creeks, just like a sea, and sometimes, when the wind blows against the current, he is no longer the solemn Nile, but a most tempestuous lake, with white horses, and turbulent little waves. But he is always beautiful. And, in general, the solemnity is given by all the colouring being of two or three shades of brown, there being however always sufficient variety of tint not to be tiresome—the brown desert, the brown Pyramids, the brown Nile. There seems to be little grown but maize, as yet.

This is a very stupid letter, my dear friends. But a sort of torpor crawls over one in a dahabieh. You feel, as you lie on the divan, and float slowly along, and the shores pass you gently by, as if you were being carried along some unknown river to some unknown shore, leaving for ever all you had ever known before—a mysterious feeling creeps over you, as if it were the passage to some other world, the invisible journey through the valley—not of death, but as the ancients imagined death, a shore where all you have known appear as shades. You feel as if in the power of some unseen spirits, who are wafting you away from all you have ever seen to the far-off land.

Since Cairo we have seen no one house, or decent building. The strange effect of the atmosphere makes the figures on the shore appear gigantic. You lose all feeling of distance. You seem to lose all feeling of identity too, and everything becomes supernatural.

But I must put up this letter for an opportunity. Dearest people, farewell.—Your "Wild Ass of the Wilderness," — but always yours.

OFF THE DESERT OF SHEIKH HASSAN

December 11th.

I always keep a letter ready and sealed in case of accidents, one of which has just occurred in the person of our friend Hassan Effendi, who boarded us on his way back to Cairo, from attending the Pacha at Minieh, and partook of brandy!

Yesterday and today, having no wind, we have taken long walks into the Eastern (Arabian) Desert, to look at quarries and catacombs. The impression which the desert makes is ever new, ever inconceivable; the oftener you are astonished at it, the more like a stranger, a mysterious power it seems. If I were to attempt to describe it, you would not feel the more acquainted with it. I myself, now while I am floating along in our smooth *Parthenope*, by the soft twilight, can hardly conceive it. It is not the absence of life, but the death of life which makes it so terrible,—of life which *has* been, as the solitary catacomb, the painted rock temple, and the distant strip of green along the Nile testify. A lifeless desert would be far less frightful than this dead desert, the idea perpetually recurring of an awful devil at work, making this kingdom his own, overwhelming every-thing by some monstrous convulsion. Perhaps it is the

contrast of the sky with the earth which makes the terror of the desert; if it were overspread with a dull, lifeless sky like ours, it would seem less unnatural,—at least, one would not see its terrors so plainly, as when glared upon by such a light as this. But while the earth in our country is rich and variegated with light, and crowded with animation, the sky above contrasts by its deadness. Here, on the other hand, the sky is radiant, the light is living, the golden light which seems to pour not only from the sun, but from all the points of the transparent blue heavens. One looks down, and the ungrateful earth lies there, hopeless and helpless, a dying, withered desert: one almost fancies one hears the Devil laughing as he dares even Almighty power to bring forth bread.

This is what gives one a supernatural, mysterious feeling in Egypt,—the looks naturally turn to the sky when the earth has no beauty that one should desire it, and the heavens have all beauty. The struggle between God and the Devil is perpetually visibly before one's thoughts, for the earth seems the abode of the Devil, the heavens of God; and you do not wonder at the Orientals being the mystical people they have become, nor at the Europeans, where all beauty is of the earth, and the thoughts turn to the earth, becoming a practical, active people.

But to return to our walk. It was Monday morning, and we landed about sunrise on the eastern coast, and went up towards some limestone cliffs we saw about a mile inland, standing high against the sky. The only living traces we saw were a pair of vultures, sitting on the topmost heights, and the tracks of jackals returning at daybreak from their feast in a little Muslim burying-ground, like ghouls. We had heard their bay at night, and thought what they were doing. The sand was not sand, but entirely composed of a little fossil *Cornu Ammonis*, the relics of a former world, older even than the Egyptian world, lying strewed as thick as dust. Through this we travelled up towards the quarries, the enormous size of which, in former times, was testified by a gigantic propylæum (hewn out of the rock, and left standing against the sky), which is now several hundred yards from the quarries. The stone is not a bit of it honest limestone, but a *Cornu Ammonis* conglomerate. I brought away specimens; as it was so brittle, I could dig with my fingers into it like a jackal.

I climbed up to the top of the quarry, and had a view of the desert on the other side. Nothing, nothing but tumbled waves of sand, as far as you could see. Round an isolated rock I found fragments of pottery, and a square hewn hole in the rock showed the entrance of a tomb,— but I had not time to go in. We returned home through the miserable little plundered burying-ground near the shore. A santon's tomb was by the landing-place, and a mat where someone had once prayed, and a ruined Arab fortress. It was quite a relief to pick up a freshwater shell by the riverside, as something that was alive.

We expected to reach Minieh that day, but there was a dead calm, and we anchored that night a little short of Samalood, on the western bank, which is the one generally chosen for the night. The next day was our first introduction to a rock temple. About midday we found ourselves opposite some catacombs, so took the little felucca, and rowed across to the eastern bank, and taking the boat's crew with us, and the Sheikh of the village, went about two miles into the desert to where the quarries stood shadowless and golden against the blue sky. We found an intaglio, larger than life, of Rameses III (of the XIX dynasty), about sixty years before Samuel, between two hideous gods, probably Athor and Osiris, with his cartouche by the side. Round the corner a small chamber in the rock dedicated to Athor, to put the quarries under her protection; the painted ceiling almost blotted out, the pillars *in antis* broken, but a figure of Rhæbenæn, the son of Rameses the Great (of the XVIII dynasty), with two gods still remaining in bas-relief over the altar. The view of the Nile was magnificently ugly from this height, — yellowish green fields on the western bank, desert on the east, nothing beautiful but the sky. There was something touching in this only trace of life which had here survived, being the Egyptians' tribute to a supernatural influence.

When we returned, we found two Effendis we knew on board our boat, waiting for us. They had devised this opportunity, as they were afraid of saluting Christians when with Pachas, which would get them into trouble. One was a poor boy brought up by Ibrahim Pacha, and sent to England to learn shipbuilding. He is now head of that department at Boulak; he took our letters to Cairo for us.

A little wind had now sprung up, and we took advantage of it to make sail, and got to Minieh, which we were to have reached on Sunday, at eight o'clock that night. We were sorry for this delay, because the Pacha had just had a review of all those beautiful Oriental troops there, and had left Minieh immediately after.

Directly after we began to make sail, the rocks on the east side became steep, and we could see staircases down into the water. Presently we saw one of our crew, who is the buffoon of the party, rigged out in a pair of white duck English trousers, and waistcoat, and straw hat, crushed in at the crown (where he got them and where he kept them the Pharaohs only know), and armed with a mallet. What this joke could be we had not the least idea, till we saw what looked like a line of the archbishop's rats swimming towards us across the river, which is here remarkably broad. The black objects approached the side of the boat, and "Bones" approached too, with his mallet. We saw the fun then. He was a Christian, preparing to receive his fellow-Christians, and these were the monks, Copts, of Mariam el Adra (Mary the Virgin), swimming across for an alms. After a mock fight with the mallet, they opened their mouths to have the piece of five paras inserted under each tongue, which "Bones" did very skilfully, and then swam off, "Bones" flying to our little felucca behind, to prevent them from getting on board her. We saw them land, and proceed stark naked up the cliffs to the convent. Alas! when I first saw the position of that convent, high on the cliffs of an impassable desert, and

Minieh

overlooking the valley of the dark and solemn Nile, it was such a situation for missionaries of the desert, ascetics of the Thebaid; and to see these wretched aquatic beggars, who, I am sorry to say, bear a shocking character for robbing dahabiehs, was such a fall. I was hardly ever so much disappointed or disgusted.

At sunrise we found ourselves anchored off Minieh. I went ashore with Mr. B. to see the place,—a miserable place, though a capital with a mosque, and the Pacha has a palace there,—but oh, the misery! However, when you hear some things, you will only wonder that the Egyptians are alive at all, not that they are wretched; for, as Mr. Lane says, they are as much oppressed as they can be and live. Our dahabieh had its berth among grain-boats, bean-boats, living boats, funeral-boats, all clustered round us. At ten o'clock we were off. I saw one curious sight,—a body on a bier, covered with a red shawl, and followed by innumerable women in blue (their mourning), ferrying over the Nile to the burying-place. The Egyptian burying-places are invariably on the other side the Nile, and it is so evidently the original of Charon and the Styx, that it seems the necessary step to set one back the 3000 years. I went ashore about noon, and saw my first field of sugarcanes, and a splendid falcon, and watched some men working their shadoofs. The shadoof is nothing but two cross-poles, with weights, working two rush-baskets, not even lined with clay, so that half the water dribbles through before it reaches its destination, which pour (or are meant to pour) the water of the Nile into a gutter made also of a rush mat, out of which a higher shadoof ladles it into another gutter, and so it reaches the sugarcane fields. Anything so inartistic it is impossible to imagine.

The men had been tracking all day (we were on the E. side of the river), and the village we had meant to make was still three miles off. We could get no further, and for the first time we anchored for the night on the E. side. Paolo was in a terrible fright lest the Bedouin tribes (for the desert is here close to the shore) should come down upon us. We sent for a watch from the village, and were ordered to put out our lights, and let as little be seen or heard of us as possible. I looked out upon the night, and saw a fire lighted upon the high bank, and five old hags crouching and grinning round it: it was like an incantation in *Macbeth*. They were backed by the solemn depths of the dark blue starry sky (it was like an Etty's ultramarine), and a tangled forest and underwood of palm trees; it was the first time we had seen palm trees really growing, not like a plantation, but like a cleared forest,—I never saw such a wizard picture. Later that night I tried to look at it again, but Paulo had caught me there. I carefully put out my lights, opened my window softly, softly, and thrust forth my head. My eyes were instantly filled with dust, and my forehead scratched against something. Paolo had put up a horrid mat, the whole length of the boat, to prevent anything from being seen from without, and taken up his own residence in the passage, carefully locking the cabin doors.

In the morning, when we went ashore, I saw an old man sitting on the ground, contemplating with esteem and affection two serpents, about four feet long, who were sitting on their bottom rings, darting out their forked tongues,—flat-headed, vicious-looking reptiles, but evidently intimate with him. He had two more in a bag, and then he thrust the heads of these into the same bag, and they went in quite contentedly. He was evidently a charmer; but, if he had not taken out their teeth, they would have been dangerous friends, charm he never so wisely. The two erect were Cobra di Capellos, the sacred asp, Thermuthis, which crowns the head of Isis, and is the symbol of royalty, Cleopatra's asp. The Egyptians call it Nashir, from its spreading out its breast. The other two were common harmless snakes. The man did not see me, and evidently was communing with the serpents for his own recreation.

We passed, coming back to the boat, a deserted Arab village, Metahara, with a Theban gateway, and a village-green of palm trees, where I saw a pair of beautiful green birds, like paroquets. There was a deserted mosque; all was unroofed and desolate.

We had a charming walk that evening at Kôni, where we stopped for the night. Sugarcanes grew up ten feet high among the wild palm trees, under which a young camel was grazing, and the acanthus was the underwood. Two men were at prayer, bowing their foreheads to the ground, and perfectly abstracted,—the first people I have seen praying since Cairo.

The Christians bear a still worse character here. They are the scribes of the whole country, and they are accused, like our lawyers, of multiplying and complicating all sorts of difficulties, to make themselves occupation, — "they gain their livelihood thereby". The Christian village, which surrounds the convent, is notorious for robbing boats; and Christianity, I am sorry to say, has put itself in ill odour among the Mahometans.

The law of inheritance here (if there were but anything to inherit) is fairer than you would expect. There is no primogeniture, and the female has half the share of the male. A man has only power over one third of his property, and that he may not leave to an heir, unless with the consent of all the others. An only daughter (if there is no son) may inherit half the whole property by the Koran, and the other half by common usage. The wife seems, wonderful to believe, to have entire command of her own property, and the husband inherits but a fourth, if she have children; and the wife or wives inherit a fourth of their husband's property, independently and over and above their dowry, if he have no children. With regard to children, the child of the slave-wife inherits equally with the child of the real wife! This sounds much better than one expected.

AT BENI HASSAN

December 14th.

Oh My People, my first real Egyptian day. Two years ago, all but a day, was the first time I saw the Sistine, my first initiation into the Michael Angelo mysteries: today has been my first initiation into the Egyptian mysteries.

I prayed for a contrary wind that we might not pass Beni Hassan, without seeing the caves, whose pillared porticoes, far in the rock above, we had been looking at the whole day from the lazy dahabieh. We arrived opposite them at five o'clock, too late to make the ascent, so anchored at Kôm; and I was promised that, if we had not a fair wind during the night, we should go up at sunrise the next day. In the morning, when I woke, we were going on, though the morning star had scarcely risen in the East. I thought they were playing me false; but no, at sunrise we put off in the little boat, crossed the Nile, and landed just below those magic holes—holes did I call them, with their square entrances as fresh as if they had been chiselled yester-day. They are all in one stratum about three-fifths up the cliff — and up we scrambled. The two deserted villages of Beni Hassan lie to the south of the fort, and what the

desolation of an Arab village, when abandoned, is, cannot be described. They were destroyed by Ibrahim Pacha, and every woman and child killed. The whole gave me the idea, not of an old town deserted, but of an old world deserted.

Entrance to the caves of Beni Hassan

We arrived at the mouth of the sepulchres, built certainly 4000 years ago, for the cartouche of Osirtasen I of the XVI dynasty is everywhere visible, in whose time Wilkinson puts Joseph; but Bunsen puts the Osirtasens at least four dynasties earlier, in the XII Dynasty, 2801 B.C., and buries them in Beni Hassan. However that may be does not signify much to me; it is certain that, *except* the Pyramids, the oldest monuments in Egypt, and probably in this world, these are the first in date of all ascertained antiquities —of all we have to see—so we very properly saw them first.

The cliff is covered with large boulder stones, which have rolled out of their places in the strata: the cliff itself is in ruins as well as its monuments. All, all the works of God, as well as the works of man, are tottering to their fall. Had St. Paul and St. John lived here, it would not have been wonderful that the Last Day and the Last Judgment, as instantly impending, should have been constantly in their minds. I should not have been surprised to have seen the angel with his last trump standing on the highest rock. There are thirty sepulchres — of most of them the paintings are gone — the columns broken — and nothing but the naked chamber hewn in the rock remaining. The columns must have been removed by main force; and there are marks, as of pistol balls, upon the hieroglyphs. But there are five still perfect with their pillared naves —the pillars are a nosegay of four lotus stalks just bound together under the chin, making thus the capitals of the four lotus buds. But this beautiful simple idea is spoilt by painting the abaci green, and the shafts banded with yellow and green, the earliest original, I should suppose, of that Lombard and Moorish architecture, of alternate layers of different col-oured marble. The rocky walls of four of the chambers are entirely covered with rows of small figures, representing the manners and customs of the day. The eastern sun did not shine into their doorways (looking west), still we could see plainly enough; all civilised trades were there—glass, iron—all the rest of it; also the trade—shall I call it civilised or not?—of opera-dancing; Pierrot, making a *jet d'homme*, with extended leg, showing that precedent is not always good, we having so closely followed our Egyptian antece-dents. Ships, with rudders exactly like those on Lago Maggiore, the men rowing, standing. The colours and even drawing of these things showed them to be good chemists and good draughtsmen at this day. The dress of the women was civilised—the ornaments and bracelets were invariably red, green, and white, the Italian colours. The only sign of barbarism was that the king was always five times as big as anybody else. The famous and much disputed procession is here, which Champollion makes that of Joseph's brethren being presented to him, while H. Martineau and others scout the idea. It is certain that their dress is Syrian, not Egyptian, and that this tomb was of Joseph's time, Wilkinson asserts. To me it seems a matter of very little consequence to decide the question: whether or no, Joseph's head is quite rubbed out, and it signifies mighty little to have a portrait of

Dan and Gad or of  and All that one

wants to know is, that on this soil nearly 4000 or 5000 years ago men stood who felt and thought like us, who cared for their brothers, and mourned over their dead with an everlasting love and a preserving memory like us — that memorials of their love have remained while all remem-brance of them has passed away—and while the sound of their names has died away into an hieroglyph, the sound of the beating of their hearts still echoes from under those dim lotus-leaved rocky chambers. They wished to have their dead continually before their eyes. The stone does find a voice, and the sand of the desert tongues, wherewith to speak to us.

But the curious part of these painted grottoes is the literal matter-of-fact delineation of all the details of everyday life—their dressing, eating, working, walking, writing, doctoring, talking, dancing, their sickness and their health, their in-doors and their out-of-doors, their business and their play, without one attempt at composition, one feeling of the picturesque or of art, one idea, one aspiration after the ideal, the supernatural. I saw nothing but representations of the dead man during life, of his occupations and his circumstances, of the highest perfection of the civilisation and organisation of everyday life, of the mechanical arts, and the arts of refinement.

Nothing could be more striking than the contrast between the Sistine and the Egyptian artist — the one all ideal and aspiration, disdaining art and earth, and transporting even the prophets of the earth back to the heaven they came from, but wild, exaggerated, and often unnatural — the other, adhering with the most scrupulous fidelity to truth and exactness in real life — so that, at the distance of 4000 years, it is of infinitely more value to us than if it had been less literal, as letting us into all his most private and every-day habits, while his ideal, when he does show it us, in his gods, is the most matter-of-fact reality possible — merely the magnified attributes of animals, their senses exaggerated. I think the Egyptian must have been very much like some of the English clergy wives of the present day, who preach out of the Old Testament, and make muslin curtains. One of the ruined chambers, with its lotus-leaved pillars, and aisles, and dim vaults, was very mysterious and curious, more from what was *not*, than from what *was* there. But I think the whole effect was more strange, more supernatural (upon one's own mind) of this magic lantern glimpse into the domestic economy of 4000 years ago, than if it had been less real petty life. After this, you will agree that you feel you would be very little the better for knowing whether those were Gad or Dan's features; all one wants to know is that Joseph did live — that he trod where you tread — that his boat floated many a time down that old river, when he went to see his father-in-law at Heliopolis: and whether his tomb was a little more to the right or a little more to the left matters little.

Coming out of the tombs into the broad sunlight, with a little knot of our red-tarbooshed, blue-robed sailors sitting in a group at the entrance (such as Europeans who sit on chairs and wear pantaloons can never form), was a pretty picture,—and the whole valley of the Nile lay below.

Σ said that the awkward architecture of the tombs was inconceivable with the perfection of the colouring. It seemed to me that they attended much more to colour than to form. The architrave, which meant to be what we should call a pediment, had its lower line curved; and no part of the curve was any part of a circle; and if it meant to be an arch, just where the strongest part of the arch should be (the centre), there was a pillar, and of the three pillars none were equidistant, and the middle was not in the middle. Even to my inexperienced eye the effect was painful, the highest part of the curve being on one side. But the sense of beauty in the Egyptian evidently was not,—I mean in the Egyptian of that age: we shall see what a later era will produce. No beauty, however, can surpass in impression what this first day has made. Our dahabieh waddled slowly across to meet us; it had not been able to move a step without us, and our Reis, with his grizzled beard, and his head swathed in shawls, looked like a Rembrandt, as he stood on deck waiting the arrival of the English sisters of Joseph and the Pharaohs. The queerest contrast of all, however, was T. sitting at the door of a tomb (for she went with us), crocheting a pattern in small of a new polka, with her back leaning against the hieroglyphs of Osirtasen, on the door-post of the sepulchre. It was less painful, however, than the childishly ignorant Arab, who stood degraded and brutified under the shadow of his magnificent ancestor's tomb. Poor Arab!—is it the end or the beginning of his civilisation?—and did God intend it so?—is what one asks continually.

Perhaps the thing which came most home to one was a Greek alphabet, sprinkled all over the wall, the letters all manner of ways. It was like surprising the man in the very act of teaching his little Greeks in this cool grot.

Another thing which struck one was the excessive prosaicness of the representations. Nothing was left to the imagination, — probably they had none. You were to see it all. If a drapery over a chair was painted, the chair was painted through. Your Egyptian artist would not have trusted, as the Duke of Cambridge did to his duchess being behind the Duchess of Sutherland in Hayter's picture of the Coronation, but would have painted her through. The *home*iness of the whole contrasted strangely with the wild scenery without.

The bodies do not lie in the chambers, but in pits in the rocky floor below; most of these now stand open, and you look down and see them running far into the rock. The place where the body lay is generally marked by a hieroglyphical tablet in the wall above. "His body shall be cast into the pit" is literal.

I must say that the Egyptian never seemed to have an idea but he spoilt it. The idea of those lotus was beautiful. They merely swelled out a little at the bottom, as if they were growing out of roots; their necks were first tied together by a fillet under the buds, which made the capital; and if they could have let them alone, it would have looked like a river-cave with natural pillars: what had they to do with painting them in stripes? Some of the painted processions were, however, beautifully done. One of a man doctoring a sick goat was in real perspective, done by an artist of genius, not of the usual Chinese fashion. So ends our Beni Hassan day, the first of many wonders, but none more curious.

We tracked but a little further that day, and anchored for the night at Nezlet e Sheikh Timay. Now it happened that Nezlet e Sheikh Timay was at war with the village of the opposite bank, Sheikh Timay, on account of some palm trees, for which N. e S. T. had killed a man of the other village, and though two men are now in prison at Minieh for it, yet "blood for blood", "an eye for an eye", is the universal

A Sheikh

56

law here; and till every relation of the murderer is murdered, the villages are not at peace, and the affair is not at an end. Now N. e S. T. would not let any boats anchor there, for fear the inhabitants of the other village should take the opportunity, and either do the boats a mischief, in order that it might be retaliated by government on the nearest village N. e S. T. (perhaps by extermination), or crawl upon the village itself, now all its male inhabitants but twelve are at Cairo. But we had seen the Sheikh of N. e S. T. at Minieh, and treated him with coffee on board our boat, and his daughter had married, *à la Capulet*, the Sheikh of the hostile village. So he gave us a letter to his village, ordering them to let us anchor there, and give us three guards, and two cats, which we wanted almost as much, for the rats in my cabin are so fierce and bold, that I am obliged to get up at night to defend my dear boots. You cannot keep clear of rats with all your care, when you are anchored near grain-boats sometimes all night. Accordingly we received our three guards; the whole boat was packed up like a brown paper parcel, both sides, with mats, to protect us from *both* Timays; and we lay like birds in a nest all night. N. Timay is on an island, so we were cheated of a morning walk. It was the first cloudy day we have seen.

OFF MANFALOOT

December 17th.

We have not had a gasp of wind these two days, and have made very little progress, — about six or seven miles a day. Our crew are not very able-bodied fellows. Today we have had a sunrise breeze, and went boldly in this morning under the grand cliffs of Gebel Aboofeda. I went ashore on the other side, when the crew stopped for breakfast, and saw the Sheikh Jacob coming into Egypt with his flocks and herds,—such droves of buffaloes, herds of camels, and flocks of brown-horned sheep, with asses in abundance. This was quite a new sight; you forget in Egypt the existence of pastoral countries, "for every shepherd is an abomination to the Egyptians", so purely agricultural is the land.

We had had heavy clouds for two days, and yet no wind; the sailors did not know what to make of it, they had never seen such a sky before without a sirocco. At last a north wind brought us gallantly through the Straits of Gebel Aboofeda, but towards noon, the river turning to the south-east, the crew were obliged to track; soon the wind increased so much that they could not pull against it. We got into a little bay, where the eddy became quite a whirlpool. Five times we tried to tow out of this corner, and five times we were swung round and back again by the whirlpool, till we were obliged to give it up. This we thought the more provoking, as five dahabiehs, which kept in the middle of the stream, passed us, going very near the wind; and one with her sail flapping.

About three, the khamsin increased; it was a wind like this which destroyed six years ago a caravan of 300 camels belonging to Mehemet Ali. The air became filled with sand. The river seemed turned upside down, and flowing bottom upwards, the whirlwind of sand from the desert literally covering it. We could not see across the river; and when we could stand upon deck, which was not often, our eyes were completely filled and our faces covered with sand. As to the critic making Thames *not* to walk between his banks, he does not deserve the credit of originality for that idea, for Nile invented the plan first, and today, instead of walking between his banks, his banks walked between him. I saw the sand blown up into a ridge *upon* the water, and it looked as if you could have passed the river on dry ground, only the dry ground was on the top. I am glad to have seen it, for I should never have believed in it if I had not, and I give you leave not to believe. By this time Nile seemed to be walking with his bed on his head; but it was no beneficent miracle, like the paralytic man's, for it looked as if earth, air, and water had been blasted together into one whirlwind of sand. We could not wash, for it was no use fishing for water in the Nile: instead of water he gave us a stone, i.e. a sand-bank. The waves were as high as when there is a moderate sea in the Channel, and the wind was hot. It grew dark, and the blast increased so, that we drove a stake into the bank and fastened a rope to it for the night.

Presently Paolo rushed in for one of the guns, which was always kept loaded. He said he saw a strange boat coming in sight. I ran out on deck after him, and sure enough, in the pitchy darkness, I saw one of the dahabiehs which had overtaken us in the afternoon, floating past us, bottom upwards; nothing to be seen of her passengers. She struck in the sand just astern of us, and remained fast there. By this time the wind had increased so much, and we bumped so incessantly, that we were afraid the rope would not hold, and we put out another. I could not help laughing, in the middle of all this, at the figure of our Reis, who had squatted himself at the bottom of our little boat (which was between the dahabieh and the bank), and sat there smoking his pipe, and taking no further interest in the question. If the rope wouldn't hold it wouldn't, and why should he be disturbed?

I did not go to bed — we bumped incessantly, and at the stern especially so hard that we thought we must spring a leak. It was so dark that we could see nothing, but in the morning we found that our boat had been astride of the poor wreck all night, which had been whirled round by the eddy under us. At dawn I looked out, she had entirely gone to pieces — nothing was left of her but a few of the cabin planks, which our boat picked up, a chest of clothes which we saved, and her oranges floating in the whirlpool. I never saw anything more affecting than those poor oranges, the last luxury of their life in the midst of death. Torrents of rain were falling — our cabin roof was completely soaked through — the sky was still one heavy mass, but the wind had a little fallen, and we struggled on, towed by the wretched crew, their teeth chattering, dripping with wet, and evidently thinking the Day of Judgment, the end of the world, was come (for to them rain is much what to us English an earthquake might be), to Manfaloot, which we reached about twelve. There we learnt that of the five boats which passed us yesterday to windward four had gone down, and of their passengers, twenty (including women and children) had been lost. Almost all their relations were in Manfaloot. We gave up the chest of clothes to the governor, to the great displeasure of our crew, who fully intended to keep it for themselves.

Watering the Oxen by Leon Belly (Mathaf Gallery)

At Manfaloot the miserable crew went on shore, and baked themselves — literally dried themselves in an oven. Such a storm had not been known since 1839, when half the houses in Manfaloot were washed down by the rain. The heavens had rained first sand, and then water, for the last twenty-four hours.

Our hold was full of bilge-water, otherwise we had no hurt. "If Nile do this," said Paolo, "him see me no more." Paolo had been up and down the Nile fifteen years, and never seen such a storm; and our Reis, who looks like Abraham, never but once. We began to think that old Nile had got it up as a little *gentilesse* for us (as Italians prepare half raw roast beef and plum pudding for English), thinking to please us by a specimen of our own climate, and gratify us by a thought of home. But if he knew what a figure he made of himself, he would not have done it.

The consternation of the Arabs seemed quite to stun and palsy them, — they were incapable of doing anything. Four days of storm we had before the sky righted itself. Whoever has seen a Nile khamsin will hope never to see one again.

The poor wretched boat which passed us so gaily in the afternoon, and came back, four hours after, a mere hulk, her mast and yardarm just appearing above the water, had been in company with us for two days, and we had seen her merry Nubians, and some of her passengers, fifty times a day, in racing with one another. They had evidently broken open the cabin in their efforts to escape; but how, even in that pitchy darkness, they could not have waded to the shoal, we could not conceive.

AT OSYOOT

December 20th.

Just arrived — for today the weather has gloriously cleared up, and enabled us to reach this, the capital of Upper Egypt, which we had been in sight of almost for four days. With rapture I found myself upon an ass again, riding like a caliph into Osyoot, a mile from the riverside, and after our return to the boat, on this the eve of the shortest day, sauntering like Pharaoh's daughter along the river's bank, to see the sun set behind the minarets, with the mountain beyond full of sepulchres in the rock.

We must stay here two days, though the wind is fair at last, to let the crew bake. They take an oven for a day and night, go to the mill, buy the wheat, wash and grind it, knead it themselves with their feet, and then bake it, spending the night at the oven, and going into it with their own bread; I suppose to keep it warm. Such is the method of providing oneself with bread here! We had been without it for four days, and could get no milk either.

FROM LYCOPOLIS

The shortest day, 1849.

We have been spending the day in the caves of Lycopolis, above Osyoot. There is nothing in them so interesting as in Beni Hassan, — no cartouches sufficiently legible to determine their date, — everything destroyed, defaced, plundered. But the position, the associations, the picturesqueness, mental and moral as well as physical, made them to me, if possible, more striking. For here the Anchorites of the Thebaid clustered, — John of Lycopolis, of course, and many others, — and the religious plays of the Nun Hrosvita, which I used to devour in the *Revue des Deux Mondes,* all came before one's imagination.

I had that strange feeling as if I had been here before, — it was so exactly what I had imagined, — a coincidence between the reality and the previous fancy, which never comes true with me. Twice I have had that feeling, — once here, and once in finding the chapel of M. Angelo's *Pietà* in St. Peter's.

Below you, far below you, lies the city of Osyoot, the capital of Upper Egypt, looking like the sort of city the animals might have built, when they had possession of the earth, as we are told, before man was created, — a collection of mud-heaps, except where its thirteen minarets cut the sky. I had read Mungo Park's descriptions of an African village, and Bruce's, and had fancied I understood them, but no description gives the idea of the debasement and misery.

Osyoot

This was the type of the savage life, while, in those caves of the rock, the saints of the Thebaid stood, each before one's imagination, at the door of his narrow cell, as the types of the spiritual life; and Alexandria stood afar, where in the Neo-Platonist school, these men, the Platonist Christians, had probably been nourished, as the type of the intellectual life. There they had seen the extreme of Epicurean refinement, of intellectual luxury, where enjoy-

On the Nile by Prosper Marilhat (Wallace Collection)

ment became a science, — and one sees how naturally the feelings of these men sprung out of such a past as that, — how they came to think prayer, and meditation, and self-denial the only good, after having been told that pleasure was the supreme end. (An immense cone of clay, into which the wild bee was flying, hung close to the door of one of the tombs. "His meat was locusts and wild honey.") Alexandria, Osyoot, and the Thebaid, — what a picture it was!

Numbers of heads and tails of mummy-jackals were lying about in their rags, — for Lycopolis was sacred to Anubis, a jackal-headed god, who was the god of Death in its *good* sense, — death in the sense of regeneration and resurrection. It was his office to preside over the dying moments, to carry away the escaping Psyche from the bed of death to the presence of his father Osiris, whose name the new-born ψυχη then took, and under which name it entered Paradise. Anubis was, in the same sense, the god of Time. But Time itself now lay dead; and the mummies, so carefully put under his protection, all lay tumbled about among the rocks. It was curious to see these things, to which a reverence for life, or even for where life had been, under *any* form, had given birth, — a reverence so great that, even in the animal, life was sacred, — to see now, not only the mummy-animals, but even the skeleton of a human being, a young woman, 5000 years ago so reverentially cared for, now handled by our childish Arabs, pulled to pieces, and thrown at one another's heads. Little she would care for it now, — still I could not bear it, — more for the feelings of those who had cared for her 5000 years ago, than for her own, — and we buried her decently out of sight, the sand with a heap of stones covering. It was little good, for five minutes afterwards we found the skeleton of her husband. But there is nothing painful in all this, — the ideas of the old Egyptians about death were so cheerful, — it was so

completely to them the portal of life, that one felt as if the god of Death must have rejoiced over his own death, now that he is gone to join his worshippers.

I shall not describe the caves, — whoever imagined anything from description? The atmosphere within is not chill or damp, like vaults or churchyards, but warm, and genial, and dry, to the last and farthest chamber in the rock. Little remains to tell their story, but some beautiful blue scrolls still covering the rocky ceiling, — blue, the old Egyptian type of wisdom, because sapphire, its favourite stone, means, as in Hebrew, to write, — so the Hebrews still call their Bible Sephir, *the* book, and the Egyptian priests wore (like the "Urim and Thummim") on their breasts a blue stone, a sapphire, with Truth engraven on it. The two breastplates appear to have been exactly similar.

Mr. B. and I climbed the mountain, through a cleft, in search of the site of the old Lycopolis, and found on the very summit the place cleared, — no doubt the Acropolis, — and a smaller round space, the Acropolis of the Acropolis; and such a view! — not beautiful, — bird's eye views never are, but all Egypt, all the windings of the Nile, seemed to lie at our feet, like a map. And the great Libyan desert here approached the cultivated land, not, as before, *rising* up from it, with a difference of level which accounted for the change, and seemed to make it natural, as being where the Nile could not reach, but level *with* the valley, like a great dragon, putting out his fiery tongue and licking up the green, fertile plain, biting into it, and threatening to encroach still more. You have no idea how frightful it looked. I had never seen this effect lower down the Nile, and the desert seemed to me more terrible than before. On the Arabian side as well, the plain was bounded with desert. That view I never shall forget.

It is good for a man to be here, — good for British pride to think, here was a nation more powerful than we are, and almost as civilised, 4000 years ago, — for 2000 years already they have been a nation of slaves, — in 2000 years where shall we be? — shall we be like them?

It is good for Christian pride, too, to be called "dog" in the street, pointed at, spat at, as we are here. No one looks at us with respect, hardly with curiosity, — we are too low. They take our money and have done with us.

It is good for British exclusiveness, too, to become so completely inhabitants of another age as we are here. Till I caught myself rejecting a Roman temple as uninteresting and modern, I had no idea how completely we were living in the time of 4000 years ago. There is no affectation in it. One says, "We will not go to that place, it is *only* Roman", or "the Romans have spoilt that tomb". One learns to distinguish the antiquity of the cartouches by their simplicity, as in heraldry, — those of the Ptolemies are overladen and complicated, those of the earliest dynasties have but three or four figures, — and to go to those tombs where the cartouches are the simplest. But I like the chambers best where there is nothing to learn, — nothing but pure plaster for the imagination! The mountain here is literally riddled with tombs and chambers. We crawled from one into the other. We rode home through the modern burial-ground, a city without the walls, rows and rows of square, white-washed, ogived enclosures, with divans round them, under which the inhabitants of the living city, which is much less handsome, lie, — beautiful palms, acacias, caroubas, filled it: — while the living city, base and dirty, with its houses windowless, of sunburnt bricks, looked degraded and hopeless. How can it be otherwise, when government *fixes the price* of produce, buys it, compels work by bastinado, and not by the natural incentive — interest — and leaves the wretched fellah nothing but taxes to live upon? The women, dirty beyond description, use their one veil for a basket. And yet they are a noble-looking race. I have never seen so many tall men, noble presences, stately heads, as in this wretched Osyoot and miserable bazaar, where the shopkeepers sit, keep their goods, and work at their trade in holes, four feet by five, raised on either side the narrow street.

The only whitewashed house is the Pacha's palace just inside the gate. A number of people were crouching at the door, waiting for audience. "He sits and judges in the gate." The ride into Osyoot is really through quite a wooded country, with yellow, flowering mimosas, and ponds, and white ibises in them. And at the corner of every road is that beautiful observance of Mahometan hospitality, the covered water-tank, long and narrow, with three little starry openings, and three little dome-lings like a holy water vessel, which is always kept filled with water for the traveller arriving at the city to refresh himself, even before he enters it. I have drunk there myself, and blest the observance towards the stranger.

Tomorrow we leave Osyoot and set our sails to Thebes, but shall not, we now fear, spend our Christmas Day there, as we had intended. Our bread is baked, and we are off. The day was from about ten minutes to seven to ten minutes past five, about ten hours and twenty minutes from sunrise to sunset today. In the middle of the day it was hot, nights cold as usual. In a garden in Osyoot the trellis was covered with vines in leaf, castor-oil plant in flower, but no attempt at flowers anywhere.

A noble cat has come aboard of its own accord, and killed two rats: I believe it is a god!

But now farewell, dearest people. And now that Nile has got up this little *divertissement* in our honour as English people, to remind us of our own climate, I hope he will give us fine weather.

God bless, and he will bless you. My Christmas love to all.

BETWEEN OSYOOT AND GIRGEH

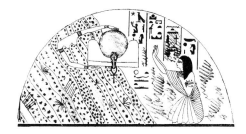

Christmas Eve.

I must write to you all, MY DEAR ONES, this holy day, and think of you with your holly boughs, as you will of us with our palm branches — your yule-log in the drawing-room chimney, and our hot sun overhead.

Tell M. S. with my love that I walked alone at sunset one Eastern evening on the seashore near Alexandria, on the very spot as I like to believe where Justin Martyr met his old man, and as I thought of their meeting I thought of ours made under auspices almost as holy. I wish she could have seen the sunset which glorified that spot; the sands of gold, the transparent green caves of the sea.

Till you see an Eastern sea you never understand the Homeric idea of Thetis and the Nymphs living in its caves. In our dull green and blue waves there seems no inducement to live; but in the transparent green caves of the East, the colour of that green fluorspar, or of chrysolite, and of nothing else that I have ever seen, you can hardly fancy that something blessed does not dwell.

But I must come back to Christmas. We breakfasted out of doors, and walked slowly under a hot sun on Christmas Eve — and what a sunset! — the Nile was like the colour of copper pyrites, or of mica when the sun is making prismatic colours on it, — not the colours of a rainbow, those are too faint, but of metal suddenly cooled, an ore run out of the furnace. Then we have had the strangest scenery since Osyoot. Those expressions "the ends of the earth", "from the corners of the world", come here quite natural. The mountains either form squares going off at a right angle, or make quite a sharp corner, so that the general ground plan of the valley is this ⌐⌐⌐⌐ A is Antæopolis. I assure you this is not in the least exaggerated. Last night when we arrived at Ekhmim, the ancient Chemmis or Panopolis, the whole river was shut in by a square of cliffs and turned into a square lake, so that it looked like the corner of the world finished off in that way! This division of the river into lakes gives one continually the feeling of some Sinbad-the-Sailor or Rasselas valley, — not in our sense of valley, but shut up, and made up at both ends from the rest of the world.

The hills are sometimes pyramids, but oftener square-headed. Not one blade of vegetation, not one cliff from the top to the bottom, but all blown over with sand. You cannot conceive the strange effect of this nature, *unnatural* to us. As to drawing, Σ declares it impossible. And when in the evening a spectral bark with its glassy white sails comes standing in silently like a phantom ship upon this molten sea, you fancy yourself anywhere but in this world. We have the lovely moon again in her first quarter, and she has brought us a fair wind.

This morning I went ashore at a village more miserable than anything we have seen. The people here did not live in huts but in half a hut, just a mere semicircular screen of mud put up with a penthouse of sugarcane stalks at the top, and underneath it squatted, half naked, eating with their hands, the whole family in the mud, with a sheep, a dog, and a hen, their two or three pots round them, their shelf a scoop in the mud wall.

The cliffs are now all blown over with hills of sand rising at their bases.

I like Osyoot much better than Beni Hassan. Beni Hassan is of infinitely more value to the chronologist; and if the twelfth dynasty lies buried there, as Bunsen says, it is

The principal Mosque at Osyoot

unique. (It seems strange, for the twelfth was the conquering dynasty, and the pictures on these tombs are all of peaceful arts and sciences, and matter-of-fact, jog-trot amusements.) Still it is only an isolated fact in chronology, while the long train of associations at Osyoot is much more interesting.

NEARING GIRGEH

Christmas Day.

You are just going to church, MY DEAR PEOPLE, in the close carriage, and we are holding our church on deck, where the thermometer (your thermometer) stands at 101, and 75 in the cabin. This morning, however, it was so cold that the windows were all crusted over with vapour; the dew was like rain at the dawn.

ON THE NILE

Christmas Night.

Many boats passed us today of pilgrims coming back from Mecca, and holy women squatting in the boat like old hags: boats, too, of slaves from Ethiopia, where you can buy one for a pocket handkerchief or a looking-glass. At the first cataract a slave costs three hundred piastres (three pounds), at the second a woman costs six dollars (about one pound) and a man eight — less than a horse.

The wind was so fair that we did not stop at Girgeh, the second great town in Upper Egypt, but sailed on, doing as much in an hour as the men can track in a day. Just before Girgeh, as the sun was going down, we came to another of those great squares shutting in the river, which disappears at a right angle. The sun came back again and again, and once again, to give his last farewell, and say a few words more, not like a child at play, but like a dying Socrates, going to his rest and unveiling his head from under his mantle once more to give his one more word of comfort to his followers. Everything in Egypt is so inexpressibly solemn; nothing ever laughs or plays here; the moon is like a melancholy sun, and the sun is like a Jupiter Capitolinus, not an Apollo.

Everything is grown up and grown old. One never sees creatures at play here as in other countries; the camel is so solemn that when he stands idle against the sky you might mistake him for a stone camel. Nothing is *pretty*. I have seen nothing pretty since we left Cairo, — yes, once, two little kids which skipped; otherwise the young creatures are as solemn as their fathers. I think no greater contrast could the world afford than England, busy England, and Egypt, solemn, melancholy, splendid Egypt.

At last the sun was dead, and Girgeh with her minarets passed in the dusk, and the moon rose — such a moon. Σ and I sat on deck till late at night, "sunning" ourselves in her *warm* beams, — think of that my people, — on Christmas Day. Not one touch of damp, not one breath of chill in the air, though the wind was high. We glided along in a supernatural stillness, for the wind being, as usual, dead fair, we were sheltered from it by the cabin behind us; and every little wave was ridden by its own silvery Jinn, like a fleet of Jinnee come out suddenly in the moonlight. Night lets her footsteps here fall so gently, one fluttering shadow on the water was all that we could see of her, while, in Europe, she comes on with such a heavy tread. The fire was lighted at the bows, and the glare from it fell upon the sail; but the moonlight was brighter, and held its own, undisputed.

The river got wider and wider, and we seemed floating out upon an immeasurable sea, the flood of *golden* moonlight over everything, for so near the tropic as we now are, the colours by moonlight are as bright as by day, and the sky, instead of being only light round the moon, and getting misty towards the horizon, as in Europe, in the East is deep blue about the Lady of the Night, and gets lighter and lighter to the horizon, all round which there is a bright band of light: let natural philosophers contradict me, and say it is impossible when the sun is so low beneath the horizon. I say it *is*.

We seemed to go on and on to unknown shores. We have long since passed the lands of civilisation, and have come to the countries of the savage. Now it seems as if we must be coming to the countries of the Jinn, which, as we all know, encircle the earth at the distance of 200 days' journey; — and they were there already, the little Jinn, each riding on his wave, his green chrysolite wave, in his little silver chariot. The Eastern moonlight looks so supernatural, because one is accustomed in Europe to see the moon low in summer, and casting an immense shadow (and in spite of all one's almanac, one always fancies this summer), so that seeing her above one's head, and the great sail casting not a bit of shadow on the water, one sits down resigned to the conviction that one is being carried away in a phantom-ship to Jinnee countries. The distant song of Arab boatmen, ending in a wild yell, sounds all supernatural; and if one of the crew rouses himself from the deck, — where they either sit motionless in little heaps, or lie covered up, heads and all, so that you tread upon them, mistaking them for a blanket, — he looks, in his striped brown-and-white African blanket, scattering fire upon the waves from his hand, like anything certainly but a man. We could not bear to go in — this our one real night of tropical moonlight. We have felt the difference of climate more these last few days than all the way south we had come before from Cairo. The days and nights are now really African — from day-break till ten or eleven o'clock it is cold.

We have never had the slightest trouble with our crew; that odious word "baksheesh" has never come out of their mouths. Whether it is owing to our having that capital man Paolo with us, I don't know, but they are so agreeable that we are only sorry we don't get on with our Arabic; they are despairingly indifferent, that is all. If Paolo says, "How far is it to Girgeh?" "God knows." "But how soon shall we get there?" "When God pleases." "But I ask you how many hours it is, because the master wants to put it down in his journal?" "God knows." One got drunk at Osyoot, and made a beast of himself with booza (whence our word "boozing"!), upon his present of five-pence; this is our only disaster, for the Arabs are temperate, oh! to a proverb: poor souls! the pleasures of the flesh, in one sense, are not their stumbling-block. The Pacha only eats once a day; and our Arabs are happy with brown bread, baked a month ago, and quite as hard as brick, and a little thin broth. We gave them a fish on Sunday, but have not yet gone the extent of a sheep.

Our housekeeping is simple; our store-room and pantry stand before us in the shape of two large chests on deck, which separate our domain from the crew's; our larder hangs overhead in the shape of a basket full of bread, and two cages full of oranges and meat; our kitchen is immediately beyond — another box, about six feet by four, and behind it is our water goullel (where the water is filtered); so that we have kitchen, scullery, still room, larder, safe, and pantry, all in a nutshell, or at least in a walnut. Ah! would that you could keep house in England so, my dearest mother. "Mustafa's womans" — this is Paolo's language — bought our provisions for us at Osyoot, and some tape! for me, which turned out a narrow muslin embroidered scarf.

The Arabs are no sailors, only pilots; they cannot even rig their own vessel. When it is rigged for them, they are as awkward about handling their own yards, though first-rate climbers, as I should be. They cannot tack; and unless the wind is dead fair, prefer tracking to sailing; the skill they show is in piloting, which is really wonderful, considering the ever changing bed of the river. Our Nubian stands on the poop, robed in his majestic folds, never wearying nor stopping to rest — if the wind is fair, steering with his enormous rudder, hardly ever getting us aground, which in a distance of nearly 1000 miles from Cairo to the second cataract, with this bed, seems miraculous. He appears to have long since forgotten all human language in his sublime solitude up there; but when he is *very* anxious there issues

Young Arab girl

forth a singular splutter from the poop, which I long mistook for the turkeys who live there too. The pigeons are not in a coop, but never try to escape. We have now four cats, the god and three others; the god is the only one who does any work, but he has cleared us of rats, and with an ornamental border of boots all round the tops of our beds we do very well. My Levinge is without price, as much against draughts now as mosquitoes.

Christmas Day produced us two ancient towns, Panopolis and Ptolemais, and our first crocodile; his great paws left heavy footmarks on the sand.

We get milk now everywhere, and bread, which is a great luxury after we had been some time without either. Butter, too, we find now at most places.

View on the Nile by Thomas Seddon (Ashmolean Museum)

NEAR KENNEH

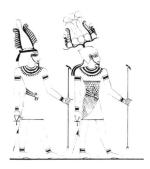

December 28th.

DEAREST PEOPLE,

I wish you could have seen the sunset last night, how the wilderness blossomed like the rose, in the last crimson tints of the dying sun. I wish you could have seen the nosegay of the beautiful yellow cotton-flower I gathered — our first cotton-plants — as we passed the island of Tabenna, where once St. Pachomius taught to pray twelve times a day, to labour, and to deny the body. Now no one prays, no one labours; and if they deny the body, it is because they have nothing to give it. Then he had 1300 followers in the island of Tabenna alone, and 6000 in the Thebaid, besides monasteries in the Arsinoite (Suez) Nome, and in the Nitria. *Then*, in the fourth century, all Egypt was Christian, or almost all; *now* she is not even Mahometan; and very zealous Christians too they must have been, to judge by the enormous percentage of religious orders to the population, and the first principle of these orders was to work; and whatever my dear Protestants of the West may say, an anchorite now appears to me an angel, in comparison with what we have daily before our eyes. In this whole wide waste of corruption, misery, and sensualism, the Christians seem to use their residence in the East not for the sake of leavening the lump, nor for doing any earthly good, but merely for the sake of using the customs of the country to gratify their own vices, and profiting by their sojourn among Mahometans to live like Mahometans (since we have been here, we have not been surprised at, but have heartily joined in, the Muslim contempt of Christians), so that when the only people whom we have seen in all this miserable land attempting to do it the slightest good, or to live for anything but their own gratification, are the Roman Catholic sisters, — I assure you we do heartily wish for a sprinkling, a little city, only a very little one, of the monks of the Thebaid, that *some* incense of service may go up to God among all these people, who know not what they are put into the world for. St. Pachomius received my warmest sympathy as we went by the now utterly desolate island, — no blade of grass, not even a stone remaining.

I should think there were few instances in history of a country being so thoroughly de-christianised as Egypt (the 20,000 Copts can hardly be considered as Christians), after having been entirely Christian, even pre-eminently so, if we are to judge by the Christian schisms which tore her in the fourth century — Athanasius five times an exile from Alexandria (I suppose Christian discord and Christianity must be reckoned as synonymous). Has Islam usually obtained such *complete* possession of a formerly Christian country?

But when one thinks of Egypt as the birthplace of Monasticism, the mother of all religious orders, as I suppose she undoubtedly was unless one excepts the Essenes, it is a curious speculation to see the very religion become an abomination. One solitary monk, a Franciscan, still exists in Osyoot (whom Mr B. went to see), the sole successor of the Johns of Lycopolis and the legions of the Thebaid. There he said his solitary mass, and had done so for ten years; wearing the very disguise of a Muslim by special dispensation from his superiors; and this in the land which, 1400 years ago, was the Rome of Christianity, uniting, like Rome, the classic with the religious capital of the world, and, unlike Rome, at the same period of time. Alexandria was then still the Queen of cities; the Serapeum, with its 700,000 volumes, was still the chief building in the world (excepting perhaps the Capitol); the Augustan age was hardly passed there; but she was also the place of all Christian learning, the arena of all Christian dispute, and the interior of her province the refuge for every man who retired from the intellectual struggle to the spiritual solitude.

But the wind has arisen, and, after two delaying days of tracking, we are at last approaching Kenneh.

We have had a good voyage of a week from Osyoot to Kenneh, 150 miles, with wind five days, which has greatly raised Mr Bracebridge's spirits, but *we* think it all too fast. If the wind is good, we shall scarcely stop at Thebes, but I hope that it will not be, that we may have just one moonlight walk there (for the moon is now full), as our first initiation to the hundred-gated city. Only imagine our being within fifty miles of Thebes: I can hardly believe it, and feel almost afraid of first seeing those awful spectres of dead Time and Space. There is nothing beautiful in Egypt to lessen the awe which one feels before these ghastly shrouds — mere shrouds, as they are in Osyoot, — those bodies petrified, suddenly turned to stone in the midst of their daily occupations, as they seem in Beni Hassan — these gigantic phantoms, as I fancy they will be, in El-Uksor, of a dead Past. If you can imagine seeing an awful spectre under the broad radiance of a meridian sunlight that is Egypt — my noble, melancholy, sublime, dead Egypt. Travelling here is nothing like the tourist seeing sights of beautiful art and sunny landscape in Italy or the South of France; it is like the ghoul haunting the tombs; that is, Lepsius was the ghoul, rifling, and despoiling the monuments, stealing the bodies; we are the poor harmless Phookas.

Abyssinian Christian pilgrim in Cairo

We have come to the region of the Dom Palms, which I think really very pretty; they remind me of my beloved stone pines of Rome, and her gardens.

We saw the post last night, walking along the river bank on his ten toes, with a bell round his neck; but I hope you will get this before I come back.

I have written all this in desperate haste, my people. I cannot make much of the goddesses at present, but hope to do better; and am always, my beloved souls, your humble, loving Phooka.

OFF KENNEH

December 29th

Past and Present are words which in Europe we are fond of using; to us they generally present a cheerful view of things, except when some rabid old Tory comes and talks about the "golden days of good Queen Bess". We read the third chapter of Macaulay and joyfully contrast our liberty and our luxuries with those of the times of Charles II. We look at *our* antiquities, the castles of chivalry, and bless our good angels that we did not live in the "good" feudal times. Here the words Past and Present are above all that you can conceive strange and painful. You enter an Egyptian tomb of, at the very lowest computation, 4000 years ago, and you see on the walls in the imperishable colours of this all-preserving climate (colours, too, which themselves prove what a perfection of chemistry these Egyptians had attained), — you see a nation possessed of almost all our civilisation, and our philosophy, and I believe most of our art and science; for much of theirs, — that, for instance, of quarrying and raising the enormous blocks of their architecture, — is entirely lost: we have had no inheritance of their mechanical skill, and but little, I suppose, of their chemical, mathematical, and astronomical science. When you see painted in the rock chambers of 3000 B.C. all the amusements of what we call the last refinement of a nation, — the dancing, music, painting of Paris and London, — you cannot but imagine the beginning of this nation to have been long before our date for the creation of man; but when you find traces of a religion so enlightened as the worship of the one God, the distinct conception of a progression through Eternity, and a philosophy so deep that all which Solomon knew of legislation, all that Pythagoras and Plato guessed of ethics and spiritual theories, seems to have been borrowed from them, and at a time, too (and for long after), when the Jews seem to have worshipped God the Creator as the God of the Hebrews, the God of Abraham, Isaac, and Jacob, not the God of the whole world, — one cannot but compare this Egyptian religion and philosophy with all others we have known.

As for their habits of daily life, their trades and arts, all before our eyes in a form which we cannot doubt (no false historian, no vanity of a biographer, can here exaggerate or extenuate), they seem to have been on a par with the civilisation of France and England. You see glass blowing, thousands of years before the young Phœnicians were said to have discovered it; you see the pen and inkstand in the tombs of the fourth Dynasty, which cannot be much less than 3,500 years B.C.; but more, much more interesting than all, you see a nation so spiritualised that death was to them more interesting than life: or rather death, as they put it, did not differ from life; life was so small a fragment of the whole to them, that the whole became of course of immeasurably more consequence, not as being different from the part, but as the axiom which nobody disputes, of the whole being greater than its part. I have often thought that there was much more evidence for a future world than there is for this. For the existence of this, we can only draw evidence from our perception (which perceptions are often destroyed or blunted); for the existence of another, we can draw evidence from our reason, our feeling, our conscience, all that some short-hand writers include under the ill-used word Faith, which means, I suppose, all that is not Perception. But the Egyptians seem to have gone farther; they seem to have said, we will consider this life as interesting only in its connection with the whole of which it is a part. I have often thought how dull we were not to see that Christ's life *showed* us this more advanced stage of existence which we call heaven; how we have persisted in calling him the "man of sorrows", instead of calling him the man who is already in the state of blessedness, the man who has progressed and succeeded.

I have left my "Past" and "Present", but it does not need my words to show what it is to look out from these tombs, this Past of a spiritual and intellectual life and see the Present, the savage, sensual, childish life. Why is there not national like individual progression? Does it not seem as if the greatest amount of progress would be secured by the *same* nation continuing to carry its own on, and profiting by its own experience? It cannot be a law that all nations shall fall after a certain number of years. God does not work in that sort of way: they must have broken some law of nature which has caused them to fall. But are all nations to sink in that way? As if national soil, like the soil of the earth, must lie fallow after a certain number of crops. And will England turn into Picts again, after a certain number of harvest years, as Egypt has turned into Arabs? Or will a nation find out at last the laws of God by which she may make a steady progression?

However that may be, I really think a traveller should consider the question, whether it is not less painful to him to travel in America, where there is no Past, an ugly and prosperous Present, but such a Future! or in the East, where there is such a Past, no Present, and, for a Future, one can only hope for extinction!

For the last hundred miles the cliffs on either side the Nile have been lined the whole way with rows of tombs (chambers in the rock), riddled with caves. The kingdom of the dead is greater than that of the living.

The evening we left Osyoot, with a splendid wind, we ran aground several times. The fact was, that the Modeer, who came to look at us, was so pleased with our boat (and it is indeed the best on the river, we have seen none at all like it), that he sent his four carpenters to measure it, which they did with their hands, and having carefully measured one side measured the other too: they admired the boat aloud. Now you know you must not admire anything among Mahometans, except by a pious ejaculation. You must not say to a mother, "What a pretty child!" but you must say, "Mashallah", or what God wills (comes to pass); you must not praise the thing, but the Creator. If you ever say, "How pretty!" you are desired to bless God; and if you don't, you draw upon the thing the "evil eye". This is so touching; I wish it would prevent us from spoiling children in England. If I take a child in my arms here, I must say, "In the name of God, the compassionate, the merciful", and if I admire it, I must say, "I seek refuge with the Lord of the daybreak for thee". Now, the carpenters had admired our boat, and the consequence was, that we ran aground perpetually.

The crew would not go on that night; and the night we were to have reached Kenneh, it was found impossible to move; the crew took out the little boat, towed her a little ahead, and then pulled up the dahabieh with the towing rope. In this way we made about half a mile, and then it was found impossible to move the boat; the crew declared there was an Efreet on board, or Sheytan (a devil), and stopped. We reached Kenneh about nine the next morning.

Mr. B. and I rode up to the town directly: at high Nile you go up by water, but now it is a mile from the river. The road to this centre of the manufacturing interest, as Kenneh is, lies up steep banks, where my donkey-boy held me on, through a water, and over a ploughed field. We stopped at our Consul's house; his two sons stood at the door, and ushered us into a square mud area, hypæthral, the walls two stories high, and at the top of all a latticed cage, which I watched in vain; no faces were visible. In this mud well two chairs were placed for us, and one for my parasol. We gave Mr. Murray's letter in Arabic, which the youths pressed to their foreheads, and they then sat down upon a hencoop. They were splendidly dressed. A tall black slave brought me coffee and Mr. B. pipes.

Presently the old father came in, our Consul, Sheikh Hoseyn, in four kaftans (or robes), one over the other, — for the Muslims dress very warm, — and three turbans; and "genteel" Muslims always wear the cloth outside, and the beautiful silks within, which is very good taste. Our Consul kissed the letter, asked us to eat bread and salt with him, repeated "Bracebridge" over some twenty times, saying "Taib" (good) at his own pronunciation every time, made his son write it down in Arabic, and took our letters, which we took the precaution to enclose to Mr. Murray. Then came in some turkeys into the Consul's drawing room for us to feel and buy, which we did, and then we rode away, I dying to dine with him, as he asked us, but we had no time: I never wanted to dine out before. We saw a dervish in the bazaar, with his tall peaked felt cap.

Abbas Pacha had just left Kenneh — he had had 101 guns fired for him — and had come on shore to visit a santon's tomb, and then gone on board again. His steamer, followed by two others, passed us today, on its way back to

Cairo. This was all that that Prince of the Faithful thought it worth while to do among his loyal people.

I went ashore at night in the most beautiful moonlight I ever saw, at the village where we stopped, and peeped into a santon's tomb. You know that a santon or welee is an idiot, and is sacred, because his spirit is in heaven, while his body only is with us. Heaven keeps it there because he is a favourite. A saint may commit all sorts of enormities, which are but the "abstraction of his soul from worldly things", which is "absorbed in devotion, while his body is left without control".

On Sunday, the 29th, we went ashore on the island of Metareh, where St. Pachomius had another monastery. Here the Christian spirit of zeal and devotion was nurtured. Now nothing seemed to grow there but a little Indian corn. If the inhabitants were Copts, as most of the people are about there, they had not even a church — worse than the Mahometans. The crew carried Mr. B. ashore on their backs, and us on their joined hands; we walked some distance, but could not even make the people understand that we wanted to see the ruins of a deir. And yet here Christianity grew up, nursed by the milk of these institutions till she was old enough to live on strong meat. If St. Pachomius can look on his island now, is he sorry?

The people were ploughing with the rudest possible plough; but the corn comes up here if you only scratch the earth.

In the morning there was khamsin; and we saw a sandbow. It was on a level with the sun, and not opposite it, as in rainbows, but about 30° from it; not the shape of a rainbow, but of a nebula; all the colours perfect. It had a most singular effect; it was about midday, so that the top of the pillar of sand must have reached to that height.

FROM EL-KARNAK

The last night of 1849.

MY DEAR PEOPLE,

Yes, I think your imagination has hardly followed me through the place where I have been spending the last night of the old year. Did you listen to it passing away and think of me? Where do you think I heard it sigh out its soul? In the dim unearthly colonnades of Karnak, which stood and watched it, motionless, silent, and awful, as they had done for thousands of years, to whom, no doubt, thousands of years seem but as a day. Would that I could call up Karnak before your eyes for one moment, but it "is beyond expression".

No one could trust themselves with their imagination alone there. Gigantic shadows spring up on every side; "the dead are stirred up for thee to meet thee at thy coming, even the chief ones of the earth", and they look out from among the columns, and you feel as terror-stricken to be there, miserable intruder, among these mighty dead, as if you had awakened the angel of the Last Day. Imagine six columns on either side, of which the last is almost out of sight, though they stand very near each other, while you look up to the stars from between them, as you would from a deep narrow gorge in the Alps, and then, passing through 160 of these, ranged in eight aisles on either side, the end choked up with heaps of rubbish, this rubbish consisting of stones twenty and thirty feet long, so that it looks like a mountain fallen to ruin, not a temple. How art thou fallen from heaven, oh

Ruins of Karnak

Lucifer, son of the morning! He did exalt his throne above the stars of God; for I looked through a colonnade, and under the roof saw the deep blue sky and a star shining brightly; and as you look upon these mighty ruins, a voice seems continually saying to you, And seekest thou good things for thyself? Seek them not, for is there ought like this ruin? One wonders that people come back from Egypt and live lives as they did before.

Yet Karnak by starlight is not to me painful: we had seen Luxor in the sunshine. I had expected the temples of Thebes to be solemn, but Luxor was fearful. Rows of painted columns, propylæa, colossi, and — built up in the Holy Place — mud (not even huts, but) unroofed enclosures, chalked out, or rather mudded out, for families, with their one oven and broken earthen vessel; and, squatting on the ground among the painted hieroglyphs, creatures with large nose-rings, the children's eyes streaming with matter, on which the mothers let the flies rest, because "it is good for them", without an attempt to drive them off; tattooed men on the ground, with camels feeding out of their laps, and nothing but a few doura stalks strewed for their beds; — I cannot describe the impression it makes: it is as if one were steering towards the sun, the glorious Eastern sun, arrayed in its golden clouds, and were to find, on nearing it, that it were full — instead of glorified beings as one expected — of a race of dwarf cannibals, stained with blood and dressed in bones. The contrast could not be more terrible than the savages of the Present in the temples of the Past at Luxor.

But Karnak by starlight is peace; not peace and joy, but peace, — solemn peace. You feel like spirits revisiting your former world, strange and fallen to ruins; but it has done its work, and there is nothing agonising about it. Egypt should have no sun and no day, no human beings. It should always be seen in solitude and by night; one eternal night it should have, like Job's, and let the stars of the twilight be its lamps; neither let it see the dawning of the day.

AT THEBES

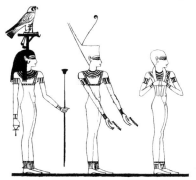

New Year's Day, 1850.

MY DEAR PEOPLE,

I open my eyes, to wish you a happy New Year, and my eyes look upon the obelisk and colonnade of Luxor, under which we lie at anchor, with the sun rising behind them. I have written in haste, because we shall leave Thebes today, if the wind be fair. We arrived here yesterday; as soon as we had passed the cliff which hid the Valley of the Tombs of the Kings, I was on the roof of the cabin, among the hens. The Nile was too low to see much, but what I *did* see!

I could not believe that we should ever see Thebes; I was afraid to die, before our eyes should have lighted upon her. I had a dream the night before, that we had been obliged to turn back before we arrived. I walked on the shore the evening before in a grove of palm trees, cactuses, vines, and cotton plants, and saw the glorious sun set behind the hill which covers the Libyan suburb; the next day we were to see Thebes, if we lived.

And how she opened before us! The wind deadened to a perfect calm, the river spread out to a perfect lake; not, as before, with a current, but a glassy breathless lake; the Arabian hills retreated and hid themselves, as if in terror to

approach the bed of death. Karnak and Luxor came in sight on the eastern bank; the heads of the Colossi and the Ramesseum appeared out of the Libyan suburbs; there lay the imperial corpse of the spirit which had gone out and animated the world. Hail to thee, poor glorious Egypt! Let

Obelisk of Luxor

our tears and our silence, and our reverence, be thine; for there are no words to celebrate such a death as this. There she lay, in the stillness of death, — even the sun had veiled his light, — and she looked the metropolis of the world, as if herself ready to be ferried over that glassy lake to the

Hades beyond. Nothing can equal the first impression of seeing Thebes. We landed, and ran up to Luxor, to see her temple before dark, her one obelisk still standing fresh, and unbroken as the day it was cut, before the propylæum, at the gate of which sit two colossi of Rameses II; but alas! the faces gone, the figures covered up to the elbows. A third colossus, a little farther, sat at the corner of the propylæum; its crown now only marks the spot, projecting above the sand. There stands the colonnade of the seven lotus columns, immeasurably vast, against the sky. The Holy Places are all blocked up, choked with huts and sand; but the cartouches, where you *can* see them, are all so fresh and sharp, that even our inexperienced eyes could read the legends of the Kings.

In the evening we went to Karnak; the night was dark, the moon had betrayed us. No one can describe the desolation of riding over the desert by night; at home one's imagination used to rest in a smooth desert: this was all, as usual, tumbled about; but we could see little. All I know is, that one man held me on behind, while another led my ass; and the blasts of sand in your face, though there was no breath of wind, were the only thing stirring beside ourselves, and the howling of the wild dogs all round us, which sounded like the spirits of the old Efreet Egyptians let loose. (With regard to danger, I must assure an anxious public that that was not the question; we had two mounted men with us, besides Paolo, and the numbers of running men I could not tell in the dark, except by their white staves. I only speak of the effect on the imagination.) In this silent procession we followed one the other for about a mile and a half, till we passed under palm trees; and a little farther, a gleam of moonlight shining out, we saw on either side a ghostly avenue, gigantic sitting sphynxes, with their faces toward us, nearly as close as they could be placed, but most of them headless, limbless, or overthrown. The intellectual and physical force (there typified) lay in the dust. Its body,

that is, lay there, — its spirit had vivified the world. This dromos used to extend all the way from Karnak to Luxor.

Then we stood under the pylon, whose top reaches heaven; then passed between the propyla into the vast atrium. One single column still stood there, not wringing its

Karnak

hands, but raising its unearthly head among the stars, and watching calmly and ceaselessly the course, not of years, but of periods. Then, climbing over hills and valleys made of ruins, you enter the immeasurable forest of columns; one, which had fallen across its aisle, dragging with it the huge stone which bridged it to the next, was the first thing which gave me the least idea of its vastness. It was too sublime in its ruin for one to dare to give pity. Opposite it, two, which had fallen together, blocked up the space: they cannot, you know, fall to the ground; their weight makes no impression on their brother giants, but the shaken giant leans against his fellow, and has probably leaned there for two thousand years, and will for many more. But there is no helplessness in their fall, they still stand immovable; what could have produced it is the only question (still unanswered). We came out at the other end where stood the double pair of obelisks, one only left of each. Around on the *horizon* you see the distant pylæ, the "gates" of the "hundred-gated" Thebes, which had, you know, no wall. Mr. B. and I mounted the towers of the propylæum and looked abroad over the world, *and* the temple; it was too dark to see much, but the vast stones which formed it. Every column, every stone, is loaded with sculpture; but it hardly attracts your eye in the overwhelming effect of the whole. Even Roberts' *Karnak* gives you not the slightest idea of it, and you know these things are buried almost up to the neck.

At Luxor stands the widowed obelisk at the propylæum gate: its fellow, which stood over against it, has been carried off, you know by whom: this one is ours, but whether from feeling, or want of feeling, I cannot say, we have left it in its own rightful home.

Abbas Pacha was here last week, and left the place as he found it; he was below all sentiment, either for the glories of his temples, or the miseries of his people. Two women sat grinding at the mill, when we were there, under the lotus capital; a calf was rubbing itself against the painted hieroglyphs; other enemies had been there — the Ptolemies had scratched out the name of the King in every one of the cartouches, leaving the rest, and the Persians had been spoiling the temple, painting their red legs over it. I stood on the ground, which is about half way above the elbow of the sitting Rameses, and could hardly reach the shoulder. From the Luxor shore you can see the Pair, — the two "Witnesses" — sitting like spectres in the Libyan suburb, where we have not touched yet.

We are just off — this New Year's morning — off for the Cataracts.

Yours, dearest people, ever in this world or the next.

OFF HERMONTHIS

January 2nd.

We left Thebes at twelve yesterday, after having stayed there a night. The view of the whole temple of Luxor from the poop, as you sail away, is beautiful, — the plan of it being less disturbed by the mud huts. What the disturbance of these is, morally and physically, no one can describe. It is not the bodily misery which shocks one: I have seen greater than that in London. On the contrary, the huts in Luxor temple were each full of calves, turkeys, hens, goats, camels, together with their men and women; the corn which the women were grinding was excellent, the breads in the oven were of the whitest, finest flour, and as well baked as yours. If it *had* been physical misery, one could have borne it, — it was the moral degradation, the voluntary debasement, which was so hideous. To see those columns lifting their heads to the sky even now, when half buried, and carrying one's eyes naturally on high, and to see human beings choosing darkness rather than light, building their door-ways four feet high or less, choosing to crawl upon the ground like reptiles, to live in a place where they could not stand upright, when the temple roof above their heads was

all they needed! In a cold climate, one could have understood it; but here it seemed as if they did it on purpose to be as like beasts as they could. There was no reason — there was plenty of room, but they chose to live all in a little yard (not even a hut to each family); pigsties and cowhouses were palaces to these. If they had been deserted, you would have thought it was the dwelling-place of some wild animal. I never before saw any of my fellow creatures degraded (thieves, bad men, women and children), but I longed to have intercourse with them, to stay with them, and make plans for them; but here, one gathered one's clothes about one, and felt as if one had trodden in a nest of reptiles. It sounds horrible to say so; but one cannot conceive how even Moses could set about his work of regeneration here — because they have plenty. Where would you find, in England, the people who had milk every day, who eat turkey and chicken? But these seem voluntarily to have abdicated their privilege as men. The thieves in London, the ragged scholars in Edinburgh, are still human beings; but the horror which the misery of Egypt excites cannot be expressed, for these are beasts.

The colourlessness of Egypt strikes one more than anything. In Italy there are crimson lights and purple shadows; here there is nothing in earth, air, sky, or water, which one can compare in any way with Europe; but with regard to absence of colour, it is striking. It was probably on account of this that the ancient Egyptians painted so much: and one does not feel the colouring of the sculptures barbaric, but necessary; for everything, ground, rivers, houses, men, camels, asses, palm trees, are the same dusty-brown "sad-colour". The houses in Luxor are built of jars, the interstices filled with mud.

We did not make much way on New Year's Day; but I was so tired that I slept all the way, though I had only run up to Luxor before breakfast. But Thebes takes so much out of one. I fell fast asleep on my ass, riding home a mile and a half from Karnak. It was no use trying to think or to feel anything, I only managed to stick on.

We looked Luxor thoroughly over twice, and climbed up to peep into the dark sanctuary. The propylæum is now a guard-house. The nuisance of these places is that one must not leave one's party a moment. On the towers of the propylæum are the most spirited chariot and horses, and king driving them to battle, that Homer ever sang. The king standing, as usual, upright in his chariot — (no charioteer), the reins tied round his waist, drawing his own bow — a noble fellow!

I must now explain that I spell, whenever I can remember it, in accordance with British prejudices; but that, as El-Uksor only means "the palaces", it is always called so here, not Luxor; as Karnak is "El-Karnak", and Kenneh "Gheneh"; which occasions a pleasing variety in my orthography not always intelligible.

Our steersman, Absheer, who had been absent at Coptos, on leave to see his friends (he is a freed slave), returned today with a sheep round his neck, — a black hairy sheep, — which he brought us as a present.

The "two witnesses", the Pair at Thebes, sit with their faces to the river. There is something uncanny about these *two* portraits of Amunoph III, as about the *two* of Rameses II at the propylæum gate of Luxor Temple. It is a truly Egyptian idea, and makes one creep as if one saw one's own self sitting opposite to one. They must have looked still more curious when perfect and fresh; but even in their present disfigured state, one cannot get accustomed to the repetition.

Egypt is like Shakespeare: we discover here whence come familiar household words, of which we knew not before the origin; just as one opens *Hamlet* and says, "I did not know it came from there".

"It would not weigh a feather in the balance." On the Egyptian walls we see the literal original of this:— the good actions of men are weighed (in the funeral scenes) against a feather in the other balance. This feather is the ostrich feather, the symbol of Truth. No doubt it at first meant a record. Alas! it has come to mean lightness. So, when one sees the great wings over the doors of all the temples (the winged disk), one is no longer perplexed by our singular

Thebes

symbol of the Saviour, — a *winged* sun, the *Sun* of Righteousness, arising with healing on his *wings*.

I could not (between ourselves) get up a single feeling of enthusiasm about the Pair, nor, indeed, about the Pyramids, from first to last: bigness does not make greatness. The difference between Thebes and the Pyramids seems to me the same as between Milton and Dante's imaginations. When Dante wants to impress you, he gives an all-material

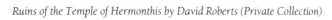
Ruins of the Temple of Hermonthis by David Roberts (Private Collection)

measurement of the size of his spirit. His head is 72 by 35 by 19; and what idea of sublimity does that give you? So it is with the Pyramids; there is nothing but size about them to make their ugliness great. Milton and Thebes knew better. But I dare say the impression will be quite different on a nearer acquaintance with the Pyramids. Recording as they do, the most hideous oppression in the world; one of them having cost its builder his house and empire; the ashes of two never having been laid in their *own* Pyramids, for fear of the people; — with nothing but horrible associations, it is no wonder that the first impression of them should be nothing but repulsive — not even interesting.

*   *   *

We went on shore this morning, while the moon was yet up, to see the Temple of Hermonthis. Before we came back to breakfast at half-past eight it was quite hot walking. The last few days have made such a difference in the climate that we dine on deck; even I hardly find the mornings cold, who the first month from Cairo could hardly keep myself alive till ten o'clock; and the days are really hot.

There is nothing very striking about the Temple: it was chiefly remarkable as the place where the goddess Reto gave birth to the god Horpire. The sacred place, i.e. the adytum, or sekos, was built over this; and great torches of palm leaves were lighted inside to show us the sculptures in the alto relievos, with which the sanctuary and an inner chamber for the oracle were covered, representing the birth and nurture of this deity. But it was to me very interesting. The Triad of Hermonthis is Mandoo, Reto, and Horpire. Mandoo is sometimes called the Sun; but he appears rather to have been the metaphysical God of War, differing from

the *physical* God of War the mere destroyer, or Mars, who occupies a very low place in the Egyptian Theology, — but representing the avenging principle, the Retribution of God, the divine attribute which attaches to evil its consequences. The name of Re-to signifies the "Sun and the World"; and in

Ruins of Hermonthis

these Triads the third member is always the result of the action of the first upon the second, generally the action of intellect upon matter, producing some created being. Horpire signifies literally "Horus, the Sun", and seems to have been the same as Harpocrates, or Horus, the symbol of the resuscitated soul, of youth, of the new birth, united with the idea of the Sun. People laugh, when they look at this sanctuary erected over the birthplace of the child-god, but why? The idea of the Triad *may* have been one purely metaphysical; viz. that the suffering attached to sin upon earth, when united with light, produces the new birth, the spring time of life, repentance. Or it may have been a physical event, like the birth of our Saviour.

Whichever it be, it is a most interesting place (though there is nothing beautiful about it); and made still more interesting by the succession of ruins, ending with a Christian church, which strew the ground. But the desire of the mind to find some law, to learn some reason, for this rise and fall of nations, is almost painful in Egypt. We take little pains in Europe to seek for it, besides a few moral reflections or pious ejaculations which the fate of nations calls forth from us; a few "How wonderfuls", in which the mind rests, when it is oppressed by the feeling of seeking a law and finding none; a few references to the prophecies. Ezekiel and Isaiah do not seem to have done the same. When shall we, instead of quoting, imitate them as far as we can? When shall we be able to say such governments had such consequences in Egypt, Assyria, Persia? — such governments *will* have such consequences in England, France, Germany? There never was such an opportunity as here, where the smallest details are laid open to us, for studying history in the future.

I should fancy that the ideas about a future state of any nation would very much arise from the natural features of its territory. The idea of a sleep after death, an intermediate state of repose, could only arise, for instance, in a northern nation. The expanse of snow, the sleep of seeds and of nature, naturally suggests the idea of *repose before* the Resurrection. In Egypt there is nothing to give this feeling, and accordingly we find no sleep after death in their Theology. For the lifelessness of the desert does not give the idea of sleep or peace, but of the burning, forced, tension of despair, — not the silence of the grave, but the silence of sullen endurance.

The valley of the Nile, on the other hand, gave the idea of the Elysian fields, and all between was the progress or retrogression of one into the other; so that the ideas of suffering *versus* enjoyment, and both progressive, neither a fixed state, but alterable, came naturally to the people of a country where too is no autumn or winter, where the leaves never fall and the frost never comes.

If you ask me whether the desert has not greatness to redeem it. Yes, it is great; at least, it has one of the elements of greatness — oneness, but not the most essential, i.e. to be without change, without unrest. It gives one the idea of being perpetually restless, of Milton's Satan, turning ceaselessly from side to side in his lake of fire.

In the sanctuary is now the prison of the Pachas. Erment (Hermonthis), not having paid its tribute a little time ago, the village was razed to the ground, and the inhabitants had their ears and noses cut off. A few columns are left, nothing else. The place is now full of soldiers. Before the revolt Ibrahim Pacha had taken away all their lands, no wonder they would neither work nor pay tribute.

That disgusting Cleopatra had been at work on the temple, making herself, Julius Cæsar, and their son, into the triad of the place. The columns of the pronaos still stand before the sekos; the reservoir lined with stone for ablution is near; and just beyond, the columns of beautiful Egyptian granite, broken and overthrown, of a Christian church, built at a time when the established religion here was Christian. Many of the columns have been carried away, and are now part of S. Paolo in Rome. A Muslim burying-ground is close to the temple portico, and a pit with a mummy goat in it a little further on. Egyptian, Roman, Christian, Muslim, what is the law of their succession?

FAR OFF SYENE

Twelfth Night.

MY DEARLY BELOVED MOTHER,

Here we are, at the island which was the birthplace and throne of dynasties; tomorrow we go up the Cataracts, and in the evening kiss the shores of Philœ, and then Nubia, no longer Egypt, is to be our home. We have won the cup; we *are* to go up to the Second Cataract, to see Ipsamboul and the Ethiopian Kings. It was a chance, but we have been successful. We sailed in this morning to Syene; sent for the Reis of the Cataracts. At first he pronounced the boat too large to go up; it was a cruel blow, but he was only making difficulties; and tomorrow, at dawn of day, with another English boat, we are to make the ascent. The wind is fair, the Nile not low, and all is favourable. Now, give us your blessing on our journey, dear mother. We have had a splendid sail of five days from Thebes, which we left on New Year's Day, and arrived here (without stopping anywhere, but half an hour at the Temple of Hermonthis, and another half hour at the quarries of Hagar Silsilis), with the hottest weather all the way, at twelve o'clock today. We came dancing in with a merry breeze; and whether it was, that to see waves on that solemn old Nile is

as unnatural as it would be to see the colossi dance, or whether it was that so much depends on the mood of mind, I was not at all so much struck with Syene as I expected. The boundary between Egypt and Nubia is well defined; the Nile closes up; the country alters all at once to black granite, sticking out of the river in a hundred little islands, hemming it in with cliffs on both sides, striped with sand-drifts, but projecting out of them the blacker and the more frowning.

Do you remember the island and burying-place of the McNabs, and the river running into Loch Tay? It is exactly like that, with every feature magnified to a gigantic size; every stone a rock; the island of the McNabs Elephantina, on which the palms grow very like firs. We anchored at Syene, and while Paolo went up to the Governor to see if there were any letters for us, rowed over to Elephantina, and landed. Not one stone remains there upon another: yes, there is the bit of a gateway, a quay, and a hideous Syenite statue; otherwise it is one mountain of broken pottery, fragments of red granite, sand, and mounds; there is not an inch of level walking.

Troops of South Sea savages received us at the landing-place, running away when we looked at them, and then running back to look at us, like a troop of jackals, with loud yells, which continued all the while we were there. The island looks as if it were a world turned upside down, and then stirred up, and that was the scum which had come to the surface. It was such a world as might have been turned out of the caldron of *Macbeth*'s Weird Sisters. I am glad to have been there, but hope never to see Elephantina again. It is impossible for anyone to come away, except with an impression of horror; there is nothing on which one can *rest* for a moment. It was as if a devil had been there, heaving underneath, upturning, tossing, and tumbling it till everything was in atoms and confusion. The yells of those children I never shall forget, as they threw up clouds of dust, not shiny as savages *ought* to be, but their black skins all dim and grimed with sand, like dusty tables, their dirty hair plaited in rats' tails, close to their heads, naked, all but a head veil. I heard some stones fall into the river, and hoped it was they, and that that debased life had finished; they

Asouan and the Island of Elephantine

were not thin or starved. I gave them all the pins I had; it was all one could do for them.

The very granite rocks looked all grown old, and were not sharp, but rounded into huge boulders, of fantastic shapes, as if they, too, were worn away, and ruined, and waiting for death — huge granite forms ground away like mortar. And here was the Elephantina which sent forth the fifth dynasty, more than three thousand years before Christ, which ruled when Mœris Apappus was turning the Nile into the Faioum — a work the world has not seen the like of, turning a desert and a marsh into the garden of the world; a time of the highest art and science, when writing had already taken the place of mere hieroglyphs; when Ethiopia, instead of being, as now, a byword for slaves, was sending out civilised kings (instead of castor oil) to rule other parts of the world. And now to look at Elephantina, and see her, not peacefully asleep, but the tumbled lair of a horde of savages. Nothing one reads of the South Sea Islanders is so bad as what we see here.

We crossed over to the other shore, where we saw, on a granite rock, the cartouche of a Pharaoh, to show the place where he had been cutting hewn blocks for his temple. It was Amunoph III's cartouche of the eighteenth dynasty, the Augustan age of Egypt, and the marks of the tools, and the wedges, by which they hewed out the huge granite blocks, were still on the rock. A boat — such a boat as a South Sea cannibal would *not* have put together, so rude and leaky, — with an old white-bearded black Charon, and a half-naked woman carrying dust on her head, put to shore. Four Ethiopian women, perfectly black, were washing in the river, dancing on the clothes like imps, not with movements like human creatures. We returned to the boat, and saw there the Kings of the East, the three Magi, sitting on our divan, talking to Paolo, with each an arm passed round his neck. They were the Sheikhs of the Cataract, or, as he introduced them, "The Great Father is dead; the two bigs are brothers"; i.e. the two eldest, "I know them, ours mans, since so high". The two "bigs" startled us at first, and crushed our hopes about the boat, but they soon came to, and promised to take us up the Cataracts, and on to the Second and back, without scathe (as the pilot of Egypt does not know any further than this). This matter off our minds, we considered our great anxiety over, and our Twelfth Day most successful. (I have just bought some ostrich eggs for Twelfth Night.)

Fellahin

A beautiful little ape came on board, not like our mangy Zoological apes, but with a green head, a back of a chaste dove colour, and a long yellow silky bib under his chin, and put his little paws on our knees; he looked so clean and so clever, and when I gave him one of my "paternal aunts" (Arabic for date), he smelt the European glove, and satisfied his curiosity before his appetites.

The followers of the Three Kings all sat round them in a circle on the ground: they are to manage our boat entirely tomorrow; our crew does nothing, not knowing the rapids.

Before dark we went out to see Asouan; traders from Darfur were passing through with skins and slaves, and stopping for the night. The skins were heaped up under the palms, and so were the slaves, most of them girls of about ten or fifteen, with beautiful little hands, making ready measures of meal, kneading it, and making cakes on the hearth, i.e., on an iron plate upon the smallest bit of fire on the ground: they took hardly any notice of us; they were sitting on their heels, some of them had three cuts on each cheek. The Ethiopian slaves are sold by their parents willingly for a couple of handkerchiefs, or a little box, and are often exposed and picked up. We passed a boatful yesterday, crammed together, all women, half naked. As we came back after dark, they were sitting round their fire for the night; they came out to beg of us, and, in the dusk, looked like skulls, with their white teeth; they set up a horrid laugh when we gave them nothing: our guide poked one with his stick, when it was sitting down, as if it were a frog.

We walked on through Syene: interminable mounds, as they seemed to us; its size must have been enormous, and nothing, not even a palm-tree now; a village smaller and more scattered than any we have seen; not even a goat, or anything that gives milk; the only living things we saw here were two camels, belonging to the traders from Darfur, and among the tombs, a bayadère, finely dressed: the most painful looking creature of all. That the only living thing now here, beside those poor slaves, should be a thing of vice! Of the old Egyptian and Roman buildings of this great capital, nothing but a few granite columns here and there, and mounds behind mounds, a perfect desert of them. Then

Island of Philœ

we climbed up to the old Saracenic wall; another wilderness of mounds lay beyond the Saracenic city, and at the top a ruin, which, by its pillars, had been a heathen temple, then a Christian church, then a Mahometan mosque, then a ruin. We peeped through a gap in the wall, and on the other side, what a scene! A vast Mahometan burying-ground, deserted these thousand years, and, indeed, there is nothing now to be buried there, and seeming to extend far into the desert: it is called the Valley of Martyrs. We had already passed through one, where the graves were only three or four fragments of granite, heaped together. Then rocks and mounds, and black stones tumbled together down to the Nile, an "universe of death", not even the usual repose for the eye on the river bank, — but the desolate islets of the Cataracts closing it in. It was a place where a ghoul could not have lived. "Among the tombs" receives, for the first time, here a horrible meaning. A ghost would have died terror-struck here in a week. The stars seemed to refuse to give their light, and it was like looking over the edge of the world. It is useless to try to describe these things, for European language has no words for them. How should it, when there is no such thing in Europe. All other nature raises one's thoughts to heaven; this sends them to hell: it makes one think of a devil (not of God), who has been following his ways out, turning up everything till he has made it to his own destructive fancy. Oh! if this is hell we have seen (I am sure there can be no worse), it is a perfect one, and enough to deter us, if fear could ever do so, from sin.

We came back, through a wilderness of stones and sand, to the river, where the few poor creatures who inhabit Syene seemed to have congregated in boats, as shunning the land.

Is the earth worn out, that she can no longer bear man? This earth, which has nourished, after a dynasty of her own (the Elephantine, in 3074 B.C.), the Pharaohs, the Persians, the Greeks, Romans, Saracens, whose memorials strew the rocks, though not one of them is standing? I saw, on Elephantina, broken pottery with Greek inscriptions, a Ptolemaic quay made of Pharaonic blocks, besides its more legitimate offspring. Is the earth sick, that she can no longer bear any but the distorted monsters she has now?

But I must put up, my friends, for I am weary, and tomorrow is a great day, — the day we touch the Holy Isle, the day of Philœ. Philœ and Iona! What a poem, for him who could imagine it! What a year (for me) which sees Philœ and Iona, the Northern and the Southern worship, both! Yet it is the same God under the different forms.

And I am whether at Philœ or at Iona, yours, and ever yours, my people.

Temple on the Nile

IN NUBIA

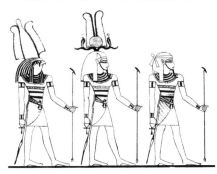

January 7th.

MY DEARS,

Well, the great feat is over; the British flag floated proudly up the last steps of the staircase at half past one today, and found herself in a position where she never had been before; and we came up stairs to another world. It was a grand sight. I would not have missed it for the world. Everybody at Cairo dissuaded us from it; but let nobody come to Egypt without going up the Cataracts: they have never seen such an exhibition before, and never will again. It is quite as interesting, in its way, as Karnak in another, or Cairo in a third, as the most wonderful development of instinct I suppose the world contains. I thought it quite beautiful; and tears fill one's eyes when one sees the provision of God for the preservation of life, always answering exactly to its need in every country. In Europe, the intellectual developments are quite enough to preserve life, and accordingly we see instinct undeveloped. In America, the wild Indian tracks his way through a trackless forest, by an instinct to us quite as miraculous as clairvoyance, or anything we are pleased to call impossible; and in Egypt the wild Nubian rides on the wave, and treads upon the foam, quite as securely as the

Indian in his forest. The strife of man with the elements, — wind, earth, and water, — and his overcoming, was as grand an epic poem as any I ever read in Homer or Milton. I should have expected to find the Triad of the Cataracts, Physical Skill, Strength, and Rapidity.

Here the poor Arab is in his element, and, instead of the sensual, debased creature you see him in his idle moments, he seems the god of the winds and the whirlpool. I think riding up the Cataract was one of the most delightful moments of my life. The inward excitement of European life is so great, its outward excitement so small, that a violent external call upon our senses and instincts to us is luxury and peace: the sense of power over the elements, of danger successfully overcome, is (to us, at least, the excitement of whose inner life has been so great) one of the keenest delights and reliefs.

We were four hours and a half surmounting the Cataracts. We left Syene at nine o'clock this morning, with all the "bigs" on board, viz. the Sheikhs, consisting of the "Great Father", his four sons, their children, and their grandchildren, four generations, and passed through "the opening" (which the name means), i.e. the rocky portals of Nubia, formed by Elephantina and Asouan. We wound our way, with a fair wind, to the foot of the First Rapid, about a mile from Asouan. Here were men posted on every rock to receive us, and we threw out our first rope. To me it would be the most interesting thing to go through every rapid with you; to describe the unerring aim with which the rope was thrown from the poop, — the man on the rock standing in the attitude of an Apollo Belvidere, watching the direction of the arrow, to receive it, his keen eye glistening with the eagerness of his watch. When a sunken rock came in view, twenty eyes had already seen it, and a dozen men had thrown themselves out upon it, and were pushing the boat off by main force, their feet only against the rock, their backs against the boat; or had plunged upon an opposite

bank, and, throwing themselves upon their backs, were pulling the rope towards them. On they sprang, from rock to rock, like chamois: I did not see one false step upon the shiny, slippery Syenite; one expected them to be dashed to pieces every moment. So the boat surmounted the First Rapid. Our rope was not strong enough, and if it had not been for a sudden puff of wind, which came exactly at the right moment, we should not have got through with our large boat; so Mr. B. said.

At the Second Rapid more men came: the divers sprang into the water, not head foremost, as ours do, but sitting, on their feet (for you must remember there is no question of sand banks here, but all hard granite), with the rope in their mouths, or under one shoulder and over the other, crossed a current which would have carried down an alligator, swam to a rock, made fast the rope *round* the rock, sitting on the noose, and holding it with their feet, while they kept their hands ready for action. Then all hands on board the boat pulled at the rope; and so we got through the Second, Third, and Fourth Rapids, which are short and straight, and the angle of pulling does not require altering. At dawn of day in the morning our decks had been cleared for action; everything carried into the cabins which could be moved, to leave space for the men; and the pantry, larder, still-room, and scullery piled up in a heap on deck, on which we were made to stand. Between every rapid comes a dead mill-pond, where old Nile rests from his labours, and where all the men came on board, they sat (as birds stand) upon the gunwale, not holding on by their toes, but the whole weight resting upon the back sinews of their legs, and balancing themselves by their ankles. They touch with nothing but their heels, and seem perfectly comfortable. I never saw such a feat; they look exactly like cormorants: our old Reis perched in the flukes of the anchor, which had been brought and laid on deck.

They do not swim as we do, but with their shoulders and arms out of the water, beating the water with their arms; and when they make a great effort, the head goes down under water, and they spring like porpoises. To see these men dive into the middle of a whirlpool, and go down where the bottom of the river is all granite, is to us like a feat of an Indian juggler going into the fire, almost incredible: or to see them come riding down a rapid upon a log, with their clothes on their heads! They come on board trembling, and their teeth chattering, where a companion receives them and wraps them in a sheet as tenderly as a bathing-woman, gives them a rub, and drags them to the fire kept burning on the bows, while Mr. B. administers the brandy. To see them watching the exact moment at which, and at no other, it will do to let the rope go, with all their senses, eyes, ears, touch, in a state as perfect as a dog's, is the most beautiful instinct I ever saw at work.

But there is a great deal beside this: the skill to seize the whirlpool exactly where, and as far as, it will carry the boat on; to profit by a counter current, and the moment it ceases to serve, and there is danger of the boat being whirled back — up with the sail, out with the ropes, forty hands overboard: — an instant, or, as Paolo calls it, a "lampo", and it would be too late. We approached the Fifth Rapid, and it seemed impossible that we could be going through that — the passage so narrow, the current so rapid, the rocks so sharp. We threw out two ropes, one on each side, for here our line of tactics altered: the rapid was too winding, the angles too numerous for us to pull to a stone; we had a line of men on each side to pull at us, and, of course, the fixed point wanting, the difficulty was greater. Crash went something: the right hand rope had broke, and the boat whirled round; but our bows caught upon the opposite rock. The other rope held, at which sixty men were pulling: the "bigs" worked like heroes, — in the water — out of the water; it reminded one of the time when chiefs were chosen for their bodily prowess, their strength in throwing, or swiftness in running — the ποδώκης Ἀχιλ-λεύς — and we

— *Warrior from Amhara* —

pulled through. By this time the rocks were lined with natives, many carrying spears and clubs. The wildness of the place is beyond expression, — not a palm, not a blade of grass; an expanse of heaps of Syenite, with rapids between them; the rocks hollowed out into the most inconceivable shapes, — some like bowls, some like boilers, some like boot-jacks, some like Etruscan vases, where little whirlpools must have established themselves in inundations. It is the most beautiful red Syenite: veins of quartz running through, mica and hornblende sparkling; sometimes layers of pure red pebbles set in rows in the mixed granite.

And here I must confess that the deafening, dizzying din of the crews takes away very much from the idea of the power. As for the "bigs" giving orders, it was out of the question; they were only understood by their gestures. One would have thought the consciousness of power would have been calm; one thinks of strength as so gentle: but I suppose it is only the intellectual that is still; and it is to remind us of the wide difference which lies between intellectual or moral power, and physical, that the latter is made so turbulent. However that be, the wild cries of these gods of the waves make the scene most grotesque, but not more impressive. At the Sixth Rapid — which is a long winding bay, where the wind fails in its help, and nothing is to be done but by sheer strength — we were put ashore, partly to see the other English boat, who, as Paolo said, "had got a stocked" (a stick, a blow), "and he leak". At the last rapid, our Sheikh had got out his new, his best rope, when the other broke: and now, with 120 (!) men pulling at this, and another rope to the stern to regulate the angle, slowly and steadily we saw her pulled up, and we floated into still water.

A mile further down we had seen a boat lost, her back broken, her yard just out of the water.

Abundance of salaams followed; we parted with our Sheikhs of four generations, and set our sail for Nubia. A mile further on, we came in sight of Philœ. There! there!

— Nubians —

Philæ on the Nile by Edward Lear (Spink & Son Ltd.)

look! it stole upon our sight gently and softly from behind its grey rocks, — such a contrast to Elephantina! It was the sleep of calm and lovely death, instead of the agony of convulsion. It was all that I had hoped and expected. The wind was not high, and we stole upon the rest of "Him who sleeps in Philœ" like whisperers, on tiptoe, just as one ought to do. But, alas! the envious wind freshened, and oh, we did not stop! I was so disappointed. But as we wore round her, for we took the Eastern passage, I saw long trains of camels, asses, and horses, with scarlet housings, on the river banks, and on the river four great boats full of worshippers, crossing over to carry these offerings; and high upon the island itself, a long procession of gaily-coloured robes, moving to the Hypæthral Temple. It was the worship of Osiris restored. We had come up stairs into the old world of 4000 years ago.

It was the Governor of Upper Egypt, transferred to the government of Ethiopia and on his way to Darfur, his seat of government, who had stopped here to visit Philœ; and one moment sooner or later, and we should not have seen this enchantment, charming back the old worship. How un-grateful of me to be disappointed.

A mile further, and we came to a ruined church, where my Padre Ryllo said his last mass on his way to martyrdom in Abyssinia. Paolo knew him in Egypt. *Not* Requiescat in pace; but let him work in glorious toil. Success not rest be with him.

Nubia (the golden, — alas! now the stony and barren) is everything as a contrast to Egypt; the river running between two rocky steeps; the rim of verdure diminished to a thread. We have a pilot who has been up to the Second Cataract four times this winter already.

A boat in sight! January 11th, near Derr, capital of Nubia.

AT IPSAMBOUL

January 17th.

MY DEAREST PEOPLE,

Here we are arrived at the last and greatest point of our voyage — greatest it is in all respects — I can fancy nothing greater. All that I have imagined has fallen short of Ipsamboul (of the great temple of the Osirides), and thank God that we have come here. I can conceive nothing in Thebes to equal this, and am well satisfied to turn back now, for we are to go no further. We arrived here on the 15th, about nine o'clock, and climbed the bank immediately to the lesser temple to see that first. There is no effect about the exterior at all, you don't know where the rock ends, and the temple begins, the slanting lines of the face of the temple (none of them parallel) are ugly, and the six colossal figures between the slants impossible to see, as the bank slopes straight down from the temple door to the river. Yet I have a love for the place; it is so innocent, so childish, so simple, so like the Athor, "the Lady of Aboccis" (the old name of Aboo Simbil) whom it represents. *Athor* means the habitation of Horus, and *Horus* means God; therefore Athor is nature, the world, in which God dwells, and which reveals Him. Her inscription calls her the "nurse, who fills heaven and earth with her beneficent acts". As such, she is identical with Isis. And her temple is so like nature, cheerful and simple, and to me at least, not very interesting, with her great broad innocent face and child-like expression, for it would not do if nature always kept us in a state of excitement. She is the same as the Grecian Aphrodite, yet how different –

The Lesser Temple at Ipsamboul

her simple, almost infantine, beauty to the more intellectual, yet at the same time more sensual, conscious beauty of the Greek Venus. It is the difference between Aspasia and Desdemona. She is also the goddess of joy, the lady of the dance and mirth, a sort of joy like that of children playing at daisy chains, not that of the feast of Epicurus. She is a secondary goddess, and her connection with the earth is more intimate than that of the real goddesses — her expression shows none of their supernatural serenity, but a simple enjoyment of her flowers and creatures.

The temple is small, the first chamber hewn in the rock and supported by six pillars, with the Athor head upon each; then a vestibule or pro sekos; then the sekos or sacred place, with her image in it. It was built by the Great Rameses, of the nineteenth dynasty, who reigned thirteen centuries and a half before Christ. The conqueror and Sesostris of the Greeks, and his figure, with those of his two queens, both evidently portraits, and one a most beautiful woman, are in "intaglio rilevato", all over the walls. Everywhere Rameses' queens occupy as conspicuous a place as himself. One only of the representations interested me much. It was the Great Rameses crowned by the good and the evil principle on either side. What a deep philosophy! — what theory of the world has ever gone farther than this? The evil is not the opposer of the good, but its *collaborateur* — the left hand of God, as the good is His right. I don't think I ever saw anything which affected me much more than this (3000 years ago) — the king at his entrance into life is initiated into the belief that what *we* call the evil was the giver of life and power as well as the good. Tell Aunt M. I thought of her when I looked at him, and of all she had taught me, and rejoiced to think how the same light dawns upon the wise from the two ends of space and of time.

The old Egyptians believed that out of good came forth evil, and out of evil came forth good; or as I should translate it, out of the well ordered comes forth the inharmonious, the passionate; and out of disorder again order; and both are a benefit. The Romans, who were a more literal people, and we their descendants, never understood this, and have set our faces against evil, like the later Egyptians, and scratched his nose.

Some people have seen a portrait of Joseph in the ass-headed god with square ears, Ombte. I myself incline to this opinion, considering him under the later idea; as I never could bear Joseph for making all the free property of Egypt into king's property, the fee simple of all Egypt into leasehold, the cause of half the evil at this present day.

But I am in a hurry to get on to the great temple, the Temple of the Sun, as he stands side by side with the modest little temple of his daughter, the mistress of the West, the lady of evening, of the morning star (Athor), who receives him every night at the end of his course behind her mountain, when he sets into her resting-place.

*　　*　　*

We clambered and slid through the avalanche of sand, which now separates the two temples. There they sit, the four mighty colossi, seventy feet high, facing the East, with the image of the sun between them, the sand-hill sloping up to the chin of the northern-most colossus.

Sublime in the highest style of intellectual beauty; intellect without effort, without suffering. I would not call it intellectual either, it is so entirely opposed to that of the Jupiter Capitolinus; it is more the beauty of the soul — not a feature is correct — but the whole effect is more expressive of spiritual grandeur than anything I could have imagined. It makes the impression upon one that thousands of voices do, uniting in one unanimous simultaneous feeling of enthusiasm or emotion, which is said to overcome the strongest man. Yet the figures are anything but beautiful; no anatomy, no proportion; it is a new language to learn, and we have no language to express it. Here I have the advantage; for being equally ignorant of the language of any art, I was as open to impression from them as from Greek or any other art. The part of the rock smoothed for the temple

face is about 100 feet to the highest row of ornament. Over the door is the image of the sun, and on either side an intaglio figure of the Great Rameses, offering, not burnt sacrifices, not even flowers, nor fruit, but a figure of *Justice* in his right hand. "Sacrifices and burnt offering thou hast

The Great Temple at Ipsamboul

not desired, else would I give it." "For what does the Lord require of thee, but to do justly."

What more refined idea of sacrifice could you have than this? Yet inside I was still more struck by the king offering justice to the God who gives him *in return life* and *purity* in either hand.

The door, which is about twenty feet high, does not reach nearly up to the knee of the colossus. Alas! the sand is now as high as three feet below the top of the door, and into this magnificent temple you have to crawl on all fours. But I am not sure that the effect is not increased by it. When you have slipped down an inclined plane of sand twenty feet high, which is like entering into the bowels of the earth, you

Entrance to the Great Temple

find yourself in a gigantic hall, wrapped in eternal twilight, and you see nothing but eight colossal figures of Osiris standing against as many square pillars which support the rocky roof, their arms crossed upon their breast, the shepherd's crook and the flagellum in either hand, for he is here in his character of judge of the dead, lord of Amenti, or the lower world of departed souls; and truly it looks like the lower world, the region of spirits; no light irritates your eyes, no sound annoys your ear, no breath of wind sets your teeth on edge; the atmosphere is much warmer than the outer air; this atmosphere, which is never stirred by anything but the beetle, the only creature light enough to tread this sand without being buried in it.

"Full of grace and truth", as his inscription bears, indeed he looks. I waited for him to speak; but he did not. Through two other halls I passed, till at last I found myself in a chamber in the rock, where sat, in the silence of an eternal night, four figures against the further end. I could see nothing more; yet I did not feel afraid as I did at Karnak, though I was quite alone in these subterraneous halls, for the sublime expression of that judge of the dead had looked down upon me, the incarnation of the goodness of the deity, as Osiris is; and I thought how beautiful the idea which placed him in the foremost hall, and then led the worshipper gradually on to the more awful attributes of the deity; for here, as I could dimly see through the darkness, sat the creative powers of the eternal mind, Neph, "the intellect", Amun the "concealed god", Phthah, "the creator of the visible world", and Ra, "the sustainer", Ra, "the sun", to whom the temple is dedicated. The heat was intense, it was as if this were the focus of the vivifying power of those attributes; and before them stood an altar, the first and last we shall see — the real old altar upon which stood the sacred ark. As to having had sacrifices here, it is physically impossible in any part of the temple; the door of the Osiris hall is the only outlet, and there is no possibility of any others.

I turned to go out, and saw at the further end the golden sand glittering in the sunshine outside the top of the door; and the long sand-hill, sloping down from it to the feet of the innermost Osirides, which are left quite free, all but their pedestals, looked like the waves of time, gradually flowing in and covering up these imperishable genii, who have seen three thousand years pass over their heads, and heed them not. In the holiest place, there where no sound ever reaches, it is as if you felt the sensible progress of time, not by the tick of a clock, as we measure time, but by some spiritual pulse which marks to you its onward march, not by its second, nor its minute, nor its hour-hand, but by its century-hand. I thought of the worshippers of 3000 years ago; how they by this time have reached the goal of spiritual ambition, have brought all their thoughts to serve God or the ideal of goodness; how we stand there with the same goal before us, only as distant as the star, which, a little later, I saw rising exactly over that same sand-hill in the centre of the top of the doorway — how to them all other thoughts are now as nothing, and the ideal we all pursue of happiness is won; not because they have not probably sufferings, like ours, but because they no longer suggest any other thought but of doing God's will, which is happiness. I thought how, 3000 years hence, we might perhaps have attained — and others would stand here, and still those old gods would be sitting in the eternal twilight. — Silent they sat and stern — and never moved; and I left them.

We shall never enjoy another place like Ipsamboul; the absolute solitude of it — the absence of a present, of any of one's fellow-creatures who contrast the past with that horrible Egyptian present. You look abroad and see no tokens of habitation; the power of leaving the boat and running up to the temple at any hour of the day or night, without a whole escort at your heels; the silence and stillness and freedom of it were what we shall never have again. At Luxor the present was such as to annihilate all pleasure in anything; and at Derr, where we stopped on the 13th for an hour, the cries and crowd were so insupportable that we saw the temple as quickly as we could, and I have no more idea of it at this moment than you have.

I came out of the penetralia and looked again upon the glorious colossi. I wish all my friends could see them once in their lives, if only for a moment; or that I could describe to anyone the look of intense repose in those faces. I think Europeans are perhaps better able to judge of them than any others, to Europeans they must be always more peculiarly affecting, the revelation of an entirely new kind of life. To us toil and excitement and restless anxiety are so familiar, that we have even consecrated them in Christianity. To the Greeks intellectual activity seemed the highest god they could frame. To the Egyptians calm of soul was the characteristic of a Divine Being. Their Osiris is never represented (at least nowhere that I have seen him) as sharing in the agitations of humanity, though he took upon him their nature.

It is so touching to come thus to the "ashes of their fathers and the temples of their gods", and even "to the tender mother that dandled them to rest", for here is Rameses' Queen — that beautiful tender face, — to descend into the bowels of the earth and find this revelation fresh and new, of a nation 3000 years passed away, that at first one is quite overwhelmed, and I assure you one is surprised to find oneself thinking of nothing at all, mechanically reading the names, which are alas scrawled over every statue, or counting the footsteps of the Scarabæus as he leaves his track upon the sand. It is like what one reads of people doing under a great blow, counting the fringe on the rug, or some such thing, instead of thinking of the event.

We went up to the top of the rock under which the temple is quarried, to look up the Nile. It is separated from the next cliff by a sand slip. I sighed for a walk in the Alps, the tropical Alps, and I walked round the valley and to the next mountain, and took a long last look south into Abyssinia, for further we were not to go. I saw nothing, met nothing, that had life, or *had had* life, but the whitened bones of a poor camel. And I reached the top of the next cliff. Oh, would I could describe that, my last real African view!— the golden sand, north, south, east, and west, except where the blue Nile flowed, strewn with bright purple granite stones, the black ridges of mountains, east and west, volcanic rocks, gigantic jet-black wigwam-looking hills. If you can imagine the largest glaciers you ever saw, the Mer de Glace at Chamouni, with all the avalanches golden sand, and all the ridges purple granite, not one blade of green anywhere, except where a sunk fence, for I can call it nothing else, bounds the river, and is cultivated with lupins, that is Nubia. It reminded me perpetually of the philosopher's stone. The people tried to make gold, and prayed to the Deity that he would turn all their soil to gold, and this must be the consequence. The banks of the rivers look like a beetle's back, green and gold, the rest of the country like one vast vein of metal ore.

They sent our Nubian steersman after their "wild ass of the wilderness"; but he found a nice bank of sand in the sun, and lay down on his face to sleep. I thought he had had an apoplectic stroke (for you can see figures miles off, as large as life in this atmosphere), and hastened to his assistance; whereupon he got up, and carried me down the next sand avalanche like a child. They help you so beautifully, these Nubians, that your feet hardly seem to touch the ground; the sand is so fine and soft that you sink at every step almost to your knees.

We came back to the dahabieh for candles and went all over the great temple. Every inch of it is covered with sculptures, perfectly uninjured except the colouring, which is gone, but the outlines are as sharp as ever. But what is the good of attempting to describe that which is now as sharply cut in my memory as in the stone, but of which I shall give no idea to you? It seems to me as if I had never seen sculpture before, as if the Elgin marbles were tame beside them! as if I had now begun to live in heroic times. The great Rameses holds by the hair of the head eleven captives

kneeling before him, in the presence of the god Ra, who decrees their destiny. Everything is done here in the presence of the gods. Rameses receives life and power from his patron Ra (after whom he is named), dedicates to him his victories, receives from him commands how his defeated

Ipsamboul

nations are to be disposed of. It reminds one of another nation and another leader, whose name only differs by the omission of the first syllable from Rameses. But the most curious part of the thing is the sublime expression of this Rameses — I never saw so beautiful a countenance. It is not a man murdering other men; it is the type of power. The captives too are not bound, but with their hands free, and some even holding daggers, so that indeed everybody has seen in it only an allegory expressive of dominion over the enemies of his country.

Three types of face in the captives are quite distinct; a negro, an Ethiopian and an Eastern, showing that, at this early period of Rameses' reign, his conquests had extended into Asia and south Africa. If it is really a portrait of Rameses, he must have been a noble creature. His name means "tried", or "regenerated by Ra", as Thothmosis means "regenerate by Thoth". The last two syllables Mss (for, in the old Egyptian, as in Arabic and Hebrew, there are no vowels) immediately recall another name — and Moses does mean "saved", "regenerate", "initiated".

The two long sides of the Osiris hall are taken up by the battle scenes, which make even a heroic age run round in a peaceful brain like mine. Rameses in his chariot, hurried along by his galloping horses, the reins twisted round his waist, drawing his bow upon the foe, in full career, preceded by his constant lion. Rameses dismounted and killing a chief whom he holds by the arm, in the exact attitude of the Pætus and Arria, so that one would think the artist of that must have seen this. Rameses in his chariot commanding. These below, and a row of Rameses in conference with different gods above, occupy all the south wall, while the north is a series of small battle-chariots standing on their heads, on their tails, in every possible position, while Rameses sitting is receiving a deputation of conquered nations. One king dismounts from his chariot and holds the reins with one hand, while he makes an obeisance to Rameses with the other. All this north wall relates to the first year of his reign; and the temple appears to have been finished early in his reign, as an inscription relating to the thirty-fifth on the south wall was evidently added afterwards. He reigned from 1388 to 1322 B.C. and Egypt is covered with his monuments — the Augustan age of Egyptian art.

All these figures are in "intaglio rilevato", very like Flaxman's outlines; the Rameses about ten feet high. But spirited as they are, I, for one, am very soon tired of them. I never made much hand of chivalry or Homer, and I returned back to my beloved adytum.

In Ipsamboul you first know what solitude is. In England, the utmost solitude you can obtain is surrounded by human beings; but there in the depths of the rock, in eternal darkness, where no sound ever reaches, solitude is no longer a name, it is a presence. In the evening we made a great fire upon the altar, and while our turbaned crew fed it, we sat in the entrance on the top of our hillock, and enjoyed the sight and feeling of the ancient worship restored. But then I knew that I liked, yes, and appreciated the Egyptian worship much more now in its desolate grandeur than then in its pomp and show. I felt as if the temple was profaned, and the solitude of the "Unutterable God" broken in upon — and I was glad when the blaze and glare were over.

Before sunrise the next day Σ and I were sitting on the soft warm fine sand, watching for the first rays of his own bright Egyptian sun to illuminate that glorious colossus. It was very cold; but oh! the luxury of that soft warm bed, without creatures, without damp, without dirt, which shakes off directly. When you are cold you bury your feet in it, and it warms them; when you are tired, you lie down upon it; when your head aches with staring, you sit and watch the scarabei with their pretty tracks; no cries for "Baksheesh", and "La Hawagee" (you merchant) pester you, and you are as happy as the day is long. But the day broke; the top of the rock became golden — the golden rays crept down — one colossus gave a radiant smile, as his own glorious sun reached him — he was bathed in living light — yes, really living, for it made him live, while the other, still gray, shadowy and stern as a ghost was unreached by the "Revealer of Life". We watched him till he too was lighted up, and then sat down over against the temple doors and looked in.

Interior of the Temple of Abu Simbel, Nubia by David Roberts (Fotomas)

The Marys could hardly have been more surprised when they saw the angel whose countenance was bright as snow, and knew that He whom they sought was risen, than we were when we saw the resurrection which had taken place there. One spot of golden light on the third Osiris spread and spread till it lighted up the cheek of the second and first. They smiled in their solemn beauty, but did not speak — a flush came over their faces for a moment — it was an awful moment — it was only a blast of sand stirring outside in the golden sunlight, but the reflection had lighted them up, and in this morning eastern light I could go over all the sculptures in the temple, and see them quite plain; but still my heart yearned for the solitary four in the holy place, whom no light ever approaches. I was surprised to find them still sitting there — they are so living — yet there they have sat for 3000 years, for 3000 years the Osiridæ have seen the sun rise as they saw it that morning, and will for thousands of years more.

*　　*　　*

In the afternoon it was announced, to my unspeakable delight, that we were to stay another day at Aboo Simbil, another sun to see rise there, another evening to watch the stars, the only thing we wanted was a moonlight.

I climbed up into the lap of one of the colossi, the southermost, who is quite uncovered, his knee is considerably above the doorway top.

To please them, I measured his middle finger, four feet. But to see my Hall of the Genii, my beloved Temple of Ipsamboul, all upon paper, with rule and line, brings it down to the level of Chatsworth in my imagination; and I won't give you the measurements of one of the colossi, I am afraid of getting like Dante. What does it matter whether Rameses' ear is two or three feet long? Champollion has dreadfully spoilt one of the colossi by whitewashing its face. I never look at that one. Imagine painting one of the pinnacles of Westminster Abbey red. It is a dissight from

The Sanctuary of the Great Temple

afar off. All that day I spent wandering about within the temple, and in the evening the new moon, like a silver boat, rested on the surface of the cliff for a moment, and then set, leaving behind it the old moon, plainly visible upon the top of the rock, after the silver thread was gone, for some moments. I never saw that sight before.

The next morning we were there again at dawn, and again saw the wonderful light, the resurrection of those colossi, their own eastern sun saluting them. In what their beauty consists it requires a wiser eye than mine to tell you — their faces are rounded, their foreheads are low, their lips thick, nothing which generally gives expression or saves from monotony, is there. The figures are clumsy, the shoulders unmodelled, the hands resting on knees like flounders, excessively short from thigh to knee, the legs like posts. Yet no one would say that those faces were expressionless, no one that has seen them, but they will live in his memory as the sublimest expression of spiritual and intellectual repose he has ever seen.

The ceiling of the great Osiris hall came out in the morning light — huge overshadowing wings crossed it from side to side. "He shall cover thee with his feathers, and under the shadow of his wings shalt thou trust." I never understood the Bible till I came to Egypt. "The Almighty shall overshadow thee;" and, "as a mother will I nurture thee." The vulture, whose shadowy wings are here portrayed, is the Egyptian symbol for a mother, and in this position, as protectress of men, she becomes a sublime representation. The king never goes out to battle, or "runs" into the presence of the gods, without this beautiful Eilethyia hovering over his head to protect him (though in a somewhat different form, with wings folded round her, instead of outspread). When she is the protectress of the country, Eilethyia spreads her glorious wings and holds two ostrich feathers in her claws, as in this ceiling. She is the beautiful head-dress of Rameses' queen, whose portrait is all over the temple, and who stands behind him in the captive picture, the most lovely countenance, her black hair gathered together with a golden fibula on the side of her forehead, and then falling on her shoulders. The second queen, a somewhat pug-nosed female, is offering to Athor in her temple, where the first also appears. Everywhere she occupies the place which the most advanced Christian civilisation gives to woman — always the one wife, nowhere

the face veiled, often the regent, the sovereign, or the co-ruler with a brother. Woman may be quite satisfied with her *Christian* position in old Egypt. The tricolor border of red, blue, and white runs round the ceiling, the sacred colours of light, wisdom, and purity.

Egypt is beginning to speak a language to me, even in the ugliest symbols of her gods; and I find there such pleasant talk — philosophy for the curious, comfort for the weary, amusement for the innocent.

The sovereign of Egypt really deserved to be a sovereign; for he appears to have been chief in every act, just as the superior of a religious order was, at first, intended to be the superior only in every act of difficulty, self-denial, or active benevolence; the king hardly ever appears carried by his fellow-men on an ignoble throne, but driving his own chariot, fighting the enemies of his country, or running full tilt on his own feet into the presence of the assemblies of the gods. This is how one oftenest sees him.

But a little representation of him there is on the side of one of the great Osiris pillars in Ipsamboul, which pleased me more than any. He is offering Truth to Mau, the son of the sun, who expresses the insight, light, or pure intellect of God, and sometimes the world, the "true image of God", but always "the highest property of God in nature as well as man". He is that property, if we may so speak, "which proves the reality of God's attributes by the truth", or definiteness of the manifestations he makes of himself in nature.

It is a beautiful idea — is it not? — this offering Thmei (Truth) to the god, but more peculiarly interesting to us from its being the original of the "Urim and Thummim". The Egyptian judges, who were all high priests, wore a breast-plate with Ra and Thmei, both in the dual (*lights* and *truths*), upon it; Ra in his double capacity of physical and intellectual light; Thmei perhaps as subjective and objective truth — i.e. truth as it appeared to the witness, and truth in an absolute sense. Now Urim and Thummim mean light and truth, the two lights and the two truths.

The judge gave judgment by touching one of the litigants with the figure as a token of the justice of his cause. I shall bring one home for Baron Rolfe. Dear Judge Coltman is gone where truths are no longer two (but all is one), and does not want it.

The king is represented so often with truth (or justice) as a fit offering for the gods; because, said the old Egyptians, this benefits your neighbours, while those pitiful other three cardinal virtues, prudence, temperance, fortitude, benefit only yourself. They knew a thing or two, those old Egyptians, don't you think so? When they spoke of a dead friend, they did not say, as we do, the "lost", or the "deceased", which is not true, as we all acknowledge in the Prayer Book, nor "poor so and so"; but the "justified" (matu); for the dead, who were found worthy, bore on their heads the feather of Truth or Justice, and took her hieroglyph.

I wish I could tell one half their philosophic ways. I must not forget the sacred boat in which people have seen Noah and his Ark, the Arkite worship, and all sorts of things, but which seems to be only a very natural emblem for a country which lived by its inundations, whose god Neph, "the Spirit of God which moved upon the face of the waters", was called "Lord of the Inundations", and was very likely, with the Egyptian want of imagination, to do this in a boat.

There are eight little chambers hewn in the rock, opening out of the Osiris hall, and covered with sculptures of offerings; but as these must be gone through with a candle, and it is impossible to enjoy anything in that way, I do not describe them. Some of them are left unfinished, as the workmen left them 3000 years ago — the line drawn but not cut.

The temple of Ipsamboul is the only thing which has ever made an impression upon me like that of St. Peter's, yet how different. We bade him adieu at nine o'clock that morning. I never thought I should have made a friend and a home for life of an Egyptian temple, nor been so sorry to look for the last time on that holiest place.

We bade him goodbye, and turned our prow north-

Fortress on the Nile

wards, for we were to go no further. Our poor yard had been already taken down, and laid along from end to end. Our proud *Parthenope* no longer floated in the Nile breeze, and we, our eyes full of sand and tears (which made mud), very hungry, very sorry, very tired, watched from the deck the last of the colossi.

ON BOARD THE *PARTHENOPE*

January 21st.

WELL, DEAREST PEOPLE,

At last I have a letter from you (dated 22nd November), sent after me from Cairo, and tumbled into our boat like one of Abraham's messengers before the door of his tent.

We went up to Gerf Hossayn with the whole village at our heels: a splendid position it is, high in the western rocks, and overlooking the whole wide valley of the Nile, from which the sunlight had just disappeared, and was kissing with its parting golden beam the eastern side. In the solemn twilight we entered the awful cave of Phthah, the God of Fire, the Creator. The Sheikh of the village, with his descendants, walked before us, carrying great serpents of fire to light up the rude magnificence of this terrible place. The serpents were thick twisted coils of palm fibre set on fire; but they looked like Moses' serpent set up in the wilderness; and twisted and flamed before this fire shrine, this God of the Hidden Fire, who has his dwelling in the thick darkness. I never saw a wilder scene. Hephaistos, the degenerate Vulcan of the Greeks, is a corruption (his name evidently so) of Phthah. I should like to have seen this dwelling of the "Heavenly Fire" (who will some day welcome back the "tired spirit" to its "accustomed home" and refine away all but the pure ore) in silence and stillness, for I can tell you very little about the temple. With an Arab holding you under each arm, for fear of your falling over the heaps of stones, a dozen others with torches, the temple perfectly chuck full, the whole population being there to look at you, and the din quite overpowering in that close cave, the whole population being there to hoot at you — it is impossible to have an idea under such circumstances — the very strangeness of the scene absorbs you. And as to understanding the ideal of the sculptures, with the flickering light illuminating them at one moment, and the next leaving them in total darkness, you might as well try to understand the poetry of the Bible, when you were picking it out, for the first time, in Hebrew. All I saw was (on either side) three figures of Osiris, so gigantic, that they seemed to crowd you in; and you could not get far enough from them to look up at their faces. Their pedestals were perfect and uncovered, which we had never before seen. The figures were so rude, the blocks so enormous, that the effect, though not so artistic as that of Aboo Simbil, was infinitely wilder, — more awful. It was like a Cyclopean cave, or a western forest, not like the art of man. Beyond this great hall in the rock is another chamber, supported by two thick, square pillars, and then the holy place, with half-destroyed deities in the niche.

*　　*　　*

I should not wish for a greater contrast than the four temples we have seen in two days — Dakkeh, Gerf Hossayn, Kalabsheh, and Beit el Welee: the philosophical minutiæ and analytic subtleties of Hermes Trismegistus, — the rude

Nubian Leading a Camel by Frederick Goodall (Fine Arts Society)

and awful grandeur of Phthah's cave, — the upstart magnificence and vulgar showiness of the terraces and buildings of Kalabsheh, — and the exquisite little gem of art of Beit el Welee! The first is Ethiopean, the third Roman, and the second and fourth of the great Rameses, though as

The Temple at Gerf Hossayn

distinct as possible. The first stands upon a sandy plain, and looks out from the top of its propylon (as philosophy, with her broad view and distant glance, ought to do). The second, with her savage, awful devotion, is a cavern in the rock. The third has great stone Chatsworth terraces, almost

like gardens, down to the river. A wilderness of hewn stones and elaborately carved capitals lies about, while the sacred place is unfinished. The fourth is a perfect little specimen of painting and sculpture, perched at the top of a rock.

We went to see it first. I never saw anything so pretty: the colours are more perfect than any we have seen; and it does not give one in the least the effect of barbarism. Who calls the Loggie barbaric? It is not at all more gay than those gems of Raphael's art. It is true that here these are intaglios, which are so coloured; but the distinction seems a fanciful one, — why should not intaglios be coloured? The place is not at all darker than Raphael's *Stanze*. There are but two chambers in the rock, the prosekos and adytum. The next is the area without. As we have the casts of the sculptures in the latter in the British Museum, and as we mean, when we come back, to take a small lodging for six months over the greengrocer's in Great Russell Street, for the sake of studying these and others, I shall not trouble you with describing them now. On one side is the Great Rameses receiving eastern captives from a nation, the Shorii, who rebelled during his father's time, and whom he reduced. Further on, he is beleaguering a negro town, and holding a captive negro *over* the town, whose legs dangle high above it, Rameses being a great deal bigger than the fortifications. On the other side he is receiving the prince of Cush (Ethiopia), who is bringing tribute; and further on himself, in a chariot, and two lesser sons behind, in chariots with charioteers, (I like this so much — the king always does the most work, he never has a charioteer) he is pursuing the enemy into the woods of *Lebanon,* where a wounded chief, leaning on his companions, is being taken home. A child runs to tell his mother, who is unconsciously cooking under a tree; another clings to its father's knees, and throws dust upon its head.

The triad, in the sacred place, is Amun Ra, Neph, and Anouke. Rameses is offering to Amun Ra, who is blue, to denote his heavenly nature. The cartouches are on a gold ground, with Ra, the sun, Rameses' own deity (a red disk), upon it; and his favourite Thmei, white — very pretty. Neph, in the adytum, is giving Rameses life and purity. But the jewel, the precious thing of the whole, is behind the door of the sacred place — Anouke, the Egyptian Vesta, and goddess of domestic purity, whispering advice into the ear of Rameses. With one hand (the most delicate, beautiful hand) she takes him under the chin, like a child, holding up his face. The other arm falls over his shoulder. She is considerably bigger than he is; yet anything like the perfect grace of the figure — the beautiful feminine grace, I never saw. And the child-like attitude of the great hero, as the goddess breathes her admonitions into his ear; the simplicity and humility of the conqueror; the youthful dignity of the virgin goddess — a more beautiful ideal never entered the mind of man. And a fond and a faithful husband it is evident he was; and in the next compartment, to show how he attended to the words of the goddess, his wife appears with him at sacrifice. They were happy women, those Egyptians of olden times, to be under the protection of such an admonitrix.

We came down from Beit el Welee (the "house of the saint": it was a Mahometan hermit's abode, Beit the same as the Bible Beth, meaning house), as soon as it was dusk; not because we had done with it, but because we really could not stay in the press and the din, and went to Kalabsheh, which is just under the cliff, through a ruined town of heaps of stones, out of which the few remaining huts reared their low heads, as if by mistake; sheep's heads, and cows' heads, and human heads were seen just sticking out of the stones. One could not divine what they were doing there.

Kalabsheh is the biggest temple in Nubia. I never saw anything so magnificent nor so vulgar. It must have been the work of some upstart *nouveau riche,* — a Roman Hudson. The heaps of ruins have struck everybody as something incredible — arch, portico, pronaos, naos, adytum, all are

full of enormous blocks of hewn stone. How they came there is the wonder, or, if they were ever put up, how they ever came down. You climb up mountains of stone, and down again, which is the only method of proceeding in this temple. One enormous block, which had roofed the

The Temple of Kalabsheh

adytum, was cracked (it must have been done by a tremendous blow from above), and now bent like a rotten beam. The ruins were like a stone builder's yard. They did not strike one with wonder or awe, but with a feeling of dreary confusion and wasted expense. The adytum was unfinished; the gods were Roman soldiers, with Egyptian animal heads on the top. Terrace upon terrace, and column upon column, lay in useless magnificence and extravagance,

The Cook by Jean Discart (Mathaf Gallery)

and a miserable Arab mud wall blocked up the entrance. Two of the crew dragged me up and down the ruins (which looked as if they had never been put up) in the moonlight; and we gladly came back to the boat, where we lay at anchor an hour, while Paolo bought a black sheep (who sits up on his hind legs like a dog), milk, and eggs, and Mustafa bought henna, with which he and two others of the crew dyed their beautiful hands red. Mustafa is the cook, and came in this morning to show his hands. I bargained for some of the women's ornaments, but they asked such an extravagant price that my mercantile British spirit forbade. I could not help thinking, had a third genus been by to have seen that deck full of Europeans and Nubians — not more separated perhaps are men and animals — with nothing to bridge over the impassable chasm between them, how melancholy it must have seemed.

After this moonlight fair, we made for the rapids of Kalabsheh, which are nearly as dangerous as those of the first cataract, and can only be passed when there is absolutely no wind, as the slightest puff either way would drive you on to the rocks, where the force of the rushing waters is tremendous. The river here is very narrow, and hemmed in on both sides with great purple volcanic walls, and islands standing piled up in the water, looking like great black monsters, — crocodiles with their mouths open, &c. — the wildest scene I was ever in. The men were rowing vehemently, as it requires all their skill to keep the boat straight. Mr. B. was in the inner cabin, Σ and I sitting on the divan on deck, watching the descent. We were floating down into a deep, dark pool, where the moonlight lay in great masses on the black waters, when we saw the whole crew start up, fling down their oars, and begin to fight violently. A confused mass of arms and legs and African blankets lay all together in the hold, howling, and screaming, and kicking, the boat of course drifting down upon the rocks meantime. In a moment, however, out

rushed Paolo with an ebony club, — which I had bought from the Berber savages coming up the cataract, and which hung in the cabin, — fell upon the mass of struggling heads, and began to belabour them with all his might, so that I thought he would have broken in their skulls. He was alone against the eleven, but he did not seem to think of it, though he was generally a great coward, nor they either; and by sheer battering he parted them, and drove them back to their oars. It was all over in a moment; but anything like the total *imprévoyance,* the savage recklessness of their own lives, I could not have conceived.

We found afterwards that one of the crew (the best man among them) had accidently struck the rower before him with his oar; the Arabs are excessively fiery, and the man chose to consider it an insult and returned the blow. The offender was a rather lonely man whom the crew disliked, and therefore the whole body except one man (who stood by him manfully) took part against him. The next day there was a great begging pardon, plenty of bruises to be plaistered, and everybody friends with everybody. It was the most savage scene morally and naturally I certainly shall ever see.

Kalabsheh is the ancient Salmis, Dakkeh the ancient Pseleis; and if I did my historical duty, I should tell you of the wars which the Romans and Queen Candace, who had but one eye, carried on here. But you know I like a law any day better than a war. Even the wars of my beloved hero, the great Ram, I have not patience to tell, though I hail his features wherever I see them. And I have never so much as mentioned his temple at Derr (the capital of Nubia), hewn in the rock, where he appears with his faithful lion. But I really don't remember it; I only remember looking out between the portico columns, and thinking that I was in the capital of the Laputæ, or of some other of Gulliver's countries — so strange, so little like the dwellings of human beings did this capital look. A sycamore by the river's shore,

Fellahin

which was the coffee-house, was the only thing human — the white domes or bee hives, the mud walls without windows, which enclosed a yard, in the corners of which were the lairs of families, the nests of little naked children, squatting between two stones (like nests of young foxes) — running away when you looked at them, and then baying like jackals after you, and looking so happy and so fat, their costume combining lightness with elegance, a string of beads round the neck, and another round the loins, small bones, well covered and well made — things which looked about four months old, climbing about like lizards, and never so much as scratching their little feet, the mothers carrying their babies across their hips, many with nose-rings; — whether I was Gulliver or Captain Cook, I don't know, — but certainly all this was as much out of our common habits of thought as if I had been either.

Yesterday we left the tropics — oh, how sorry I was! This morning I parted with my three pets, the chameleons which I have had ever since we were in Nubia. I grandly sacrificed them, and would not tear them from their beloved tropic, as I was torn; so set them ashore this morning, instead of going to see a temple. We bought them of some Arabs at Ipsamboul. Three belonged to me, and one to the crew, who gave him to me to take care of. Mine were very aristocratic, however, and tormented him so dreadfully that he died: they were all sadly quarrelsome. One was a capital shot, and shot all the flies, for his own use, at the first blow: he was slight and agile. The largest was very stupid, and a bad shot besides. They were of a greenish yellow, the colour of the mimosa leaves. I used to sprinkle a mimosa bough with sugar, which brought the flies, and then the chameleons came round and shot them with their tongues. When they were angry they became bright yellow, and when afraid, brown, with purple spots. Their use in the world is to free it from flies, and they will kill fifteen in a quarter of an hour sometimes. They are three inches long as to the body, three inches as to the tail, three inches as to the tongue. They used to hang themselves up by their tail and pretend to be dead, that the flies might come and settle on them; and my three would do it in order to entice the one belonging to the crew close up to them, and then beat him.

Island of Philœ

Today we leave Nubia, where we have been just a fortnight — tonight we shall be at Philœ.

24°5′N. LAT.

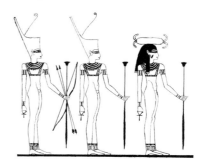

January 28th.

Goodbye, Philœ — φιλη indeed to me: Goodbye, dear Philœ, beautiful Philœ, whose very name from this time has a magic in it to our ears, to make sad moments joyful — to people solitary moments — to make us young again when we are old. Oh, Philœ, whom I shall never see again, may she be to many others what she has been to us during the happy, happy week which we have spent there; and may she live again some day herself, when Egypt is a happier world. Fare thee very well, my dear and holy Philœ. I never *loved* a place so much — never felt a place so homey: thank God for all we have felt and thought there. Every moment of that precious week, from before sunrise to long after moonlight had begun, I spent upon the Sacred Island, most of it in Osiris' chamber. This morning we came away at daybreak, rushed down the cataracts, and found ourselves again in the nether world, after having been in a place so curiously raised up and bounded in by nature, that our three weeks in Nubia seem to us as if they had been spent in another star. Sorry enough we were to leave her, and to come down again: but there is a time for everything, as Solomon says.

I cannot describe to you the feeling at Philœ. The myths of Osiris are so typical of our Saviour that it seemed to me as if I were coming to a place where He had lived — like going to Jerusalem; and when I saw a shadow in the moonlight in the temple court, I thought, "perhaps I shall see him: now he is there".

The chamber of Osiris was like the place where *He* was buried; and after our little service on the Sunday morning, I went and sat there, and thought *I* had never sat in any place so sacred, nor ever could, except in Syria.

The position of the island, high above the water (the Greeks called it *abaton*), the calm, shadowy *lake* around (which the Nile becomes there), the "Golden Mountains" (the Hemaceutæ), which hem it in, the stillness, the tufts of wild palms, which grow out of the clefts of the rocks all round the island, the solitude — for all its Arab inhabitants have deserted it, — there *can* be nothing like Philœ in the world! The first moonlight night that I sat on a broken colonnade *in Philœ, by the temple of Isis, within the roar of the Cataract,* I kept repeating those words to myself that I might believe them, and felt how far the reality surpassed the words. Excepting a solitary sakia, which often goes the whole night round, the Cataract's roar is the only sound which rocks the rest of him who sleeps in Philœ, and none disturb his sleep. The full moon hangs her lamp over his solitary bier, but no other funeral lights are there.

And, first of all, I must prepare you for the fact that everything in Philœ is *ugly*. The hypæthral temple is hideous: the sculptures (after what we have been accustomed to in Nubia, of the times of the great Rameses) would disgrace a child — ill drawn, ill cut, ill painted. Not a building remains, excepting one pylon (the first), in the temple of Isis, of a time earlier than that of the degenerate Ptolemies, and everything is in as bad taste as all that the Ptolemies did. The Puritans — I mean the Persians — have destroyed every vestige of the old part. There is nothing left which the most enthusiastic lover of the Egyptians could call beautiful; but the spirit that reigns over all is divine; and I think that this very failing effort of the fading nation to embody their old spirit makes it the more affecting. It is like the last leaping up of the light in the socket, which shows the dying face you loved, of which the spirit is still beautiful, though the body is disfigured and agonising — it is like the last dying words, the farewell. I am not sure that I did not love Philœ better for her struggle to say one thing more to our watching ears, to teach us the great truths *she* felt so deeply with her last failing breath. Now rest in peace, dear Philœ. She has done her work, her mission is accomplished; — it is finished.

Many times the last night did I put my head out of the window, and saw by the full moon the palm trees waving over the temples, the tomb of Osiris, till I knew every line by heart. Now our Passover is over, our Passion Week is at an end; but I shall always think of it as my Holy Week.

But I must come to "meaner things, my St. John". We found the —— there. He is making a series of drawings of the temple of Isis, and is a picture himself; he always wears the Turkish dress — a blue gubbeh, white kaftan, red turban, and a long white beard: his wife, a nice little woman, young and pretty, always sits by him. One night in Philœ we "dined out" in their princely tent at Mahatta. A *diner-en-ville* in Nubia is charming. Carrying our chairs with us, our carpet and cushions, and having put on everything we had in this world, we went, about moonrise, in our little boat, threading our way through the defiles of the Nile, piles of rocks towering over us in grotesque shapes on every side, and with the current we floated down in about half an hour, till we landed at a sandy place, and, preceded by our Arabs carrying the furniture, we scrambled along Brook Street, which was a bank of sand intermingled with very large stones, from the top of which a lady, who wanted to sell her silver bracelets, threw them down at us (which is the

The Temple of Philœ by David Roberts (Mathaf Gallery)

method of traffic in Nubia). I bought those same bracelets for thee, my dear P——; they came from Darfur, and are the only pretty things I have seen here.

Then we went through some palm gardens, by some sleeping camels, and were announced at Mr. and Mrs. ——'s by our Arab (with our two chairs on his back, and our carpets wrapped round his head) crawling upon his face under the ropes of the tent, and into the tent upon his knees. Mr. —— came out, like a rather fine gentleman as he is, and expanded himself in compliments. He had got a young Englishman to meet us — he was so happy — we were so kind, &c.; and Mrs. ——'s Cairene woman, trowsered and veiled, stood like an Oriental slave while we took off some of our blankets. The tent was, however, bitterly cold; our dahabieh is more comfortable. I must tell you that the thermometer varies here 90° in 24 hours, from 30° at night — for it has actually frozen — to 120° in the sun; and this, in a country where there is no possibility of protecting oneself artificially, excepting by clothes. When one is cold in Egypt, one waits till the sun is hot.

The dinner was very much like a London dinner: Mr. —— was fine and courteous; Mr. —— was stupid and silent; Mrs. —— was nice and *naïve*. They have just had their house in Cairo burnt. The Pacha next door wanted the ground for his garden, and sent a slave *to burn it,* the method of purchase in Egypt. No drawings, however, luckily, were lost. His figures are beautiful — his buildings commonplace and literal. After having drunk as much coffee as we could, we walked down to the beach, in preparation for going home — Mr. ——, shuffling first, in Turkish slippers, and losing one among the sand; his Nubians following with our chairs and carpet. We came home again by a counter current in ten minutes, cutting in through the rocks by the moonlight. But these late hours destroy one's health: we were not home till nine o'clock.

Nubians

Another day I went with Mrs. —— to Bidji, the neighbouring island, to see her little friend Zehnab, a child of four years old, the daughter of a widow of sixteen. Zehnab's aunt, of ten, who is just married, and who showed us her house with great pride, the nicest in the island, swam over to see Mrs. —— at Mahatta this morning: everybody swims here. Bidji is almost entirely peopled with one family, the original grandfather and his posterity. We asked Zehnab's mother how old she was. "How *could* she tell? Her mother knew." They all slept out of doors in the summer, in the winter on the clay divan at the end of the hut. But everybody had their own hut; and Zehnab's swimming aunt had two cushions!! There was no other article of furniture, however, but the clay divan and the jars in hers or in any other house; they were swept out very clean; you could not stand upright in them; there was always, however, one room for the family and another for the chickens. But, alas! the chickens, and the eggs, and the doura bread are all kept for the men; and the women live on the leaves of the bean, raw and boiled, and on doura cakes. They wanted Mrs. ——'s wedding ring, and listened with great attention to her story of our marriage ceremony. Then they asked if her husband beat her, and were astonished to hear he did not; next how much he had "given for her" — as in Egypt the husband gives the dowry, not the father; and when she said thirty shillings, they said "it was very cheap". (The thirty shillings was true, for she was obliged to be married before the cadi; and Mr. —— gave away thirty shillings to the poor to satisfy the cadi's question.) That one man should keep faithful to one woman his whole life, and not send her back to her parents, and marry another, is more unheard of among the poor than among the rich, because the rich man maintains all his wives by etiquette — the poor man just sends them back.

Zehnab had a little row of beads round her neck, and another round her waist — nothing else. I tried to persuade Mrs. —— to take her and educate her, and send her back to educate the island. The women never pray; no Mahometan poor woman does, excepting the haggs or pilgrims. On the island was a little heap of stones, where a man mounted (the elder of the village) to call to mosque on Fridays, in the open

Ruins of a temple on the Island of Bidji

air. The belief among the women in a future state seems to be very small; if they express any feeling about it at all, it is that they shall be servants there to the men.

I walked across the Island of Bidji, such a wild, but not desolate walk, through a wilderness of rocks, to a solitary burial-ground (each grave marked only by a little circle of stones), in a valley on the *top* of the island, and down to a deep green pool or tarn left by the Nile, on the other side, with a tuft

Portico of the Temple of Philæ by David Roberts (Fotomas)

of palm trees, a hut or two, and a little oasis of green in the middle of that chaos of piled rocks. Another day we walked along the eastern shore of the Nile to the ruined Christian church, where Padre Ryllo said his last mass. The huts are not so sordid, and the population not so "rubbishy" near Philœ as elsewhere.

Mr. ——, to whom we had a letter, came the evening before we left, with his Abyssinian daughter, the child of an Abyssinian woman. I liked her much; a really sensible nice girl — black. He is very learned and very queer.

On Monday morning we left our beloved mooring place. I cannot tell you *why* Philœ is so dear. It is like a friend of whose face one does not think whether it is ugly or beautiful — one does not *know*. So different, too, from Ipsamboul, with its depths of stillness, which I loved as much, in a different way. Philœ is cheerful, living, sunny, compared with Ipsamboul, and yet the roar of the Cataracts is not like life; it is like eternity, and everything in Philœ seems like another world.

*　　*　　*

If the going *up* the Cataracts was strange, it was nothing to the coming *down*. We set off before sunrise, as it is necessary to have no breath of wind, with the "bigs" and all their men on board. Our boat is the largest that has ever been up the Cataracts, and we came down a passage which is very rarely used, as the tossing rapid would swamp a smaller boat. It was widened for Ibrahim Pacha's steamer. Σ went on shore, but I stuck by the old boat, and truly it was a sight worth seeing how she gradually accelerated her speed as she approached the rapid, which, foaming and tossing, with scarcely two feet on either side our oars, seemed as if no boat could live in it, then took the leap like a racehorse, so gallantly, and went riding down the torrent as if she enjoyed it. Three times her bows dived under water (I don't mean that the waves broke over the boat, — that they did all the time, and half filled her with

The Hypœthral Temple at Philœ

water, and all our biscuit, too, which was of more consequence), but three times she dived under water up to the kitchen, and rose again; twice she struck, but gallantly triumphed over all her enemies, and long before I have written this one line we were at the bottom, and swung round at the end of the rapid — the first time this feat has been tried, as boats are generally run ashore on the bank at the foot of the Cataract, as the only alternative. Of course, everything depends on the steering, and the oldest "big" of all, the "Great Father", mounted on the poop by his steersman, whence they did steer like masters. The boat obeyed, and we verged not an inch to the right or the left. Σ, who watched us from the shore, thought that we could not be going down that place, that the boat had not minded its rudder, and that they had run her down there as the only resource. I suppose such a feat of steering is without parallel in any other country. The Cataract by which we came down runs into the main stream at right angles, like water out of a cock; we were steered on the edge of the gush, on the left edge, so that when we came to the bottom, by the motion of the rudder and a vigorous pull of the oars on one side (our men were rowing with their whole might all through the descent), the bows were got out of the current on the left, which caught the stern, and the boat turned on her centre like a pivot, and swung round into still water; this is a new feat.

Mr. B—— and I sat on the pantry, embracing our water jar, on the top of which we received the congratulations of all the "bigs" and of all their men, who all shook hands with us, and cried "Salaam!" the moment it was over. There was but one more little rapid to pass, and when we arrived at Syene, and were quietly at breakfast, the great "big" came in, and then the pilots, and solemnly applied my hand to his lips and forehead, and kissed Mr. B—— on the top of his head, and then asked for Baksheesh. The dignity with which an Arab shakes hands with you and begs is charming.

The old Sheikh ended by presenting me with his *pillow*, which I hope you will not mistake for a gigantic brown beetle, with many legs. It was not, though, for its curiosity that he gave it, but as a useful piece of furniture — a wonderfully large piece of hard wood such as could not be found nearer than Abyssinia.

But the fun of funs was to see us riding up to Mahatta in the afternoon to pay a series of morning calls *at the Cataract*. We came down the wildest of rocky passes, walking (it was too steep for the donkeys, who followed), and there lay the English fleet — six boats, in a little creek of the Nile below the Cataracts; they had not been up; it was exactly like a wood-cut in one of Captain Cook's voyages — the savage scene, the neat English boats and flags in the little bay. So we scrambled down, in company with three camels; while the men of Mahatta pop out upon us, brandishing their spears right in our faces for fun, and making our asses to turn aside, but we insist upon going on, and so make our calls.

We found Mr. Murray at Asouan, just arrived; but there was such a "ruck" of English boats there — all the N —— party, and a thousand others — and nothing to eat, for they had devoured everything like locusts, even all the rice and milk of Syene, that we turned savage and sailed before sunrise. This animal (that's us) it is impossible to tame; it can never be domesticated, but remains in its savage state in spite of all the kindness (and constraint) that can be lavished upon it.

I was glad enough to get away from Syene, which I cannot bear; and would not so much as go over again to Elephantina.

I have seen the mirage once, and except that I knew it was impossible that the Nile could have got into the place where we saw it, should not have been much struck with the sight.

I must not forget to record that we saw a few drops of rain on the sand one day in Nubia, preserved by the sand as a curiosity in its natural museum in little round holes made for the purpose.

NEAR THEBES

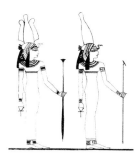

February 3rd.

MY DEAREST MOTHER,

We have been a week coming from Asouan to Thebes, owing to a strong north wind against us, and bitter weather, such as Paolo, who has been up the Nile twenty-five times, says he has never felt the like of. The wind is like March, and the whirlwinds of sand such that you feel like a hippopotamus in your skin, and the air is nothing but a sand rain, and the river a sand bank. We have been forty-eight hours at Esne, from sheer inability to get on, scarcely going on shore because of the blinding sand, though hardly able to keep ourselves alive in the boat. Everything in the boat looks as if it had not been dusted for a month, and my paper is so covered with sand that I am afraid you will hardly be able to read this.

Tonight the wind a little fell, and we immediately took advantage of it, to pull all night, hoping to be at Thebes tomorrow.

We have had twenty-four days of this wind, — a thing quite unprecedented in the annals of Egypt, where three days' wind is the calculation, and then calm.

We have seen, on our way, Kôm Ombo, a stupid temple, and the quarries of Hadjar Silsileh, the same afternoon. They are sandstone, like our own in Derbyshire. It was a beautiful day, and a very pleasant walk; the next morning Edfoo, a Ptolemaic temple; the people did not beg; the breed of cows, with heads like antelopes, was the most beautiful I ever saw;

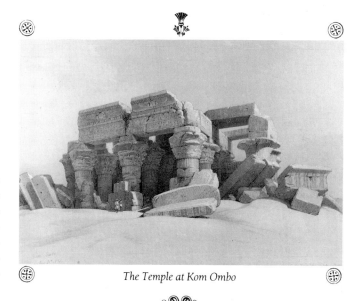

The Temple at Kom Ombo

and the brown sheep, with large ruffs round their necks, holding their heads erect, and with lively, intelligent manners, like dogs, came to look at us and speak to us. A donkey on the roof of the temple must have walked upstairs: the whole roof was crowded with huts, the scale of the building magnificent, the propylæum 120 feet high; but we did not even attempt going up, the atmosphere was in such a state with sand.

The Tailors' Shop by Benjamin Constant (Mathaf Gallery)

The next morning we rose up early, saddled our ass, took our young men, and rode three miles into the desert to Eilethyia, the oldest ruins in Egypt. The donkeys had no bridles, but a cord round their necks. I could choke my donkey, but I could not stop him. However, they knew their business much better than we did. The desert was not an ugly desert, but a beautiful valley with isolated rocks standing up in it, and rocky sides; no verdure, of course; it was like the gigantic bed of a dried-up pre-Adamite river, not like a crumbling desolation. In this vast valley we found a "lodge in the wilderness", a little chapel built by Amunoph III, the last king but one of the XVIII Dynasty, 1638 B.C. with the colours of the sculptures as fresh as if they had been just done. Here the people must have come out from Eilethyia for evening sacrifice; and it looked like a place of worship, so still and holy, sitting on its little stone platform. It is dedicated, of course, to Eilethyia, and on the door is a little sculpture of the great Rameses, attended by his son, a priest, in the office of fan-bearer. His fan is a feather of the sort which Eilethyia, when she covers the roofs of temples with her wings, bears in her claws, meaning that with her fans she shall thoroughly purge her floor.

In the northern hills are the famous painted tombs of Eilethyia, about one of which (that of the Admiral of Amosis, the restorer of the empire after the Shepherds, 1638 B.C.) everyone has heard. I think they are very curious but very tiresome. They give Sir Charles Grandison of old Egyptian life, and it is such a bore going over all those details, that one of them is quite enough, and that we had at Beni Hassan. There is one comfort, however, to be drawn from them, that the conventionalities of social life are the same in the two ends of Time and Space — the master and mistress sitting before dinner, with the company in rows, the ladies smelling at their nosegays, and a little music to amuse them, is exactly what 100 mistresses of 100 country houses endure every day in an island

the Egyptians had never heard of, and at a time near 4000 years off.

The crude brick wall of the old town of Eilethyia, which lies below its tombs, and at the mouth of its valley, is gigantic. Imagine a square of about a third of a mile to the side, with walls thirty-five feet thick (Mr. B. measured them), and inclined planes twenty-five feet more, leading to the top, as is the case in the old Egyptian towns: the square seemed thoroughly cleared out, scarcely a vestige of a ruin in it; but these colossal walls, the colour of them, the awful size, make one think of a time before the Ichthyosauri.

On the top of an isolated rock farther up the valley, which we passed, all the modern population of Eilethyia, women and children, collect on their New Year's Day, and spend the whole day there, taking their food with them, for prayer — those who can. Such a pleasant plan.

The next day we were at Esne, the centre of the manufacturing interest, with a royal palace and gardens.

We were astonished when we went ashore to see blue linen dyeing and hanging across the streets, so that the passengers had to lift it up as they went along; shops, and a market place: and, passing into the bazaar, we saw — oh, what a moment! a bale of Manchester goods! Here we burst into tears — no, we *ought* to have done so, but didn't: no emotion did the Manchester mart produce in my mercantile soul. But stop, do not condemn me, it was Sunday, and my Sabbatical habits forbade even to *feel* anything at the sight of cotton on the day of shop-shutting. I thought of the streets of Manchester on a Sunday, made a rigid face, and passed on. We went to the Pashalik garden; mint its only produce; into the Pashalik palace. A sarsenet French bed (of tawdry gilding mixed with dirty blue, not so good as what you would see at a small theatre), its only furniture. The guide showed Mr. B. *what it was for,* and how to use it! as we had, of course, never seen a bed before! No other article of furniture was in the room, but the wooden divan against the wall, with a heap of cushions; and I suspect the Pacha gets off his bed and sleeps there. No Arab can lie except in a heap. There was not a semblance, there was not even a *possibility* of occupation all over the palace, except in the bath — the "hama". We went out upon the roof. It shook under our feet. The guide showed us a factory from the roof, and made a Lord Burleigh nod, which Mr. B. construed to mean "that it had been a flourishing manufactory of the finest Malta web, but that the workmen had been removed to Cairo, and the place closed". The poor gardener picked me a nosegay. I am glad to have seen a royal palace.

This was the Esne, where, as we came up the river, at the same time as Abbas Pacha, he, finding something not to his liking in the preparations made for him, ordered the governor 500 lashes, and displaced him. Who the new governor was I cannot say, but yesterday we saw him go on board his beautiful dahabieh for Cairo. The wind was so strong that his Reis remonstrated. He ordered the Reis to be bastinadoed, and the boat to proceed; 500 yards further we saw him run aground, and on the bank he beat about the whole night; and we gladly endured the worst night we have had for the pleasure of knowing that the same wind kept *him* there, stuck for twenty-four hours. Little Beys have great Beys upon their backs to beat them, and great Beys have greater Beys; and so ad infinitum. But I am not sure how long this praiseworthy spirit of retribution would have kept us warm.

We went to the Temple. Mehemet Ali excavated the portico, which is like a great well; the rubbish cleared out was removed (apparently) into the interior of the Temple itself. The consequence is that the portico, which is gigantic, three rows of six columns, is dark, dank, and damp (I don't know if the Infernal Regions have a portico, but if they have, this is surely it, — I never saw anything so Stygian). The earth in the Temple looks ready to pour down upon you and overwhelm you: you go down to the portico by a formidable flight of narrow mud steps; the portico itself is black as Erebus; the ceiling is covered with infernal beasts.

We walked through this extraordinary centre of commerce and manufacture again today (the first town we have

The Temple at Esneh

seen since Osyoot), and felt shabby among genteel Arabs. I saw a school — the first time we have ever seen one — master, ushers, and children, sitting in the dust in a yard; a tin plate their copy-book, a page out of the Koran their reading-book. They would not let us touch the sacred page, but were not uncivil. In this great emporium we were actually able to buy candles; at Esne they burn lights; we had bought the *whole* stock of the town of Osyoot (there were no more in the place), and they had long since come to an end.

Tomorrow, dear people, please God, we mean to wake in Thebes, and to wake there every morning for a fortnight (at least). Think of a fortnight in Thebes!

I am so glad I put my poor little chameleons on shore in Nubia, they would have died in this cold.

The colour of Egypt strikes us so much after Nubia, or rather, the no-colour; the difference between the two sands is that of a dusty, dirty floor, and gold dust.

The cultivation of Egypt looks like vast plains, after the sunk fence of Nubia.

I have been quite glad of this delay from the winds, and this week's rest, to recover from the pleasure of Philœ, and prepare for that of Thebes.

AT THEBES

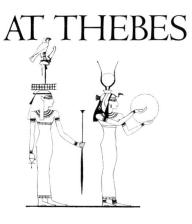

February 4th.

Thebes! Thebes! We are just arrived, at twelve o'clock. We made no way in the night, owing to the wind, and so I got my wish of coming in by daylight; but the Nile is so low that there was nothing to be seen.

Just as we were sending off a courier fifty miles, to Kenneh, to get our letters, we were told that the "Lord Lieutenant" here had them, and we have spent this afternoon at El Karnak reading them, with a glorious sunset to do honour to this noble plain — the first real sunset we have seen for many weeks.

While we were waiting at El Uksor for the letters, with a crowd round us, who called us the Cabiri (the Great), a woman passed by with a fish on her head nearly as big as herself, which we stopped. Then the Lord Lieutenant, like a red flamingo, came out with the letters, and we asked the Lord Lieutenant's opinion about the fish, which he said was a good fish, so we bought it. Then he told us there was nothing to pay for the letters, as he had made an Englishman, who came for his that morning, pay for the whole batch at once.

Behind the Lord Lieutenant's door was a post, and to the post was fixed a chain, and the chain went through a door by a hole, to which hole Mr. B——, applying his face to see what the chain was going to do, saw that it was fastened to the neck of a prisoner inside, who smiled, and Mr. B——

Luxor

smiled, to show that they were very glad to see one another; the prisoner had four friends to chat with him, who were seated on the ground round him.

AT THEBES

February 6th.

WELL, DEAREST PEOPLE, here is your daughter really in Thebes, though I can scarcely believe it. How beautiful it is, after the extreme ugliness of Egypt, and even of our beloved Nubia! How pleasant it is to find oneself in beautiful country once more, in this glorious plain, all surrounded by those violet-coloured hills, with rich fields bordering the blue Nile, and groves of palm trees and acacias, and tamarisks (quite a new sight), overshadowing the ruins of a world. It is not the deathbed of a *city* which you come to visit here, it is the death of a *world*. And what a world! As we crossed the river yesterday morning, and rode for the first time on the western bank, there she lay, the Libyan suburb — there stood the two Colossi, her gigantic portal — there hung the frowning, overhanging cliffs, which make the grand western barrier between her two worlds — her world of life and that of death. There is nothing melancholy about this great plain of death (excepting that miserable Luxor), as there is about the rest of Egypt; the people pasture their flocks and herds, and the women walk, spinning, at their heads; and it is more

126

Twilight Scene on the River by Charles Theodore Frere (Mathaf Gallery)

like the old life in the Bible, than any very sordid life of poverty. As we sat on the pedestals of the Colossi yesterday, they came and surrounded us with great flocks of sheep and goats, and a few camels and oxen, but they did not beg or howl; and I heard a baby in a tomb afterwards (most of them

A canja on the Nile off Thebes, the temple of Luxor behind

live in the tombs), making a pretty little noise, the only pretty noise I have ever heard a human being make in Egypt.

There is nothing horrid in this deathbed of Thebes.

When I see the evening sun making golden the tips of her violet crown — her amethyst diadem of hills, which sits so royally upon her noble brow — the words perpetually come into my head —

Her destiny's accomplished, — her time of work is done, —
She dwelleth in the golden home, her faithful toil hath won.

And the pastoral life of the few Arabs here, looks more like a new world which is beginning — an infant world springing out of her ashes, than a dying and helpless old age.

Well, we climbed up on the pedestals of the Colossi, and copied a few Greek and Latin inscriptions, which told how, in the times of this Emperor or that Ptolemy, I "Camillus", or I "ΗΜΟΔΩΡΟΣ", heard the Memnon "once in the first hour". But, as I am only writing my real and individual impressions, I must confess that I cannot understand people raving about these Colossi. The faces are so utterly gone, that to talk about any expression is absurd, and to compare them with the Rameses Colossi at Aboo Simbil, is to compare the Torso with the Apollo Belvidere; if size is the object, the Aboo Simbil Colossi are two feet the biggest; but I don't see how an ugly thing put into a solar microscope is made handsome. At Thebes one can afford to be disappointed in one thing — even in a great thing; otherwise I should be mad with myself at having felt so little about these Colossi. But they are such sightless, shapeless ruins, they look like sightless Lear after the storm, — as if the lightning of heaven had rested upon them, and made them the awful ruins you see; as if Amunoph had been the author of some fearful secret crime, and this was the vengeance of God making all secret things manifest, blighting them with some Macbeth's doom.

However it may stand with poor Amunoph's conscience, his Colossi don't look at all colossal; on the contrary, they look quite in keeping with everything about them, as if *they* were the natural size of man, and we were dwarfs, not they giants. One of our Arabs climbed up to the shoulder, to take up our tape, and looked like a fly perched upon him — a Lilliputian upon Gulliver. While we were pursuing these avocations, a large circle of these grave Arabs collected, and sat smoking their pipes at the bottom, while the women brought their flocks to come and look at us, walking at the heads of them with their distaffs, which Arab women in Egypt are not much given to.

The Colossi of Memnon

From the Colossi we went up to the tombs of Sheikh Abd-el-Koorneh, and went into several. This is the place for Fetichism, for visions of Domdaniel, of the road to the *Città dolente,* the gate of the *gente perduta,* the spot to see images of the dead rising up about you — to see "the possessed" inhabiting the tombs; and verily some of these poor Arab children do look like the possessed. When you have seen these places, you no longer wonder that the Egyptian's word

for the Western Region and Hades was the same, that he believed these to be really doors into the next world. I could believe it myself. The private tombs are generally a transept for the entrance, and a long narrow chamber running far into the rock behind. The tombs of the kings are passage after chamber, and vaulted hall after chamber and passage; and then hall, chamber, and passage over again, which we, who have pored over Belzoni in our youth, can well imagine, but which nobody who has not read Belzoni as a *child* can conceive. But these vaulted halls, deep in the rocky girdle of the earth, what are they like but the entrance to another world? And the heat, the intense heat of them, how unlike this — the stillness and heaviness.

But to return to the private tombs in Sheikh Abd-el-Koorneh. Every one of them is now inhabited; and you see a wild pair of Arab eyes with the blue whites peering out of the darkness at you. "Go not among the tombs, there is a wild man there"; while the transepts are full of the victories of Thothmosis III over the Ethiopians, of doura jars and dove cotes, these poor people's only furniture. You know I am no friend of these tiresome processions and banqueting feasts, the Grandisonian life of these tombs. A funeral procession here and there is most interesting, but you have to look at most of them with candles. Now you see a face, a sculptured face, whose earnest expression of intense devotion startles you, as the torch glimmers by. It is a king, perhaps, sacrificing, or a priest; or it is the dead man of the tomb in life, with his wife's arms thrown round him. One tomb which has just been opened, and which Mr. B. and I crawled into upon our hands and feet (it has not yet been blackened with torches or cut by names), looks as if it had been painted last week. The white ground with the gilding and colours looks like the most beautiful porcelain. It is too gay to be pretty.

After the tombs we went up to Dayr el Bahree, the last temple at the foot of the cliff (where it joins the plain), and

Entrance to the Tombs of the Kings, Thebes by David Roberts (Fotomas)

which even runs far into the cliff, and looked down upon this glorious bier. There were the two colossal ruins of Karnak and Dayr el Bahree, on either side the solemn Nile, facing each other, probably connected by a dromos of sphynxes the whole way, except where the river divided it, — we saw traces of such an avenue for a long distance; if so, it must have been upwards of three miles long. On the El Karnak bank, El Uksor on its promontory, on our side, the Ramesseum, below us in the plain, the two Colossi; temples and palaces as far as the eye could reach, and everywhere, in every hill and mound, the square portals showing that it was riddled with tombs within, the worlds of life and death were here so near together.

Then we rode down again to the little temple of Kasr e Rubahk near the river. The sculptures in its chambers are beautiful; but I was weary, and while they went over it I sat down on the broken base of one of the columns in the colonnade in front, and watched the sun set. Never did I see so beautiful, so poetic a scene, but no one could draw it, for when Martin or Danby try, how hard it looks. The beauty of it was all new to our Egyptian eyes. Imagine, looking abroad through a grove of palm trees and acacias, and seeing under them the temples of Luxor on their promontory, brilliant with the setting sun (such a sun as only Egypt can show), so clear with gems of living light; and behind them those violet mountains (not purple), with a little border of gold — the whole western sky looking like a scene out of the Revelations, so bright with "celestial jewelry", and the green plain, no longer hard and raw with *this* background, already in the darkness of twilight. No symptoms of ruin were here, — Luxor looked as she might have looked the day she was finished; in that sunset light all signs of decay disappeared, and in the stillness of that evening hour, with no sound but that of the flocks and herds going home, I felt like a Theban maiden sitting there in the colonnade of that solitary temple, where she had come for the evening benediction, and

looking out upon the glories of her native land, fair and fresh in the evening light, and yet sublime at the same time; there she sat, looking up to the attributes of the "Unknown God", as I too saw them sculptured above me in the colonnade; and (it is astonishing how alike the human heart is in all periods and climates — I see the same feelings we have in every sculpture and tomb and temple here), thinking probably very much like me. I felt quite friendly with her.

We rode home; our asses took to the water without difficulty, and landed us safely in the boat, which took us to our own dahabieh. The guide here rides before us on a horse with scarlet housings and high Turkish saddle, carrying a spear. Now and then (all these Arabs, even our cook whom I saw prancing about this morning, ride like Centaurs) he takes, partly because a wild fit seizes him, partly for our admiration, a gallop in the plain, to the amazing discomfiture of our asses, who mistake him for Balaam's angel, and turn their faces out of the way.

I wish I could give you the least idea of the situation of this city, unparalleled in the world, I should think. Imagine a plain about ten miles diameter, surrounded by these lovely hills, — a river, at low Nile, about twice as wide as the Thames at Westminster — the western mountains' rocky cliffs, with deep precipitous winding valleys, or rather ravines, between them, shaded by overhanging rocks, and without even the coloquintida, much less a blade of verdure among them, fit only for efreets and ghouls to live in the clefts of the rock, — they look like the circle of mountains, the abode of the Jinn, which, we all know, surrounds the earth, — and this within a mile of the city of temples and palaces. In these they buried their kings — surely there never was such a spot, by nature fitted for an imperial city.

The "Valley of the Kings!" — what a scene that name conjures up now in our minds of the great ones of the earth, not lying at rest, but stirred up to meet another at his coming. There we spent yesterday in the tombs of Rameses IV, Rameses V and the Queen Faosiri. But what can I compare the plain of Thebes to? The situation of London has a river, but it has no hills; and then there are so few grand landmarks in its city, such as Karnak, Medina Tabou,

plain, that there is a place to stand from and see it near, and that all is to be seen. No wind visits this great bay, — the hills are not near enough to make a draught, and high enough to shut it out, and from the moment we came in here it was calm.

The boat is going, which takes this letter. Farewell, dear people.

The Libyan chain of mountains, from the Temple of Luxor

Luxor, and the Ramesseum make here. Rome is more like it for its plain and for its great monuments; but then these monuments are concealed from one another by the hills, while here the folds are all gathered up in the girdle, and leave the plain smooth and spread out, so that, if it were not for the heaps of rubbish, almost every monument might be seen from every other, and all at once from the hills. It is this, I believe, which makes the especial grandeur of the

AT THEBES

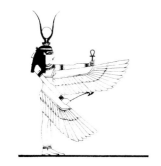

February 10th.

DEAREST PEOPLE,

The Queen's wedding day, I think — what a long way I do seem from Victoria's wedding day! Nofriari's I feel much more at home with.

We shall have been a week in Thebes tomorrow, a week of absolute despair, for to come to Thebes for a fortnight is what going to Rome for a fortnight would be. We feel at the end of a week that we know less about it than we did before we came; not that the individual things of Thebes require so much time; for (said in the lowest whisper) there is nothing here to compare with Aboo Simbil. The Osiridæ in the Ramesseum have not a head among them all, while our Osiradæ at Aboo Simbil had each a head piece. The Colossi are not to be named with the four Rameses, and the sculptures on the outside of Medina Tabou are small and confused. Karnak is such a mass that it perplexes me with its gigantic fall; but at Thebes one feels that detail matters little — it is the grave of a world that one has come to see.

The Valley of the Kings seems, though within a mile of Thebes, as if one arrived at the mountains of Kaf, beyond which are only "creatures unknown to any but God" — so deep are the ravines, so high and blue the sky, so absolutely solitary and unearthly, so utterly uninhabitable the place. One look at the valley would give you more idea of the supernatural, the gate of Hades, than all the descriptions, sacred or profane. What a moment it is the entering that valley, where in those rocky caverns, the vastness and the gloomy darkness of which are equally awful, the kings of the earth lie, each in his huge sarcophagus, with the bodies of his chiefs, each in their chamber, about him; and where, about this time, they are to return, to find their bodies (where are they now?) and resume their abode on earth — if purified by their 3000 years of probation, in a higher and better state; if degraded, in a lower. I thought I met them at every turn in those long subterraneous galleries, — saw their shades rising from their shattered sarcophagi, and advancing once more towards the light of day, which shone like a star, so distant and so faint, at the end of that opening — the dead were stirred up, the chief ones of the earth. If their belief is true, they are now returning, but they will find that they do not want their bodies (the destruction and ruin there will not be so terrible to them as they would have thought it beforehand), for God is able of these stones to raise up bodies for them. Well, these Pharaohs are perhaps now here, again in the body, their 3000 years having just elapsed to some of them, — that is, if they have philosophised sincerely, or, together with philosophy, have "loved beautiful forms"; if not, they are, as we saw one of them, in the form of an animal.

If they are but ordinary beings, I believe Plato thinks that 10,000 years will be the time before they come again. But at the end of every 1000 years, they will be able to choose what life they will have next; and upon this choice depends much of what they would become, for if they choose a philosophically virtuous life three times in succession, at the end of that time "they recover the use of their wings"; but the soul "which has never perceived the truth cannot pass into the human form". And if I were a Pharaoh now, I would choose the Arab form, and come back to help these poor people; and I am going tomorrow to a tomb of a Rameses, 1150 B.C. to meet him and tell him so.

In the tomb of Rameses V (the second we went into) we

Interior of a tomb

met one who had *not* been able to choose; he was revisiting the earth in the form of a pig, having lived a sensual life, and extinguished within himself the spark of eternal life. At one end of the wall he was slowly mounting into the presence of Osiris; next, standing before him, himself weighing his *own*

deeds, and then being "found wanting", he was leaving the divine presence, in the form of a wretched pig, driven by two monkeys. There was nothing ridiculous in this representation of the natural effect of sensuality; you could not laugh — you felt it as the inevitable necessity. If a man has allowed all that is divine (or human) within him to die out, how can it be otherwise? Poor pig! I shall always think of it, if I ever see another pig, which of course one does not here.

In the same tomb of Rameses V (who was one of the twentieth dynasty, but not quite late enough for my purpose) there are the Hours, each with a star on her head, to signify the hourly review the deceased king ought to have taken of his life; and which if he did not during his life, dedicating each hour to the deity, or the occupation, of the hour — he must do when he came to weigh his own deeds before Osiris. You never see these deities in the temples, which shows that they were not intended as divinities to be worshipped, but simply that these Egyptians thought that each hour was worth religiously consecrating to its object — each was a "genius in itself", "a fraction of the divine essence which pervaded it". The dead man makes an offering to each in succession.

It is curious how entirely without effect the outsides of these tombs are; they are simply doors cut in the cliff, generally with an Isis and a Nephthys, the Beginning and the End, cut on each side the cartouche, nothing else. But indeed in all Egyptian buildings you are not less struck by this, — they seem to have thought nothing about effect; their buildings are hardly meant to look at from the outside.

The tomb of Rameses V appears to go an interminable length in the rock, passage after passage, till at last you come to the strange vaulted chamber at the end, where, gold and red and black, the ceiling is covered with astronomical records, fresh as ever, bright as if just from the alchemist's hand, who seems to have made those magical characters on

View at Karnak by Augustus Osborne Lamplough (Mathaf Gallery)

the roof, in this the centre of the earth, the farthest of Domdaniel's caves.

In the tomb of Rameses IV the ceiling is painted with the goddess of heaven encircling the firmament with her arms; the figure of a man is upholding her with outstretched hands.

The sarcophagus stands in the middle, broken and empty, but in this case not overthrown. In that of Rameses V it lies on its side broken to pieces, and the fragments strewn about: how such a block could be broken is the wonder.

All these tombs slope rapidly downwards as you go in.

I have never seen in all these representations any hint of a belief in repentance; it does not at all follow that it is not there, — this language is so new to us.

The pre-eminence of the schoolmaster, the spiritual and intellectual teacher, and of his trade above all others, is what recurs to one oftenest in these tombs; the king himself was scarcely equal to the teacher. It is what we have so often sighed for in England, when we have said that, till the schoolmaster's vocation was considered, as it is, the highest after the statesman's, instead of being, as it is now with us, inconceivable as it sounds, almost *infra dig,* the training up the soul almost a lower profession than the curing of the body, education never could prosper in England. Here, in Egypt, the spiritual teachers were before everything, and above everything; nay, the king must himself be admitted as one, before he could be the rightful monarch; and in their hands was evidently all the education in Egypt. It was a fatal error to these poor Egyptians, but surely it was a noble error, — surely they erred on the right side, when they so ennobled their spiritual instructors, instead of degrading them, and experience only could teach how terrible would be the consequences. Meanwhile, those consequences almost reconcile one to the disrepute of the office of schoolmaster in the country which calls itself the most civilised in the world.

We went into one other tomb, that of the last of the nineteenth dynasty, which seemed to have held two kings in succession, — for it had *two* vaulted halls (the last unfinished) divided from one another by long suites of chambers. The first had a gallery round it, as most of them have, divided by square pillars from the hall, the walls covered with sculptures — walking serpents, serpents in coils, covering a whole side, and now and then a funereal subject, the most interesting.

All the furniture of the king was painted round this one, which was much less to my taste.

After seeing three tombs, which was quite enough, we rode over the rock, or rather climbed, for the asses followed us, and down upon Thebes.

One day we spent in the Ramesseum, where lies the granite statue of Rameses II, broken and overthrown, the wonder of the world, and the largest colossus even in Egypt, larger than the Pair, larger than those at Aboo Simbil; but here size has almost defeated itself, for it is too large to take in the whole of any part at one time, and so destroys its own effect.

The most extraordinary thing in these temples is the union and representation, side by side, of the most vulgar warfare, and of the highest state of civilisation in private and religious life. After the temple, we rode to the Valley of the Tombs of the Queens. It is, if possible, more perfect, as a place set apart under the shadow of death, than the Valley of the Kings; it is much smaller, more compact, more shut in, so that you can take in the whole at once with the eye, and see that there is no outlet. It is a complete chasm, more than a valley, for you do not enter by the mouth, but climb over the sides. At the farthest end, a dark cleft in the rock looks like an entrance into Hades; other outlet you can see none. We were too tired to go into any of the tombs, which I am sorry for now; but the view of the valley is enough.

AT THEBES

February 11th.

DEAR PEOPLE,

Do you want to know how we pass our days? We rise up early in the morning, and are breakfasted perhaps by eight o'clock. Then we cross the water in the "sandal", which is a small "dingee", to western Thebes; the asses rush into the water to meet us, or the crew carry us ashore; we mount the asses, and with a great multitude — for in Egypt every attendant has his ass, and every ass his attendant — we repair (preceded by a tall man with a spear, his wild turban coming undone in the wind), like a small army, to a tomb; the tomb instantly fills — we suffocate for two or three hours, the guides having, besides, lighted fires and torches therein. When nature can sustain no more, we rush out, and goollehs, bread and dates are laid upon a stone. Those who have strength then begin again, till dark; those who have not, lie on stones in the valley.

Then begins the delightful ride home, the quiet, the silence (except that no Arab is ever silent — the donkey men and the guides talk without one moment's interruption, if it is ten miles or if it is one, the whole way home), the sunset tints, the goats coming home, the women spinning at

the head, the gamous (the great Nile buffalo) crossing the little branches of the Nile in large herds on their way home, two little children perhaps riding on the neck of the largest, a stray jackal coming out, and the Pair looking golden in the western sunlight; the evening picture is all beautiful. Our asses enter the river and slide us into the sandal, and home we come to the little fleet of European boats moored under the colonnades of Luxor, which really from the river are almost beautiful.

We dine, and after dinner, when we are all hung up by the tails, like the chameleons, pretending to be dead, and waiting for half-past seven, or at latest eight, to bury us, lo! a dreadful plash of oars, or Paolo puts in his head, with an abominable grin at our mute misery, and says, "The Hungarian count!" or "the German professor!" and so on. Mr. B—— immediately retires to his own room, whence he is generally heard to snore Σ and I unwillingly, but nobly, sacrifice ourselves to our duty, sit up (in the brown Holland dressing gowns we are sure to have on, having been much too tired to dress), and talk; but we never give one drop of tea, which has greatly limited these visitations, for, in our street, the doors stand always open, and the people have nothing to do but to spend their evenings on board each other's boat. One night, and one night only, we were got out. Capt. ——, good-natured man, came himself in his sandal, and positively carried us off; and one day the ——'s dined with us, and with all the devotion of Arab hospitality which distinguished us, we killed — was it not beautiful of us? — no, not our horse, we had none, but our dog, for dinner. I think I told you of our dog — a turkey, "as big as donkey", as Paolo said. Oh what a loss was there; how he used to walk majestically up and down the beach in front of the boat, which he believed it his duty to guard, bastina-doing the chickens when they made a noise. He killed two cocks the day he died. No man could get him into a coop (the crew were afraid to go near him), yet he never strayed.

Loading Dhows on the Nile by Eugene Fromentin (Mathaf Gallery)

No dog ever ventured near our boat while he lived; the moment he was dead, the hungry Luxor dogs used to come on board every night, till Mustafa, like Cuddie's lady, greeted them with boiling water; and after his death, we never could keep a quail a single night, though our numerous acquaintances kept us well in quails, for our four cats had parties every night, and bared the larder: and we killed him!

As soon as our guests were gone, sometimes before, we went to bed. Don't think us grown quite savage and uncivilised. It is very hard to be all day by the deathbed of the greatest of your race, and to come home and talk about quails or London.

What do people come to Egypt for?

Without the past, I conceive Egypt to be utterly uninhabitable. Oh, if you were to see the people! No ideas that I had of polygamy come near the fact; and my wonder is now, not that Sarah and Rachel were so bad, but that they were not a great deal worse. Polygamy strikes at the root of everything in woman — she is not a wife — she is not a mother; — and in these Oriental countries, what is a woman, if she is not that? In all other countries she has something else to fall back upon. The Roman Catholic woman has a religion — the Protestant has an intellect; in the early Christian, in the old Egyptian time, women had a vocation, a profession, provided for them in their religion, independent of their wifedom; here, she is nothing but the servant of a man. No, I do assure you, the female elephant, the female eagle, has a higher idea of what she was put into the world to do, than the human female has here. I never knew of a religion, ancient or modern, that I could not have some points of sympathy with, — but with the Mahometan, how few.

*   *   *

I suppose you have some idea of Karnak — more at least than I can ever give you — of the vast propylæa, looking towards the river; then the immense propylæum area, so vast that a moderate-sized temple, built by Rameses III *into one side,* scarcely disturbs the eye; then two propylæa ruined

The Great Hall of Karnak

from top to bottom, vast stone quarries; then the Hall of Columns, of which no one can speak — they are like him to whom they are dedicated, "ineffable". Then comes a transept, gone, all but one obelisk; the pair was placed there by Thothmosis I whose cartouche I saw upon it, every line as clear as the day it was cut. This part is much older than the Hall of Columns. Then comes another transept, and another pair of obelisks — one is standing, raised by Queen Mephra (Amun neit gori, wrongly called) to the memory of her father Thothmosis I and mother Amense. Mephra reigned successively for her two brothers, Thothmosis II and III, who were engaged in driving out the Hyksos; the latter only finally expelled them from Egypt, whence they went to Palestine, and were called Philistines. On the prostrate obelisk I could read the names of Mephra and her youngest brother T. III (though it lies in fragments): perhaps it was a memorial of her gratitude for his success. She seems to have been a gallant regent and a loving sister.

Then come the sanctuary and ruins innumerable; behind the sanctuary, the oldest part of the temple built by Osirtasen I, of the old empire and the twelfth dynasty, 2775 B.C. carefully preserved by the new empire, and older by more than 1000 years than all the rest of Karnak or Thebes. Then comes the columnar temple of Thothmosis III, the place where his invaluable table of Karnak (now at Paris), which gives the lists of kings, his ancestors, was found; and pylons and accessory temples, enough to make one desperate, extend beyond the Temenos.

I suppose you know that on Karnak is the famous sculpture of Shishak, of the twenty-second dynasty; opposite him, the god holding Rehoboam by a string, among other prisoner kings. There could be no doubt of it, I could read the letters on his cartouche quite plain, IOUDA MELEK, king of Judah. Oh, I was so sick of it, people seemed to think it a holy pilgrimage, like a visit to Jerusalem, to go and look at it. I suppose I have been there fifty times with different people, and we don't know anything which makes Rehoboam so very interesting to us. But people seemed to think that Rehoboam was the only thing that was true, and that all the rest of Karnak was the work of the Phookas, or something worse, — the devil perhaps. At last I hated Rehoboam, and vowed I would go no more; besides that Egyptian history, art, religion, ceases to be interesting long before Shishak the Bubastian's time. So, enough of Rehoboam.

I possess an antiquity though, which I really do value, an official seal, of the time of Rameses the Great, my hero, with his cartouche upon it. An undoubted reality. Who will dare to open letters, sealed with the great Rameses' own seal?

And now I must go to *délasser* myself at his Ramesseum, which, not so overpowering as Karnak, is yet grand enough to be awful, beautiful enough to be pleasant, and large enough to hide one. How many hours I have sat in that small hall of the eight columns, where the sacred library of Hermes' books was laid up, and felt as much reverence as ever Egyptian did before those treasures, which trained the men who trained Moses, who trained the world; those books, which taught us, – us whom the Egyptians had never heard of, — the name of God.

On the walls are four sacred boats or shrines, familiar to us through Moses' imitation of them, in the Ark and Tabernacle. The two foremost are the shrines of Maut (mother), or Nature; and Khonso (Hercules), or Strength; the two behind are of Rameses II and his beloved Nofri Ari (the good Ari), his wife. They are all coming to do homage to Amun, the Unknown God. (*Amun,* as you know, only means "Come", as Hecatæus tells us, and is therefore a mere name of entreaty or love for the God whose real name was too sacred to be pronounced, who was, as Manetho says, the "Concealed God".) The shrines are distinguished by the heads of their respective masters at the prow, and each is making a prayer.

Khonso says, "We come towards thee to serve thee; grant a *stable* and *pure* life to thy son (Rameses) who loves thee." Having thus introduced the hero, Rameses simply says, "I come to my father."

But his queen's prayers for her hero are much longer, the

good Ari says, "I come to do homage to my father; my heart is joyful with the love thou bearest me; I am in joy when I consider thy benefits. O, thou who establishest the seat of thy power in the dwelling of thy son (Rameses), grant him purity and stability."

The Great Colossus at the Ramesseum

It is rare to see any but spiritual prayers on Egyptian walls.

On the roof of the library is the celebrated astronomical ceiling, which decides by the Sothis cycle, the heliacal rising of the dog star, the date of the death of Rameses, 1322 B.C.

But where was I? Sitting on a stone in the eight columned hall of the Ramesseum. There is a harmony in the Ramesseum, which you do not find anywhere else in Thebes; it is so compact, so well proportioned, so intelligible — it is the very image of grace in strength, and strength in harmony. It is not that the intaglios are particularly beautiful — they are not; but the whole is so beautiful. At first you are rather disappointed — is that all that people have talked so much about? But every day you admire it more and more, while every day you like Medina Tabou less and less. It is just on the edge of the desert, the tombs being immediately behind, — taking up no superfluous ground, not trenching on the cultivated land. Oh, bright Ramesseum, how like the spirit of thy builder thou art! He never spent time in superfluous words, I am sure — the compact, energetic, muscular-minded man; not an artist, like his father; a warrior, a devout spirit, and a philosopher, but not a mystical one; not such good company as his father, but a brave honest heart, and a learned head. I feel more acquainted with him than I do with Sethos; and he was so fond of his wife, and his father, and his grandfather, who no doubt deserved it well.

He was a bit of a *littérateur,* too, it is evident — as indeed all the kings were, for they were obliged to be skilled in all the wisdom of the priests (the most learned body of the world of any age), before they could become kings; it being the maxim of the Egyptians, that the nation was not made for the king, but the king for the nation. All the occupations of the king were therefore laid down by law. He was to rise early — to perform all the business of the nation, from daybreak till the third hour; then he proceeded to the temple, and performed the sacrifice, when the high priest read him a sermon on the duties of kings, and so on. He was to have no servants about him, but only such sons of the priests as had profited the best by their education, that he might have none to minister to his caprices: the law was to will for him, and he was to have no power but by the law. He was to drink no wine — his very diet was regulated for him by law, and how long he was to sleep. Everything in

Egypt, Diodorus says, was calculated and regulated for the public good. A little too much calculated and regulated, and a good deal too much done for them. However, it certainly was wonderful what kings they turned out — at their deaths any man might accuse them and deprive them of burial. As Diodorus says, the state never could have lasted so long, defying time and its usual regulations, if it had not been for these laws. In Egypt the law was king, and the king was only the first subject of the law.

Another digression from the Ramesseum: before the entrance into the Great Hall of Assembly sat the two small (or "young") black granite statues, now overthrown, of Rameses (of which we have one head in the British Museum). I marked his tail, and wished he had his head again. The other head stands broken off upon its chin. The wondrous Colossus, which sat before the entrance into the inner propylæum, the great (or old) granite statue, is nothing but a ruin. But how I have sat and peopled and rebuilt those ruins. How beautifully one evening the setting sun streamed in among those columns, and the mound of Medina Tabou in the west looked like an Acropolis, or anything but the dirty ruined crowd of huts it is; and I saw Rameses descending on the beams of his beloved Ra — now really the "tried" and purified "of Ra", to see what his temple was doing after this long lapse of years.

Those three kings, the grandfather, father, and son, — the poet, the artist, the philosopher, — are at last returning now; their thirty hundred years of trial done, how altered they will find their Thebes — the Thebes they loved and dressed with the most precious things they had — the Thebes they worshipped with such true devotion; but with what various thoughts each will look upon her desolation.

*   *   *

One evening and one morning I have spent at that exquisite little temple of Koorneh, and each time more in love with it. I cannot describe the beauty of its position, with its crown of palm trees; its long low portico, with lotus columns; with a few (not many, nor confused) of those beautiful simple bas-reliefs, representing Sethos I pouring libations before the gods of the future state, in honour, no doubt, of his father, or the great Rameses, kneeling before the gods, his grandfather ("justified") looking on at his reception among them: for this temple was built by Sethos I to his father Rameses I's memory, and finished by *his* son Rameses II to *his*. The names of Rameses II and his father are lovingly enclosed in the same asp-frame on the columns, which I have never seen elsewhere; and the dedication says — "The friend of truth, the tried of Ra, has executed these works in honour of his father Amun Ra, and completed the palace of his father Sethos." This palace temple, or rather the Great Hall (into which you enter from the portico), supported by its six lotus columns, served for popular purposes, as well as religious and regal. Here the tribunals of justice sat — here the Great Assemblies were held, the object of which is unknown to us, but over which only the king could preside (and President of which was his highest title on earth); and here politics, the incarnation of religion, had her discussions.

Upon the steps of that colonnade I have sat for hours, moving with the shadow of the columns, as it turned with the sun, and looking out upon that matchless view under the different lights; the distance to the west over the green corn fields — then the palm garden — then the eastern hills on the other side the river — then more palms, and, between their stems, the great colonnade of Luxor on its promontory, which becomes higher and higher, as the Nile sinks rapidly, and which one night was like a colonnade of chrysophrast shafts in the sunset; then more grove, and, under it, a tall black veiled figure moving among the

Valley of the Nile with the ruins of the Temple of Sethos by Prosper Marilhat (Louvre)

palms, with a vase upon her head; and here the birds sing — the first I have heard in Egypt, — and there is water and sakias.

This temple is the only place in Thebes I really cared for — for it is impossible to love Thebes: one stands in awe of her; one feels a wonder-stricken reverence before this marble headless statue of the philosopher of the world, but not a tender respect as for Philœ and Ipsamboul. There is no place I wish to linger in, there is nothing I can love, except perhaps this little temple of Koorneh.

We have been most unlucky in our weather at Thebes. The sunsets I can reckon up — one the first night at Karnak, one the second at Koorneh, one at the Ramesseum, one more at Karnak, and that is all in three weeks; and for the ugliness of a sand storm give me the orangest fog in London, and I don't think it is uglier.

We have been anchored for three weeks within a hundred yards of Luxor; and I have been up to the temple but once, it is such an odious place. We climbed into the adytum, which is like an oblong box set on end; and into a number of dark chambers. All the old part is built by that Amunoph III, the Memnon of the Colossi, the great conqueror, who carried his arms into Mesopotamia, during which time his mother Maut-m-Skoi was regent. The prettiest feature in the temple is the infinity of chambers dedicated to her, and the number of times she occurs in the sculptures. Two figures of Nilus, one red to indicate the inundation, one blue the subsided river, present the infant Amunoph and the infant god Haska (one of the minor protecting Triad of Thebes) to Amun, the mother being present. Everything about the temple seemed to speak of Amunoph's devotion to nature, to the principles of nature and natural affection. You seldom see Nilus in so conspicuous a position — his immense conquests seem to contradict this; but I believe Alexander was a very similar character, or would have been, if he had lived, like

Amunoph, to be old. The sculptures are nothing; art had not yet reached its simplicity. Amunoph II was only the great-grandson of Thothmosis III.

The propylæa were added by the great Rameses, with the two obelisks, and four colossal sitting statues of himself in

Grand Entrance to the Temple at Luxor

front. One bas-relief of the enemy's camp, and him taking it, is curious; but those battle pieces are so tiresome.

That the Egyptians believed, like the Jews, that they were really building a habitation for the Lord in a temple, is evident from the dedications, where the king entreats the god to come and take up his abode in the house he has prepared for him.

In that same chamber of Amunoph, you see Thoth

choosing his name for him, "Lord of Justice", a mistake as old as the world and as young as our time, to suppose oneself called to a power one has not, to do a thing which is not one's business.

There is something in Karnak so expressive of him to whom it was dedicated (Amun, the "Concealed God"), that one begins to think, as I have often thought in St. Peter's, that architecture is the only way to speak of Him — the best mode of religious expression. St. Peter's and Karnak are the only two worthy expressions of "Him that is ineffable" which I have ever seen — yet how different: Karnak, like the thoughtful metaphysical Egyptian faith; St. Peter's, like the fervent Roman Catholic — in Karnak you think; in St. Peter's you feel. In that intricate hall of columns you see how the Egyptian has thought out, through the mazes and difficulties and intricacies with which the government of the earth is full to our minds, the Deity who would answer to the phenomena he saw, the attributes which would explain those difficulties. In the long uninterrupted space through which the worshipper of St. Peter's looks from the door to the altar, from the altar up to heaven, you see how the feeling, unthinking, ardent heart has rushed at once to its Creator, careless of all problems which it has regarded as temptations to its faith, and has left to a devil to solve. The Egyptian loved his God with all his mind; the Roman Catholic, with all his heart. The Egyptian would never have made a missionary, I suspect; the Roman Catholic has never made a philosopher. The Egyptian mind, with its satire and subtlety, reminds one of Pascal, and shows, as he did, how truly earnestness may be allied with these.

How Karnak contradicts all the tales that have been fabricated by Greeks and Romans about Egypt. "Oh, Egypt, Egypt," says Hermes (in the prophetic spirit of Ezekiel), "a time will come when in the stead of a pure religion and a pure worship, thou shalt have no longer religion and a pure worship, thou shalt have no longer aught but foolish fables, incredible to posterity, and there shall remain to thee no more than words graven on stone, the only monuments which shall attest thy piety." But they do attest her piety. The very name of the king who built Karnak is unknown: one reads it Sethos, another Osirei, a third Menephthah; what does it signify to him now? The ideas he has left us are imperishable: on his monument alone remains, uninjured and legible, that much denied truth, which he has embodied by causing himself to be represented with the Good and Evil alike pouring life upon him.

I have never said anything about the private tombs. They are vexation of spirit, for they have been cruelly mauled. One in Sheikh Abd-el-Koorneh had interminable processions of tribute bearers, presenting themselves to Thothmosis III, 1557 B.C. the King of the Exodus, according to Bunsen. But, *caro Totmose, che fate là?* I do not know what business he has there, as it is a private tomb, and I think the owner had much better have been engaged in saying his prayers than in thinking of his sovereign's glories, and his workmen and manufactories. But, as Lepsius says, what an irresistible "Trieb" these Egyptians seem to have had to work for history, when they made their graves into a book of trades!

I bring home some little figures found in the tombs. Each carries a hoe in one hand and a bag of seed in the other; the arms are crossed on the breast, in imitation of Osiris, whose name the dead took. The old Egyptian idea of the resurrection of the body seems to have been very like St. Paul's. The body was the seed. The hieroglyphs on the little mummied figure are, "Let all that the deceased has done be reckoned and told — how he has dug the fields, sown the fields, watered from the wells, and brought the grain of the West to the East." This is a quotation from Hermes Trismegistus, out of the Book of the Dead. One of the prayers of the dead is that his name may *germinate* in heaven

Ruins of Luxor from the South West

by the divine sun. In one of the king's tombs, Osiris is rising again out of a heap of cornseed.

One of the last days of our Theban stay, Mr. B —— and I rode round the whole of the Libyan suburb — past Medina Tabou, past a little Ptolemaic temple beyond, and all round the site of the immense ancient lake, over which the dead were ferried, and which is now only marked by the mounds, which were once thrown up in its excavation. The distance

was longer than we thought. The sun set, there was no moon, and it became dark; but just at twilight we came to the most perfectly desolate spot I could have conceived — an utterly arid mound of sand, strewed with whitened bones of men — little depressions showing in the sand where once they had been buried. It looked like a cursed place; as if no foot but a vulture's claw had pressed it for thousands of years, and the dew of heaven had never visited it. These were the graves of those who had been refused burial for some act of violence or treachery, some secret crime which had been brought to light against them, when the Forty-two sat in judgment by the shores of the Sacred Lake. There they were thrown into the ground, and there they seemed to have lain whitening ever since. I am sure it never entered into the heart of man to conceive of so desolate a place; and if there their spirts were doomed to wander, it must have been a weary tramp. One or two of their bones we could not help bringing home.

Dayr el Bahree is the most beautiful position in Thebes, and the strongest, backed by the Libyan cliff, and overlooking from its heights the whole plain and the river. It was built by Thothmosis III, fifteen centuries and a half before Christ, that Thothmosis who finally drove the Hyksos from Egypt, and expelled them from Avario, their stronghold (which was twice as large as Aurelian Rome), out of which they marched 240,000 men into Syria, with all that they had. This was the Thothmosis too under whom the Israelites slaved and suffered. And curious similarities struck me at every turn between the doctrines they afterwards professed and his, if we are to judge from the small remains left of his mighty temple, — the *glory* of God — God, a God of hosts and battles, — His object to slay and exterminate his enemies, — the only difference being that Thothmosis exterminated the invaders of Egypt, and the Israelites were themselves the invaders. The great and universal mistake about God seeking His own glory seemed to me to have inspired that temple, set out, as it were, upon a tray to make a show.

In the old part of Karnak, next door to the sanctuary, he represents himself offering to the "unknown God", the two obelisks, and all the service of the temple, the number of each thing which he gives written under each, — dishes 244, other ditto 300, rings 214, vessels 94, with the sign of gold over the gold ones, that the god might not mistake them for plated, and the number, for fear he should not be able to count. The numbers I noted down on the spot for the oddity of the thing. A ground plan of the temple which he dedicates follows. Some of the vases are beautiful, quite classical.

One hardly knows whether to admire or to smile, — to admire the richness of the gift dedicated by the king, not to making *himself* but *the god* a palace (in those days people built temples, not palaces; and I must say, if it is a mistake, it is a much finer mistake to beautify and magnify God's house rather than your own), or to smile at the anxiety of Thothmosis, that the god should understand and value his gift. Thy glory, O God, and a little of my own too, — lo! a very little. I always think how abundant must be the vanity of those people who think God is so fond of His glory; but we all judge, each, his own God, by himself, and think He likes what we like ourselves.

In the sanctuary of Dayr el Bahree (the only part which remains, because hewn in the living rock), Thothmosis is making an offering to his deceased ancestor Thothmosis I. Another similarity with the Jews, who are always raving about their ancestors, the God of their ancestors; and indeed, before Christ, no nation seems to have risen to the idea of a God of the whole world. Have we now? Do we not still believe England to be His chosen nation?

Thothmosis has surpassed all the Kings of Egypt in the multitude of his temples.

One day we went through the huge fragments which lie prostrate and half buried behind the Pair. There are above eighteen Colossi whose enormous limbs lie strewn about. In a direct line, some hundred yards behind the two, are two gigantic stelæ, with their faces to the earth, some thirty feet long, covered with inscriptions, most delicately cut. Champollion says these were probably the backs of the seats of two other Colossi now buried under the earth, and that all these enormous fragments belonged to a building called the Amenophium, built by that Amunoph III whose portrait the Pair represents. These must have stood before the front propyla as the four statues of Rameses II before Ipsamboul. The deposits of the inundations are gradually immuring in muddy forgetfulness these consecrated fragments as effectually as ever nun was walled up in convent wall.

By the space covered with these vast blocks the Amenophium must have been at least as large as Karnak. At the side of the Pair, in the same block, is the mother of Amunoph, the same representation that you see in the Temple of Luxor.

I wish you could see Lady M. A.'s drawings — she has made a sketch of the Colossi by sunset, which is worthy of Amunoph himself, it is quite heroic. I never saw anything finer than her daring dashes of gamboge and vermilion; her genius is really Homeric.

AT THEBES

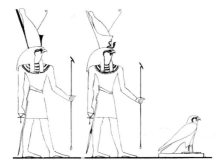

February 12th.

Ugly Medina Tabou — how I hated you, with your gaudy colours, your squat columns, as round as they were high — your coronation scenes, more vulgar than Hayter's, more profane than his *Communion of the Queen,* — your modern-looking three-storied palace, not forming a part of the temple, as if it belonged to the king to live there as minister of the gods, but stuck up in front like an impudent Blenheim porter's lodge, as if to say no one comes in here but by paying twenty-five shillings, or three enemies' heads; its very balconies made of captives' heads, not like the work of the great Rameses, but that of a common Pacha tyrant, his battle pieces represented in the very area of the temple, not decently exiled to the outer walls, as at Karnak; the king's chariot, with three prisoners tied under the axle — a piece of savage cruelty you never see elsewhere — degrading the very sacred place.

If Karnak is the St. Peter's of Egypt, Medina Tabou is its Madeleine. It is just such a temple as Napoleon would have built and the apotheosis of that vulgar tyrant in La Madeleine is not more indecent nor inappropriate than the battle and coronation scenes of Rameses III in Medina Tabou. It is the very sanctuary of low Oriental despotism, baseness, and pomp. It reminded me of Napoleon throughout, with his Josephine and his Marie Louise, his notions of women, and his coronation of his wife. You see Rameses

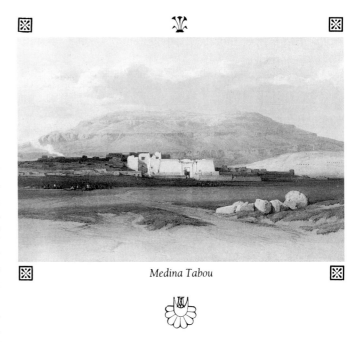

Medina Tabou

surrounded by his ladies (how unlike the loving Nofriari and her hero at the Ramesseum — "lovely in their lives, and in their death they were not divided"); you see the queen put out of the way, on a shelf, in the coronation scene, like the miserable wife of a Louis Quatorze. The empire was falling, and barbarism beginning, which could produce a Medina Tabou.

The very shrines (in the sacred boats) at Medina Tabou

seemed to me degraded; the cherubim were still the same, they could not be deprived of the crowns of light and life in their hands; but instead of the symbol of truth, they held that of power and dominion; instead of the heavenly kingdom, which is truth, they held the earthly kingdom.

From the time of Rameses III (1290 B.C.) art and power suddenly declined, and the glory of Egypt departed for ever. It is no wonder; the connexion between freedom and art, between purity of morals and religion, and a high state of national prosperity, seems very evident.

The ugly Gothic battlement of Medina Tabou is peculiar to the reign of Rameses III, and the whole affair looks more like the feudal castle of a savage chief than a temple of the philosophical Egyptian.

But there is nothing to rival the gorgeousness of its courts and colonnades, with their painted processions, brighter than anything in Egypt, except Karnak. It does not look like a place of worship however, it is full of priests' rooms and dark places; standing against its finest procession is a handsome Christian stone altar, as in a London church, which it reminded me of, though deserted these 1200 years. But it is very curious, very interesting to have seen, though never a place to become bewitched with, to have favourite corners to sit in, and ruminate, like St. Peter's and Ipsamboul, and my dear Philœ. Its magnificence strikes one, not its devotion — its riches, not its religion. It is a place for kings and priests to worship in, not for philosophers and simple-hearted people. Rameses the Great was magnificent, but out of piety — this man out of ostentation

It was dedicated by Rameses III (not the Great, not my Rameses — how different was the spirit of his places of worship), the second king of the twentieth dynasty, upon his return from his immense Eastern conquests in Asia over nations whose names we scarcely know. He was the son of that Proteus or Nilus (the contemporary of Menelaus and the Trojan war) who gave a refuge to Helen, and lived about 1290 B.C.

There is an enormous hieroglyphic inscription (not yet decyphered, I believe) relating to the conquests of the seventh year of his reign. Art was evidently already

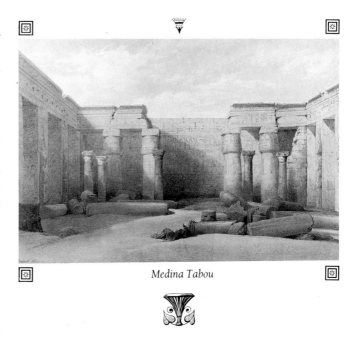

Medina Tabou

beginning to decline; though the sharpness of execution and the vigour of the drawing are still as great as ever, yet the composition is more laboured, the gods more pedantic — unlike the time of the great Rameses already. The coronation procession is curious for its magnificence, not interesting from any *feeling* it betrays. Thoth, the god of letters, and Horus, binding up the king's throne with water plants, is one of the prettiest representations, showing that he considered an intellectual support to his throne necessary as well as that of terrestrial prosperity; and a number of spirits of the earth, leading him into the presence of the great Triad of Thebes, is interesting. If it were not for one's familiarity from one's youth (thanks to the Books of Leviticus and Chronicles) with every line and utensil of those processions, they would be tiresome beyond measure. But there is the tabernacle I used to fancy when I was a child; there are the mercy-seat and cherubim, some crowned with *Truth*, and others with *Light*, the feather and the disk (and there is much that is beautiful in this, the spirits of light and the spirits of truth); some kneel by the ark, some stand with protecting wings; one kneels without with outstretched wings, "truth as a frontlet", and life in her spread hands. A little figure of the king ministers before the sacred shrine; emblems of goodness form the pillars on either side.

The battle scenes I suppose are splendid — the triumph afterwards, the appearance lastly of the king before the gods, presenting to them his conquests and his captives as a tribute. How many tributes equally unacceptable have been offered from times immemorial (and will be offered till the world grows wiser) in all sincerity and singleness of heart to God, like this of Rameses! He has not, however, the expression of his great ancestor while doing this. In one battle piece, he sits after the heat of battle on the back of his car, while his chiefs lay at his feet thousands of *hands*. His four sons, who all succeeded him and reigned, successive Rameses, attend him, and carry him in the coronation procession, — this is rather pretty, his children the support of his throne. Here, too, the good and evil spirit alike pour life and purity over him – the evil spirit being more carefully obliterated than I have ever seen it, and with those war scenes opposite I do not so much wonder at his exciting abhorrence.

The columns of this court, which is the inner vestibulum or propylæum, are gorgeous, eight square columns from which the Osirides are gone, on either side, and five round pillars at the two ends. On the north side is a splendid, or what Sir G. W. calls "an elegant portico, in which the circumference of the columns is 23 feet, and the height 24 feet", covered too with painting.

From Medina Tabou you can see the whole circumference of the vast lake across which the bodies were formerly ferried on their way to burial, the judgment being previously held even in the case of a king, whether he was fit to pass over; many were "found wanting", even kings; and the desolate tombs are still visible, where, on the shore of despair, the other side of the lake, across which there was no more passage, no more entrance, the miserable men were buried.

Medina is Arabic for city, and Tabou the old word for Thebes; so that Medeenet Haboo, as it is wrongly written, only means the "city of Thebes".

It is not a temple one cares to go back to. The beautiful little temple of Koorneh, old and untouched, I long to see again; but the sacred place here is built up and covered up with the ruins of a deserted crude brick village. What sacred place shall we ever see again though like Ipsamboul?

I am writing in the greatest possible haste for a steamer (!) which has just brought Mr. Murray, and is going on to Cairo. I would not go in a steamer on the Nile, if I were never to see the Nile without it.

AT THEBES

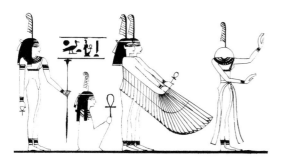

February 1850.

One temple I have never mentioned, because it was only Ptolemaic — though it deserves to be of my beloved Rameses: it is called Dayr-el-Medeeneh, and belongs to Isis. It is built just under the western cliff, which is supported by a wall of layers of crude brick in wavy lines, and has a little hidden nook of its own among the rocks. The way to it leads up behind what was the Amenophium. It is very small, has only a little area, a pronaos, and the sekos, with side adyta, the one to the right consecrated to Athor, and the one to the left to Thmei; the principle of beauty thus identified with that of truth — a new idea in this worship — to make the artist one with the philosopher — a most rare conjunction, — for he who pursues truth generally despises beauty, and the ordinary followers of beauty find truth dry and ugly. But here Thmei appears as a second form of Athor. Truth is herself beauty.

In Athor's sanctuary, the king is offering to two figures of Isis or Athor at once, the one as an animal (a cow's head), the other as a woman. If this means animal and intellectual nature, the sense is very beautiful. How, in Europe, we have dwarfed instead of educated our animal nature — and through it, perhaps, crippled our intellectual! The European has seldom fancied any other course of discipline for his body but that of indulging or tormenting it, poor thing!

In Thmei's sanctuary sits Osiris in the prætorium of Amenti; before him the lotus, the emblem of the material world, and, standing on it, the four Genii of Amenti, who were also the genii of the four cardinal points. Cerberus stands behind them, whose Egyptian name signifies "the Devourer". And then comes Harpocrates, sitting on his father's crook, and holding in his hands the flagellum, and a kind of instrument (of which I bring home a bronze specimen): he sits there to show that the human being must pass through a Regeneration before he can see God or the Divine Goodness (Osiris). Behind him is Thoth, the "lord of the divine words", the "*colonel* of the pure spirits", noting down the result of the moral life of the tried. Then come the scales, in one of which is the feather of truth; in the other the heart of the dead man. Anubis and Horus watch the scales. The *two* Truths, or Truth and Justice (over Justice being written "Thmei, who dwells in Amenti, where she weighs hearts in the balance; none of the wicked escape her!"), appear behind, leading the dead man himself, in prayer, pressing the feather of Truth to his bosom, as if to say that whether she condemned him or not, Truth was what he henceforth desired. Over him is written — "Arrival of a soul in Amenti!" and in two rows above the heads of these sit the forty-two assessors — a figure of the dead man kneeling before each row. Over each assessor is written his name; but to figure them to the minds of those who could not read, they were necessarily represented with different heads, the heads of animals, to characterise to the *eye* of the foolish the different sins. Diodorus Siculus says that in the Ramesseum the judgment of the hero Rameses is represented, and the appearance of his soul before these forty-two judges. I should like to have seen that. Alas! it is gone.

I am afraid you must find my triads and my temples tiresome, dear people; one comfort is, they are all coming to an end, and you will not be troubled with them long.

I bring home nothing pretty or curious for you. I thought in England one had nothing to do but walk into the tombs and dig out *the newest jewellery!* whereas there never was a place like Thebes for the impossibility of getting anything, — unless one brings away the base of the young Memnon to unite it to the head we have. But I hope you have not found Thebes quite "flat, stale, dull, and unprofitable". I am afraid you have an "idiot's tale"; you do not know how difficult it is to write anything about such a subject, it is like getting a genie into a bottle; and when I have succeeded in getting him in, I could sit down and cry to see what I have made of him. It is not because I have failed that I cry, but because I have profaned Thebes, and I would so gladly do something to show you what a land you have sent me to, what recollections you have secured for my whole life. I have seen no book which has been worthy of Thebes — the primæval, the pre-Adamite world! How little idea I had of her — how little I have given you!

OFF KARNAK

February 1850.

Karnak is the history of a race, the greatest race, perhaps, that ever existed — a race of giants, who illustrated themselves in their successive generations in this temple palace — it is the political, ethical, and religious manifestation of the "Unknown God" — it was the residence of his viceregents, the kings — the sanctuary of his wise men, the priests — the place of justice. In Egypt, where religion was the basis of everything; where politics were but one incarnation of it, science another; where the king really believed himself God's viceregent, and submitted to have his very time and occupations laid out for him by what was conceived to be divine law — in the actual *faith* that he was a servant and not a master — where we know that these things really entered into the very belief of men's minds, that they felt as well as knew them, there is nothing repulsive in finding the temples consecrated to *every* form in which God manifests himself.

From the twelfth dynasty, nearly 3000 years before Christ, to the Ptolemies, 300 years before Christ, you find in Karnak illustrations of the race.

Those in the Great Hall, the hall of assembly, of the time of Sethos, are the most beautiful in Egypt, — quite equal to those of Ipsamboul itself.

On the wall of the propylon, to the left, entering from the first area, is Sethos, kneeling, and offering *himself* in the form of a little figure, which is eagerly bending forward on its knees. Immediately beyond this, as if in answer to this devoting of himself, the Good and Evil Spirit are pouring over him life — as if to say, Give me thyself, my son, and thou shalt learn to draw life out of evil as well as good — out of all experience — "all things work together for good to them that love God". The Agathodæmon or Trinity hovers over head, not as usual with wings outspread, but a little depressed, as if to "cover him with its feathers". The whole conception is beautiful. In the upper compartment his farther Rameses I is rushing into the presence of Amun, quite different in his expression and character; and even without the cartouche, which always gives the name of the man, you could not mistake the different kings, so different is the character of their devotions.

Beyond, is a bas-relief in the second row, which quite puzzled me. Sethos is standing before Amun Khem, the union of the Wisdom and creative power of the Deity; between them is a sceptre standing erect, and leaning against it, two other sceptres, with little figures climbing up, some with two feathers, some with one on their heads. Whether this meant that the God gave the king undivided sovereignty, and that the little fellows were climbing up and trying to take it, or whether they were aspiring sons or what, I cannot find out.

Farther on Sethos is sitting at the feet of Amun (with his back almost leaning against his knees) who is blessing him. Thoth stands in front recording. In the previous compartment Thoth and Atmoo are leading in the eager Sethos, perhaps meaning that he has *completed* some business *wisely*, whom you see in the next, comfortably ensconced at the feet of the God. Succession was a great element in the Egyptian pictures.

Alas! that all this is being corroded rapidly by the natron, with which the soil is filled, which is heaped half way up the wall. One hundred pounds would clear this magnificent

Karnak

hall, in this country, where the people in the manufactories work for 30 paras (¾ of a piastre, 2½d.) a day, but the Pacha spends his money in bribes at Constantinople and in the lowest sensuality. The monuments of Egypt are going fast, — all that can go. One head of Sethos is just above the heaped-up soil on that propylon wall; the rubbish reaches to the chin, and soon will cover it entirely; and it is not here as in the other monuments, where the sand is a preserver, this natron soil is a corroder: this head is the most wonderful ideal of sublime serenity and childlike trust and confidence I ever saw. Σ went back to look at it, that last day, again and again. I tried to compare it with Guido's *Speranza*; but it is too different from the Christian ideal, though one can hardly tell in what — there is a purity in these heathen (?) expressions which is not in the Christian; in the heathen, it is the first fruits of a spirit soaring to God, in the Christian it is the *returning* spirit. There is that absence of the doctrine of repentance which has struck me so much in these records of a nation's religion. The Christian ideal has sinned and suffered — there has been struggle, asceticism, the cheek is pale with vigils, the eye stained with tears — it is resignation, not serenity — meekness, not trust, — composure rather than happiness — the spirit has weaned itself after long effort and weary suffering from the love of sin and earth, and placed its joy alone in the beyond, in the far away, in the future. The heathen ideal is quite different. It is purity, in opposition to repentance. There is always something of the Magdalen in Christian representations, there is always something of the Virgin in the heathen. It is the sinless soul, which has never left the bosom of its God, which finds him, the Omnipresent, as near in one spot of his creation as in another, which does not wait for another world to enjoy His presence. The Christian looks for *comfort* in His society hereafter — the Egyptian for *happiness* in it *here*. There is no asceticism in the Egyptian ideal, — all the gifts of its Father it will accept from the Father's hand — there is no struggle, the soul has never loved anything better than its God — there is no hope, it is all trust, trust that the present is as much its Father's blessing, its Father's gift, as the future can be — there is no resignation, for where evil is to give life as well as good, it is absurd to talk of resigning oneself to a benefit. Then it is love, not resignation.

But I must go on to the side wall of the Great Hall of Assembly (on the N.E.). Here Sethos is kneeling before all the different deities, making the offering to each which to each will be acceptable. This sounds monotonous. But it is not. There is the greatest variety of attitude and expression — sometimes eager — sometimes devoted — sometimes submissive. To the lioness-headed Goddess Bubastis, he is offering a little Typhon. I cannot guess the meaning of this. Farther on, enter Sethos kneeling; he is evidently advancing upon his knees, and very fast; this is before Horus. I don't know what he is in such a hurry about.

I saw on this wall a very perfect sacred boat with the shrine in it — so perfect that I could write down every part, which I did for the curiosity of it. Over the shrine or "mercy-seat", was the Agathodæmon or Trinity (the globe, asp, and wings). Then came a hand pointing the way, a Thmei and the symbol of life, "I am the *way*, and the *truth*, and the *life*"; then the three emblems of stability, purity, light, and a hand giving the sign of Set, the Evil.

Below these were two cherubim kneeling, crowned with Light, and holding *Life* in their hands, with their wings (one stretching upwards, and one covering their bodies, like Ezekiel's cherubim) protecting a Horus, also crowned with Light and holding Truth. Upon the prow of the boat were Neph (the spirit), the two figures of Truth and Light — a sphynx, or the union of physical and intellectual power, offering the hieroglyph of "chosen" — i.e. its most chosen offerings — and the king kneeling.

The rubbish, being heaped up to nearly the top of the wall, allowed me to examine this boat and help my eyes with my fingers; but it was so very plain that there was hardly any need. I was very glad to see it so distinctly, because it explains many things in the Bible — "truth as his frontlet", and "life in his hands" — "righteousness" or truth "upon him for a garment", &c. The form matters little, the shape of the shrine, it was these curious emblems which made it so interesting.

Egyptian women

The whole of the 134 columns, which support this hall, are covered with bas-reliefs, either simple intaglios or alto rilievos, as the light required, the effect being given, Σ said, by the varying depth of the cutting. They are by very different hands; it seemed to me that all those in relief were very inferior to the intaglios.

The ruin of these columns is something supernatural — here and there it seems as if one of the millstones, of which they are formed, had been twisted out of its place by a Jinn, while the one above and the one below it have not been disturbed, so that the parts of the figure no longer fit. In others, the whole column has fallen bodily, and leans against the next architrave, which yet it has not disturbed, dragging its own architrave with it. We climbed upon the roof, and walked along the lines of architraves, most of which still remain in their places, looking down upon the forest of columns below. The construction of all the Temple roofs is the same. The middle aisle of columns is nearly twice the height of the others: the two nearest aisles are raised by blocks to the same height, and the stone beams laid across, so that the roof of the three middle aisles is level; and clerestory windows are left, which lighted the Hall. The blocks of stone are sometimes enormous, but measurements never give one any definite idea. On the roof are the remains of what must have been another story, perhaps two, as no one could have carried the stones up there for purposes of warfare.

The architraves which are fallen give the opportunity of studying the cartouches: there is as much variety in the execution of these as of anything else; and though, in a cartouche, there does not seem much room for the imagination of the artist, yet there *is* variety — some seem to have taken the Gods literally — others poetically — others artistically — some set to work with earnest belief, and you see their good faith in every line — others did not believe much in the Gods, but made them as pretty as possible. We crawled under one huge block, to study the Evil Spirit (Set), in Sethos' cartouche, after whom, of course, he was called. Sometimes it is drawn with life in its hands, sometimes with a shepherd's crook; the expression of its ugly face is as various as possible. In one place Thoth is writing Sethos' cartouche. I must say Thoth made a good choice there.

Of this Sethos I, Lepsius thinks that Joseph was the Premier. Bunsen puts him a great deal farther back in the old empire (twelfth dynasty). I had rather it should be Sethos, because I feel so much more familiar with him than with the Osirtasens, and I like to think of Joseph walking in the Great Hall of Karnak.

The south-west wall of the Great Hall, and propylon towers, are so ruined, and the rubbish so high, that one cannot see much; but they belong to the reign of Rameses II who completed his father's hall, and as they are very inferior in point of art, it does not signify much. I was very glad, however, to find an old representation (of the time of Rameses II) of what I had seen at Esne (but did not care about, as that is only Roman, and therefore it was no proof) of the "fishers of men". Here, Horus, Rameses II, and Neph, were drawing a net, in which were enclosed a number of birds, "pure spirits". Thoth stood behind with a pair of scales upon his shoulders. At Esne, the net contained fish as well as birds.

Everywhere in Karnak you can see old sculptured stone built into new walls by successive generations.

But how useless it is to try with words to give any idea of the ruins of that hundred-gated Karnak. I cannot even count its approaches. By one of the secondary entrances, but which I liked the best, to the left of the great avenue from Luxor, you approach through a dromos of sphynxes, and four great pairs of propyla, one after the other, three of which are standing, all with colossi sitting before their gates, each of them a moderate sized temple. Then round all the plain, at every step you stumble over a half-buried sphynx, or a granite colossus, or the substructions of some subsidiary pylon, or mount your ass upon a broken hand, gigantic enough to make a step. The view by this approach through the three pyla of the palms beyond, which now fill up the avenue of sphynxes, is beautiful.

Am I to tell of the two sacred lakes, their shores lined with quays and ruins, and their waters reflecting propyla and towers? — of the great entrance from Luxor, which leads to the mightiest pylon of all; this has a temple of its own, and a large one too, built by Rameses VIII and Bocchoris, which you hardly notice as you approach the Temple of Karnak itself. From the first propylon of *the* Temple, which overlooks all the plain, you have a glorious view of the whole of the entrance from the river, of the plan of the ruins, of the pyla for miles round. You look across the river, and on the highest summit of the Libyan ridge beyond, you see the comitia being held for the election of the king, the God invoked under his blue canopy of heaven (they were always held in the open air), and then the whole train descending the steep cliff, winding its way by temple and palace, terraces and gardens, perhaps down the dromos, which led from the Temple of Dayr el Bahree to the river, never resting till it had crossed the river, ascended the dromos on the other side, and consecrated the king in the temple palace of the Unknown God. The train passes under the propylon on which you are standing, and fills the immense area within. I thought I heard their shouts, the triumphal march. I looked: alas! what do you think it was? An army of Arabs harnessed to an enormous stone, and dragging it away to build the house of the governor. So is Egypt losing her ruins day by day — her temples, the only thing she has left. And Mehemet Ali cleared out the two Roman temples of Esne and Dendera, and left Karnak to destruction.

The Temple of Karnak is entirely enclosed by a temenos wall. Near the sacred lake, where a little temple of Sabaco once stood, I had a glorious view of the Great Hall, with the light shining in *between* the seventeen aisles of columns and showing their shadows, and not looking down too much upon their tops. The whole of the outer walls of the Great Hall is covered with battle scenes out of the life of Sethos on one side, and of Rameses II on the other, tiresome beyond measure, I thought. And now I have ridden all round the Temple, and wish I could have taken you with me. I see the rich plain round the belts of palms, the narrower strip of cultivation, but very green, on the Libyan side. The Nile could never have come up higher on that side than it does now, as the tombs begin immediately behind the now cultivated line; and the Egyptians wasted no ground; besides which, they never allowed their tombs to get wet. I see the sun setting behind the mud village, which, before his glory, itself looks glorious, and seems to send up a cloud of incense to heaven in its evening smoke. I see the violet hills. But how can I make you see them? as I did on that last night, our farewell to Karnak.

OFF DENDERA

February 25th.

Dendera is a vulgar, upstart temple, covered with acres of bas-reliefs which one has no desire to examine; built without faith or purpose; but cleaned out by the Pacha to the bottom, so that one can walk about it but too well. The only impression one brings away from it is, that the people who built it thought that there must be gods, and that the god of the Egyptians would do as well as any other — it did not signify — take him into the Pantheon. So, without really believing much in any god, Dendera was built; and the consequence is, one never wishes to see it again; and while there, one has no wish to examine the miles of sculpture; one does not want to become better acquainted with them or with it. It is the very sanctuary of priestcraft, a wonder of holy artifice; the walls so thick that no sound can go through them — the sekos, and its two auxiliaries, entirely surrounded by a broad passage; beyond that a hedge of priests' apartments, and, finally, the whole outer wall, hollowed like a honey-comb, with secret passages, riddled with staircases, and one or perhaps two stories deep provided for beneath, in the substructions. Into these

157

Interior of the Temple of Hathor, Dendera by William James Muller (Spink & Son Ltd.)

passages you crawl through a hole, which just admits your horizontal body. We found three such in the priests' apartments; they could evidently be made up with a stone from within, so that no external trace should remain. We saw other stones, which had been insufficiently put in,

The Temple at Dendera

betraying other holes. These passages were wide enough and high enough to walk comfortably in, and led from story to story by staircases, and the whole was lined every inch of it with bas-reliefs. They had probably served for initiations, mysteries, &c. They must have been rather stuffy. Besides these, there are all sorts of wider processional passages, from roof to floor and from floor to roof. The portico of Dendera, as you know, is magnificent. I think we found the columns

to measure twice (in diameter) those of Philœ. Dendera is, of course, Roman. The earliest name which you find there is of that vile Cleopatra.

The only room which interested me was one in the roof. It was while I was there that I heard the most supernatural noise, like the sighing of spirits in hell, rising from one place, and spreading over the whole temple; evidently some effect produced (and provided for) by the wind in the secret passages.

In this chamber there was a poor imitation of Philœ; an Osiris half raised on his bier, Horus giving him life, and the soul, a human-headed bird, sitting on a tree at the head.

There was, too, an idea copied from the older monuments — all the gods, with Amun at their head (Thoth, &c. inclusive), making offerings to Osiris — a beautiful idea, that all the attributes of God are but the servants or ministers of His goodness, which animates them all. Horus, piercing the serpent, and all the usual representations were there. One new to me was of boats, with a radiating sun at the prow: but a mere list of these would not interest you, and I have no inspiration about Dendera. Outside was a frieze of kings' souls, the sun between each two, with three beams coming down to earth in the form of lotus buds, to show his fertilising power, I suppose.

There is also a little temple to Athor there, peripteral, with rather a pretty frieze on the inner side; Horus on a lotus between Typho and Mors. We rode into the sacred place — a process one does not feel a profanation there, but which is an abomination to me in general, that we, upon our asses' feet, should be treading the place too sacred in their eyes for any but the high priest, cleansed and purified, to enter — the place of all their aspirations and all their love.

The ride to Dendera through long halfeh grass and doum palms is very pretty. To the astronomer Dendera is dear, for upon its portico is the famous Zodiac, and in the Zodiac the sign of the Lion comes first, showing that the summer solstice was then in that sign, instead of, as now, in Cancer, for the summer solstice began the Zodiacal year with the Egyptians, which we begin with the vernal equinox. In the Zodiac at Esne the sign of Virgo comes first, instead of Leo, showing that then the summer solstice was in Virgo. Now this proves that, in Egypt, the precession of the equinoxes was already known, and it may prove more. But as both Esne and Dendera are only Roman, all that is certain is, that the Egyptian astronomers wished to represent in those two Zodiacs two successive states of the heavens — that in which the summer solstice was in Leo, and consequently the vernal equinox in Taurus, instead of Aries — and that in which the summer solstice was in Virgo, and consequently the vernal equinox in Gemini. Now we know that it was before the date of Dendera that the summer solstice passed into Cancer, and the vernal equinox into Aries; therefore it was not, at all events, the *actual* state of the heavens which the astronomer wished to represent, but a recorded state; and if, as Champollion thinks, both Dendera and Esne are copies of much more ancient monuments, of which the present were simply restorations, and that this proves that Egyptian astronomers were acquainted with the precession of the equinoxes at the time those monuments were made, to what a period does it not bring back that knowledge? Doctors disagree.

One does long in Egypt to know more of this wonderful race of men, the Egyptian priesthood. That promotion and power was held from the civil authority by it, as well as by the English hierarchy, and that theirs, as ours, was endowed by the state, is evident; but the duties they had to perform in return were enormous in comparison with ours.

The power of the Egyptian priesthood was evidently given them by the spirit of the people, to whom religion was everything. All their insurrections (even in Roman times) arose from insults made to their gods, and the nation invoked the gods upon every possible occasion, public and

Under the Portico of the Temple at Dendera

private. The priests being a caste, of course, all the offices and all the lands were hereditary.

But the great difference between their priesthood and ours, and the way to define it, seems to be, not that the priesthood had got hold of all the offices political, legal, religious, scientific, and administrative, but that, *all* knowledge and science being holy, the profession of *any* science made the priest. It was a national state of mind, of which we can have hardly any idea. Religion and law were its two characteristics. It was not as if a great and ambitious body had by degrees worked itself into all the power and influence in the country; it was as if the power and influence of knowledge, being sacred, made their possessors sacred. It was a part of religion as much to take care of your health as to go and sacrifice in the temple, therefore the doctor was as much a priest, or a sacred character, as the Hierophant or the Sacrificer. The priest was not the doctor or the lawyer, but the doctor or the lawyer was a priest.

Greece, where religion played so small a part, where there was so poor an idea of a priesthood, and where the service of the temples was its only occupation, can give us no true account of the real feeling which surrounded the Egyptian priesthood; so that we are almost in ignorance about it. But you find the priestly caste in every office, disdaining none, extending from the king, who was often a high priest, down to the porters of the palaces. Always with the head shaved, and the linen tunic, you recognise them in the monuments, from the scribe, with his pen behind his ear (there is a precedent 4000 years old), to the panther-skinned priest of Osiris.

The women, too, had offices and vocations in the church — as in every church except ours — the wives of the priests, the daughters of the kings were so employed. In the very tombs of the Queens you read some title of the kind.

What the education of the *highest* order of priests was, we see by that of Moses, who was prophet, legislator, general, politician, and philosopher, all that was necessary to make a king, as the Egyptians said: and we see how he beat the Egyptian wise men at their own weapons. Clement of Alexandria says that he studied in the colleges of priests, and particularly the hieroglyphic and symbolic art.

How entirely we have mistaken the character of the institution of the priests in Egypt is wonderful, though after all it is not wonderful, for how can *we* conceive a nation who wrote its religion upon its public monuments (fancy the statue of the Duke of York inscribed all over with the belief in a future state), to whom religion was what politics, what railroads are to us? There is something very beautiful in all knowledge being so religious that the very professing of it consecrated a man. To the Egyptians Sir Isaac Newton would have been as holy as St. Augustine; the one kind of knowledge was as much inspiration as the other. In this kind of priesthood there is nothing repulsive, though its later degeneracy has taught us what seeds of danger there were in it, and how to avoid them (by having none at all) — has taught us that priesthood but too easily becomes priestcraft — and we have reversed the lesson, and said that priestcraft is priesthood.

Champollion says that he has measured 50,000 square feet of sculptures on one temenos wall. I suppose there is no parallel to this in any land, and in Egypt every monument is its own interpreter; it bears its own date, its own history, its own faith engraved upon itself. There is no occasion to go, as in Greek and Roman history, to a number of traditions, all of which we know to be false, and uncertainly to grope for the truth only by comparing the false. Would we but study the language, here we have the contemporaneous history of every monument written upon its own self. Who will come and read it? For the philosophy of history, what country stretches out its hands to press such facilities upon us as Egypt? In every other one gets one's knowledge out of books — here, even we, in our ignorance, feel we have read what we know from the monuments themselves.

There is, too, this certainty, that though the Roman and Ptolemaic monuments are often disgusting from their style of art, yet Champollion says he is convinced that the ancient gods of Egypt were still reigning the day their temples were closed by Christianity; that the inscriptions of the Roman and Ptolemaic buildings are exact copies of the Pharaonic, as is proved by all the many cases where the blocks of the pre-existing building were used for and built up in the restored one. The Triads never changed. On the site of the Roman temple of Kalabsheh, which I was so disgusted with, there was a previous Ptolemaic one, and another before that, of Amunoph II — the creed the same in all, as proved by the inscriptions of the old blocks.

Homer, like Pythagoras and Plato, studied in Egypt, — the things he revealed in his poetry to Greece he did not learn there — he found them here. As Champollion says, how feelingly he puts in Ulysses' mouth "It is not a good thing, the government of many, let there be but one chief, one king." Having had the opportunity of comparing the prosperity, philosophy, and religion of monarchical Egypt with the rivalities and ambitions of Greece, — having seen in Egypt one faith, one hope of a future state — kings bowing their heads before it and their religion — law ensuring order throughout a vast empire — the highest classes submitting to it, and the rest following, — monuments which no work of man has equalled, — writing, i.e. the Demotic, in general use, — no wonder Homer was captivated with Egypt: — he spoke *avec connaissance de cause,* when he made comparisons in his own mind, odious, of course, at that time.

OFF CHEMMIS

February 27th.

We breakfasted in haste, mounted our bridleless asses, and were off before eight o'clock, to see a tomb at How, about a mile inland, which has a Judgment Scene. It was a most interesting ride: an immense plain, with cultivation about a mile in depth, then, without warning or apparent difference of level, or tongues of sand encroaching, but only divided by a sharp straight line, began desert, which reached to the foot of the square of mountains or rather cliffs; — the whole of this desert under our feet being evidently but the lid of a subterraneous city of tombs. Σ and I sat down on the sand, and were surrounded by the Sheikh and all the elders of a neighbouring village, draped and coloured like Guercinos, — red, blue and brown, — (that heap of brown drapery they wear upon the shoulder is so like his pictures) — the Sheikh looking like a St. Peter, with crimson turban and white beard: they seemed a well-to-do village, and did not cry "Baksheesh"; and there was nothing of the usual sordid look about them. But conceive our desperation when we found the tomb we came to see positively carried away bodily, — the stones, the painted stones, gone to make a

Sunset on the Nile by Augustus Osborne Lamplough (Mathaf Gallery)

Egyptian men

sugar factory at How, where Mr. B—— saw them afterwards: — not a public enterprise, but a private speculation of a son of Ibrahim Pacha.

This sugar factory employs 200 people, who are paid thirty paras a day (1¾d.). It goes day and night; an Englishman directs it.

How is very pretty, when the sugar chimneys are out of sight — acanthus and sycamore round it, and wells for the passer by.

Girgeh, with its seven minarets, looks almost like an European town from the opposite shore. The Modeer's boat anchored there at the same time as ours, he having arrived on business — that business being, I suppose, to make the miserable villages pay twice over; there can be no other here. We went to the Latin church, which, to judge from its size, must have a congregation; but the Latin father was gone to Osyoot. But with what joy I entered a Christian church again! — really my heart leaped within me! The mass-book was in Coptic and Arabic.

Girgeh is the second town in Upper Egypt; and we saw a school with six scholars, who wrote on a tin plate very tolerably.

There were no candles to be had in all the town of Girgeh, and the Coptic clerk of the above church promised to *manufacture* some for Paolo, his particular friend. In about eight hours they arrived, — pure wax with the honey in it they certainly were; but, unless appearances are *very* deceptive, they were stolen out of the church's store; and we are now burning the ecclesiastical candle. I hope our friend is filling up the gap, and now manufacturing for the church. Fancy us going to the second town of Egypt to feed, like David, on the shewbread. There was no path up from the river to the town; and all day long the unfortunate water-carriers were coming down a perpendicular steep bank, with their skins to fill, and climbing up again with a stick. But Girgeh itself is crumbling into the river bit by bit.

Here I saw four-storied houses, every window walled up with unburnt bricks, and every appearance of being *uninhabited*, — save by a woman on the roof, or a blue-veiled face sticking out of a hole in the third story. Anything so forlorn as the brown mud walls which make the streets of Egyptian towns, without windows, without any openings but the door, is impossible to conceive. One thing I must say for the poor women one meets walking alone in the streets, they never peep, they never try to show their faces, but are always most conscientiously covered; you never see anything but the oldest most withered hag unveiled.

A ruined mosque in Girgeh is the most desolate thing I almost ever saw.

We left Girgeh at night, but, when we had gone three miles, were obliged to put back for the wind. The next day we struggled on to Ekhmim, the ancient Chemmis, and *modern* (i.e. Roman) Panopolis, but there is nothing left but enormous mounds, dividing the wretched village into three.

AT OSYOOT

March 9th.

We have been just a fortnight coming from Thebes to Osyoot, owing to the north wind blowing like a tempest; whereas the whole distance from Thebes to Cairo is generally done in eight days. This has been very aggravating, as all the time that we have been lying at different places we might have spent at Thebes, and been just as forward on our voyage, and what would not another week at Thebes have been worth to us!

Arrived at Osyoot, we went straight up to Lycopolis. The view and the place were as interesting as ever, but our grand eyes rather disdained the more-than-three-quarters effaced sculptures, and the cartouches, which did not determine their age. However, my noble mind was bent not upon tombs, but upon hareems, upon Mustafa's (our cook's) "womans". I do not care a doit about seeing Abbas Pacha's hareem, one never gets further than the sweetmeats and the fine clothes; but I do want to see the common hareems. So, armed with needles and pins, we went to Mustafa's house, nominally to thank for some bread they had presented us with on our way up the river. Oh! what a curious sight it

On the Banks of the Nile by Charles Theodore Frere (Mathaf Gallery)

was — the incongruities! — the principal lady, the married sister, dressed like an oriental queen, but without a shift or anything which could be washed, next her skin, and sitting upon the mud floor — no furniture, but a slave — and the square holes for windows stuffed with mats. The second wife, in a blue shirt, stood on the threshold. The mother was baking downstairs; and two slave wives peeped in at the door. I never saw anything so beautiful, so really beautiful, as the woman's dress — of course it was her only one: — Cachemire trousers, of a delicate small pattern, — a "yelek", with hanging sleeves, of an exquisite Brusa silk, crimson and white, trimmed with gold binding, — a "tob", with immense sleeves, of lilac silk, — and over it (for the Arab never wears her gayest clothes outside) a purple gauze drapery embroidered with silver, and veil of the same colour, embroidered in silks; and, withal, she had the carriage of an empress, as she pointed to the carpet she had spread for us, and invited us to eat. The kitchen, where she had been baking, was a mere tent, screened off from the yard by mats and poles, and there was no other furniture but a few pots and pans, and one very old clasp knife, made (apparently) by Tubal Cain, which was given us to eat with. The house was a large one for an Arab, and the room we sat in was upstairs — room it was not, but a shed. Of course the woman's dress was not a fair specimen, as Mustafa, having asked us to go, had been up and in the town since daybreak preparing for us, and was himself so fine we did not know him. But there was not the slightest fuss or vulgarity in their way of receiving us when we did come. You never see an oriental in a fuss. When a Sheikh asks you for a baksheesh, he does it like an emperor.

Female fellah

167

OFF GIZEH

March 18th.

You are Dear Good People. I have found here no end of letters from you. All good news.

We arrived here on Saturday morning, 16th, and Mr. B. said we would send into Cairo for the letters, and *we* would go up the Pyramids, because then, if anything *had* happened, we should at all events have secured them. This, though said in joke, I believe pretty much expressed the feelings of all, viz., that it was a very good thing to have the Pyramids to occupy our attention while waiting for the letters. However, a greater than Mr. B. decided — the khamsin — and it made its decision with so loud a voice, that to the Pyramids we could not go. So Mr. B. and I mounted our asses and rode into Cairo for the letters, which we found after a world of trouble, and after frequently hearing there were none. Many and thick and happy ones, thank God; you are very good people. Nothing, however, decisive as to whether it is possible for us to go to Greece; so we came back again for Σ, and wandered about old Cairo in the afternoon.

Sunday we went in to church upon our asses; and meeting the Murrays, just landed, went in to luncheon, and then to call upon the L——.

You have no idea how strange it is to come back again into the world of life, and civilised wants and customs, after having been for three months and a half in the land of graves — amidst death and a world of spirits. But the spirits of the old Egyptians are such good company, and preach such nice cheerful sermons upon death and a hereafter.

I never shall forget the strange feeling, as we sailed up to Cairo on Saturday, of hearing a band of military music in the distance — we who have heard nothing but the music of the stars, or the still small voice of the dead, for a whole winter.

This morning we set finally and resolutely out for the Pyramids; but we had not reached the shore before it became invisible for the sand clouds; the wind covered us with water — it was hopeless. We said to the asses, wait — a welcome word to the Egyptian, who will wait for twenty-four hours without moving, if you tell him — and came back, and at this moment I can hardly write, and cannot even *see* Roda. We are keeping on the boat, till we have accomplished these unaccomplishable Pyramids, and are lying off Gizeh, as it is too far to go from Cairo.

And now for Memphis — beautiful, poetic, melancholy Memphis. No one had prepared us for its beauty. We thought of it as a thing to be done; tiresome after Thebes. We had three fair days of sailing from Minieh, and had not been ashore. The last night a storm arose, and we were obliged to anchor; but rain — three drops! — fell, and the wind was so terrified that it fainted away. By dint of tacking we got on the next day to Bedreshayn, but took the little boat to get there. Paolo went up to the village for asses, we starving and shivering meanwhile in the boat; and shortly we saw Gad return, driving before him a troop of asses, about thirty or forty (Gad, if I mistake not, means "a troop"). After some delay we mounted (no ass having a bridle), and rode along a causeway till we came to the most beautiful spot you can imagine. I have seen nothing like it except in my dreams, certainly not in Egypt; a palm forest, the old palms springing out of the freshest grass; the ground covered with a little pink flower (of which I have tried in vain to preserve a plant for you), and the most delicate little lilac dwarf iris. Here and there a glassy pool and a flock of goats and kids, the long sun-light streaks and shadows falling among the trees. It looked as if nature had spread her loveliest coverlid, had grown her freshest flowers to deck the pall, and throw on the grave of Memphis. I have seen nothing like this palm forest in the East. And in the middle, in a grassy hollow, by the side of a bright pool of water, lies a statue of the great Rameses, the most beautiful sculpture we have yet seen. I must even confess that there is nothing at Ipsamboul to compare with it. I never felt so much the powerlessness of words. There he lies upon his face, as if he had just lain down weary; you speak low that you may not wake him to see the desolation of his land, yet there is nothing dreary, but all is still. It is the most beautiful tomb-stone for the grave of a nation I ever saw. I felt as if God had placed it there himself, and said — "Very dear to me thou wert, my land of Memphis, and thou shalt have a fitting monument — the sweet green grass above thee spread, and one of the most glorious statues in the world to mark the place." I could have cried when I heard them talk of turning it round upon its back, — as if God had placed it there, and it should not be touched by man. This statue was given to the English. It is well indeed we did not take it. We went down into the hollow to see the features; they are composed, serene, purified beyond anything I ever saw; with such a smile on the mouth, and such an intellect in the brow. I had rather look upon that face again than upon anything in Egypt. The art is so perfect that the stone has all the softness of flesh: you are really afraid to touch those colossal stone features, the high blood nostril, the short upper lip, the moulded brow, for fear of insulting him; and

he lies so calmly upon his pillow — the pillow of his mother earth. Nothing is broken but the legs. In either hand is a papyrus, with his cartouche upon it. Though the eyes are open, there is the most perfect appearance of repose. But I am ashamed to speak about the art, when such an expression is there — the spiritualised, transfigured expression, not indeed of a Christ in his transfiguration, but of an Æschylean creation, a Prometheus, or an Abdiel of Milton. This was the colossal standing statue, which perhaps stood before the great temple of Phthah.

At some hundred yards distance is a cluster of three mounds, about a mile round, with walls of crude brick, varying from twelve to twenty-four feet thick. This we fixed upon in our own minds as the site of the temple of Phthah, that wonder of ancient times. I brought away (for the school) a crude brick, full of straw, which mayhap the Israelites may have made. At all events, it is part of no Arab building, but of a real old Egyptian one; but I felt as if I had lived so intimately with Moses and Rameses for the last three months, that I did not care much about their bricks, when I had themselves.

Today I walked with Moses, under the palms; through the desert, where he killed the Egyptian — about the palace, where he lived as the grandson of the king — round the temple, where he derived his ideas of a pure worship, and (sifting the chaff from the wheat) thought how he could retain the spirit of the religion, while getting rid of the worship of animals. I forget whether it is Manetho or Strabo, who says that "Moyses" was a priest of Heliopolis, who wished to change the worship of brutes in Egypt; and I have often thought he may have tried the Egyptians first, and failing, gone to the Hebrews. I looked at the line of hills and of Pyramids which he had looked at, and thought that probably the hills were more altered than the Pyramids. How grieved he must have been to leave Memphis, — guilty of ingratitude, as he must have seemed, towards his princess-mother, who had so tenderly and wisely reared him, and given him the means of learning all he valued so much, as the way of raising his brethren — that great, that single instance in history as far as I know, of a learned man, a philosopher, and a gentleman, forming the plan of himself educating savages, and devoting himself to it. It was like Sir Isaac Newton keeping school among the Nubians — Charles James Fox turning missionary. There was more of the Roman Catholic, of the Jesuit, in Moses, than of the Protestant. *We* should have said, what a waste! to squander such talents among miserable slaves, who won't understand you; keep in your own sphere; you will do much more good among educated men like yourself. I do not know any man in all history with whom I sympathise so much as with Moses — his romantic devotion — his disappointments — his aspirations, so much higher than anything he was able to accomplish, always striving to give the Hebrews a religion they could not understand.

Well, we rode on through palm groves and corn fields, and by a small lake where once the famous sacred lake of Memphis was, over which the dead were ferried, to the edge of the desert, where once was the necropolis of Memphis, and which we call the desert of Sakhara; a desert covered with whitened bones, mummy cloths, and fragments, and full of pits; not here and there; not in one place and then in another, but strewed like a battlefield, so as really to look like the burial place of the world. Of all the mighty world not one living man has remained to us, only this valley of their bones. Here Ezekiel might have seen his vision of the dry bones, and passed by them round about; for there were very many in the open valley, and lo! they were very dry.

Here the Pyramids lost their vulgarity — their come, look-at-me appearance, and melted away into a fitting part and portion of this vast necropolis, subdued by the genius of the place. Hardly anything can be imagined more vulgar, more uninteresting than a Pyramid in itself, set up upon a tray, like a clipt yew in a public-house garden; it represents no idea; it appeals to no feeling; it tries to call forth no part of you, but the vulgarest part — astonishment at its size — at the expense. Surely size is a very vulgar element of the sublime, — duration, you will say, is a better, that is true; but this is the *only* idea it presents — a form without beauty, without ideal, devised only to resist time, to last the longest; and age is an idea one is so familiar with in Egypt, that if a thing has nothing but age to recommend it, you soon learn to pass by it to the children of Savak and Athor, of Time and of Beauty. No, the Pyramids are a fit emblem of the abominable race they represented and overthrew. Have they a thought in them? it is a thought of tyranny. And what earthly good they ever did to any human being, but upsetting the wretches who built them, I never could find out, — except determining, by the mathematical accuracy of their position that, in 6000 years the axis of the earth has not changed an iota of its direction. As a monument of time, then, the earth is as good as the Pyramids.

Well, I had been very loth to see the Pyramids; but here we stood at the bottom of the oldest monument of man in the known world, the large Pyramid of Sakhara, which is now believed to have been the family tomb of the first of the third dynasty, Sesorchris I, 3500 years before Christ. There is nothing left to testify of man's existence before this. It is not above 300 feet high, and has a chamber excavated beneath it in the rock 100 feet deep, into which you descend by a well. I should like to have seen this mysterious cave, but it was impossible. This Pyramid, unlike the others, is made of five great steps.

I ran up a mound near it, from which I could see the whole of this necropolis of the world. Sprinkled about the churchyard stood the nine Pyramids of Sakhara. On my left, to the south, the two of Dashoor, of which the nearest is almost as large (by thirty feet) as the Great Pyramid of Gizeh

Dromedary and Arabs by Thomas Seddon (Fine Arts Society)

— both these are supposed to be of the third dynasty — near them the two brick pyramids — mere ruins. On my right, to the north, the three Pyramids of Abousir, of the three last kings of the third dynasty, and beyond them, but seeming quite near, the two Giants of Gizeh, with the smaller one of the Holy Mycerinus (all of the fourth dynasty, 3229 B.C.). Above my head was the great Pyramid of Sakhara, 3453 B.C. But their ugliness was softened away by the

The Step Pyramid at Sakhara

shadow of death, which reigned over the place — as moonlight makes everything look beautiful. I could have wandered about that desert and those tombs for hours, but fatigue and those screeching Arabs, the two great Egyptian evils, drove us away.

We stopped as we went at the tomb of Psammeticus II, a modern of 600 years before Christ, the predecessor of the Pharaoh Hophra of the Bible — who was the predecessor of

Amasis, the patron of Pythagoras and Solon, and friend of Polycrates, of the twenty-sixth dynasty. This was a series of chambers, excavated in the ground, to which you descended by a pit. The chambers were vaulted, and had pits in them. The hieroglyphs were clear; they were of the decadence.

A granite sarcophagus here, an ibis pit there, stopped us, as we rode away from the Arabs, and back to Memphis, by the long palm grove and village of Sakhara. Again we stopped, and had a long look at our Rameses, whom we found still sleeping on the turf of the valley. I never saw anything which affected me so much. I do not believe there is anything like it in the world, except the *Santa Cecilia decollata* in Trastevere at Rome. We clambered over the mounds, and thought we made out two gigantic clusters of what must have been temples. Here and there we found an Athor capital, a granite figure of an official, bearing on his shoulders one of those staves with king's heads, which were carried in processions. Otherwise the city of three thousand six hundred and odd years before Christ, founded by Menes himself, lay asleep under the green sod and the palm trees — "At her head a green grass turf, at her feet a stone."

The difficulty of writing about Egypt is, that one feels ashamed of talking about one's *own* impressions at such a deathbed as this; and yet, to describe the place itself, — one cannot — there are no words big enough. Memphis has wound itself round my heart — made itself a place in my imagination. I have walked there with Moses and Rameses, and with them I shall always return there.

I told you how Saturday morning Mr. B—— and I rode into the town from old Cairo, about two miles (I always feel so

proud when mounted like a caliph on my ass); how he deposited me with Madame François, my friend and hotel keeper; how I walked up and down the dreary sandy large high room, with no furniture, but mosquito curtains, and getting impatient looked out of the window into the white *un*windowed street; how one solitary individual came down the street, who, looking up at the same moment that I was looking out, turned out to be the mad Count we met on the Nile, who gave us birds and books, but whose name we never knew; how I was very near jumping out of the window, but remembering I should have to give back the books, refrained; how Mr. B. came back with only one letter — how Mr. Legros followed with a new pair of primrose-coloured gloves, put on for us, in which he looked like a dear old bear in satin shoes; how he fell about our necks — how he wanted me to go and see the hippopotamus — how I, getting uneasy about Σ, wished to go back — how he mounted us on our asses; how Mr. B., at the door of our consulate, remembered he must go to the Greek merchant; how I rode into the consulate, ass and all, taking her with me as a sufficient chaperone, and a quite maternal protector, even though she could not speak; how at this moment two handfuls of letters arrived — how I snatched — how Mr. Legros said, "Won't you get off to read your letters?" — how I did it, but remembering in the house the gross impropriety I had been guilty of in leaving my ass, and coming in without her, implored to go into the garden; how I climbed up upon a white wall to be modest and retiring, and read my letters; how shocked I was when wine and biscuits arrived, and were deposited by a dumb Arab in beautiful trousers before me (if it had been coffee I might have had fewer scruples); how I crawled down again, and remounting our asses, for Mr. B. had by this time come back, we embraced Mr. Legros, and ambled away to old Cairo at a pace caliphs might have envied.

Well, we fetched Σ and spent the afternoon in Fostat (old Cairo), very interesting, though differing from Memphis. First, we went through narrow, narrow streets, with threads, not gleams, of sun through them, where the Moorish balconies not only met, but overlapped, overhead, to a Coptish church in the Roman fortress, where a Coptic funeral was going on — women couchant on the floor and howling — the coffin a mere shallow tray with the body in it, covered by a pink gauze — a priest chanting; and when he had done, the finery torn off the corpse, which galloped away, followed by the women howling.

Below the church we went down into a grotto or crypt, supported by four slips of columns on either side, making three aisles, very small and low, about eight paces by seven, certainly the oldest Christian place of worship I ever was in, without excepting the catacombs of Rome. Mr. B. thought it older than any church at Jerusalem. Here, it is said, a serpent was worshipped by the Egyptians, till the Virgin and Child made it their abode, when it disappeared. Certain it is that all sects, however inimical, Copt, Catholic, Greek, Maronite, believe in the tradition, and each says mass there. I cannot help, like Robertson, believing in tradition, with one's own reservations. It is astonishing how much more difficulty we have in believing in an antiquity one thousand eight hundred years old than in one of six thousand. We have lately been so intimate with buildings of thousands of years, and cannot now believe in one of hundreds.

But however that may be, it is certain that many martyrs suffered here — that it served as a Roman dungeon in Diocletian's time. It is within the Roman camp of Fostat, and near the gate where the Prætorium was. It is certain that Mary was in Old Cairo, and I shall believe that it was here she lived till further notice. —— says it could not be, because it is so near the Prætorium; but it was much more likely that Mary should put herself under the protection of the Romans, who cared for no religion (till the Christians persecuted them), than under the enthusiastic bigoted

Cairo street scene by John Varley Jnr. (Mathaf Gallery)

Egyptians, who, like us, hated and despised every nation but their own. The insignificant Mary could be of no importance to the Romans, except as a Roman subject; for what were they likely to know of Herod's quarrels?

From hence we went to a Coptic convent, still on the site of the Roman fortress, of which the church is of the third century, full of beautiful Moorish screens and ivory work, with saints which work all sorts of miracles — one a "patriarch Abraham", who with the help of a believing shoemaker saved the Christians' lives by making a mountain move, to convince a hardly believing caliph. They showed us his and the shoemaker's picture, and the mark on the pillar where he rested his head when he prayed. Is it not curious? Evidently some mixture of the visit of Abraham to Memphis, with "Christians" substituted in the tradition; also a picture of the Virgin and Child by St. Mark, and a St. Onofrio, whose shrine was covered with bits of hair nailed under his picture by believing toothaches, who, having done this, are cured. We went to the rooms at the top of the convent, where sick Copts (among others, Dr. Abbott's wife) come to get well, and the Roman Catholic odours savoured sweet in my nostrils. But I never remember so strange a feeling as looking through a chink in the convent wall (in a great state of rapture at finding myself really again in something like Catholic precincts) and seeing the pyramids as large as life in the plain. Strange incongruity!

After alternating Osiriolatry and Mariolatry (on my part), we took a third dose in the form of Amrou's Mosque, which he built when he took the Roman fortress sixteen years after the Hegira for the Caliph Omar, calling the place Fostat, from his leather tent. He was seven months taking the place: he made it the royal city. Now, his mosque stands among mounds and ruins, desolate to see. But oh! what a beautiful thing it is; an immense open quadrangle, with the octagonal well and water "de rigueur" in the middle; at the further end a colonnade of seven aisles, so light and airy that they look

as if they were there for their amusement and were dancing with their shadows, not at all burthened by a sense of their responsibilities, but laughing merrily with the sunbeams. The adjoining side has rows of columns, three deep; the other two one. You never saw anything so pretty, or so gay. The pulpit and reading place, the niche towards Mecca, and Amrou's unhonoured tomb in the corner, are still there. But it looks to me like the place of worship of the Cluricaunes, or where Titania's mischievous elves make their devotions; not at all where a reasonable Mahometan, like myself, could do so.

We rode home over those desolate mounds — the ancient Rameses of the Egyptians, where the Pharaonic palace stood, only a little more to the south, in which Moses met Pharaoh — the Babylon of the Persians (who christened the re-built city after the Babylon of the East), whence Peter wrote his first epistle (there seems no doubt that this *is* the Babylon he mentions at the end, and that he came here with Mark, whose stay at Alexandria everyone believes) — the Fostat of Amrou, who built *his* city at the northern end of the vast Babylon. Then came Salah-e-dien, my old friend Saladin, 500 years later, and moved the city still farther to the north, to Masr-el-Kahirah (the victorious Masr), which we have degraded into Cairo, and upon the citadel are *his* ruins still seen.

All this story the mounds tell, besides the Roman one; for all the convents we saw are within the Roman fortress, which now contains a Christian village; and five steps away is the Jewish synagogue, which you can only go into on a Saturday, where the oldest copy of the law is found, and which is called the synagogue where Jeremiah was when in Egypt. I think it matters little to the spirit of the thing to verify the exact spot, whether five feet to the right or left, where these men walked and talked. If I can believe that here Jeremiah sighed over the miseries of his fatherland — that here Moses, a stronger character, planned the founding of his — that here the infant eyes opened, which first looked beyond the ideas of "fatherland", and of "the God of Abraham, Isaac, and Jacob", and planned the restoration of the world and the worship of the God of the *whole earth*, is not that all one wants? There is no want of interest, you see, in Cairo, even after Thebes.

And now, my dearest people, I must put up — very much more comfortable in my mind, I can assure you, since I have had my letters. If you can read this — it is in spite of the khamsin — at this instant the floor of the cabin is a quarter of an inch deep in sand — our faces are covered like the hippopotamus, and I could write much more easily on the table with my finger than on the paper with my pen. It is almost dark, and to sit in the sitting cabin, which is the outer one, is impossible. Let an European wait till he has seen the Nile in a khamsin before he speaks uncivilly of a London fog. We are come over to the island of Roda for shelter — where the cradle of Moses stuck — but have not been on shore yet.

As to our plans, Zirinia, the great Greek merchant, says there is no difficulty in going to Greece.

In three weeks everything at Athens must be settled between the fleet and Otho, and this dreadful wind over, which will most likely last now all through the equinox.

However, all this is *en l'air*, or rather *en sable*, at present. And if you were to see the "sable" on the paper, you would think it a sandy foundation. And the moon has just become visible, all covered with sand. She wants her face washed. We lie here because we are in mortal fear of a party to the Pyramids. People in Cairo are always making parties thither. All the boats from Thebes are coming in. There was such a shaking and bowing after church yesterday, and at Shepheard's Hotel.

THE HOTEL D'ORIENT

March 23rd.

Greek affairs go ill. I cannot very well tell what we shall do. European politics are disgusting, disheartening, or distressing — here there are no politics at all, only hareem intrigues, and deep, grinding, brutalising misery. Let no one live in the East, who can find a corner in the ugliest, coldest hole in Europe. Give me Edinburgh wynds rather than Cairo Arabian Nights. And yet they are such an attaching race, the poor Arabs, *vide* the tears of our crew at parting with us, their round merry faces a mile long, sobbing outside the door. And all for what? Merely for not having been maltreated. I am sure I could not have imagined what real sorrow it was to part from them. If I had not been crying myself, I should have said what a pretty picture it was yesterday. When they all came up to the hotel to bid us goodbye a second time, they begged to see me, else I should not have done it again, and when I went in they were ranged in two semicircles, all their shoes left outside, one black face leaning against the white drapery of the bed, even the stupid old Reis cried, and my particular friend Abool Ali, arrayed in a beautiful new brown zaaboot and clean white turban, was spoiling all his new clothes with wiping his eyes. Then they all pressed forward to salute us, Arab fashion, which kisses your hand and presses it to the heart and to the head, and then they would do it all over again, and after that we parted, and shall never see one another more.

In the evening, three of them, who had done us particular services, came by appointment for a particular conversation. And Abool Ali who is very anxious to marry, but cannot have the 150 piastres necessary to buy a "tob" or garment for the lady, — a saucepan, a mat, and two tin dishes, which is all the father, or any father requires, — agreed with me that he would really save 75 piastres within a year, if I would leave the other 75 piastres with the Consul for him. He further promised he would not beat his wife, which he said he should not have occasion to do, as she was not a Cairene, but of the country, and very steady, and that he would not put her away when he was tired of her; he was not profuse of words, and I believed him; and then he swore, not by my request, but by Allah and his two eyes. Another hand-kissing followed, and so we parted. A crew of more native gentlemen never existed; they never showed any curiosity — never peeped into our cabins, and though not only always kind, but *empressés*, they yet never intruded themselves. The only thing that disconcerted them was that Mr. B. sometimes left us with strange gentlemen at Thebes, and kept them with him, instead of sending them to mount guard over us.

But I ought to begin my story in order. I must kill a few of these flies, though unlike Sir Isaac, before I begin. I am getting just as bad as the Egyptians, and let them settle all over my face in black clusters, resigning myself to the will of Allah and the flies.

Well, I have disturbed the flies; but now you must wait another moment while I check the saltatory exercises of a few dozen fleas; but it is of no use, I might as well devote myself to the pleasure of the chase at once and for ever.

Nubian and Fellah

On Tuesday it was still khamsin, but there was so little, that all of a sudden, at eight o'clock, we made up our minds to go to the Pyramids of Gizeh; we were tired of playing hide and seek with all our acquaintance at Cairo, who wanted to make a party there; tired, too, of having the boat off Gizeh. Paolo was too ill to go with us, but we thought we could manage with two of our excellent crew. The road from Gizeh is very pretty (though not equal to Memphis), with fields of corn, and acres of that exquisite little dwarf lilac Iris. We went along a causeway between an avenue of tamarisk, — the remains of the old causeway are quite perceptible in it, built to convey the stone, which cases the inside of the Pyramid; the *outside* is built from the Libyan quarries (refer to your Herodotus). Presently those forms of perfect ugliness loomed upon our view, through a grey fog of sand, not unbecoming however. We reached the desert, — as usual without the slightest warning, and, an Egyptian donkey's wont, my ass immediately lay down to roll, — an operation he frequently repeated. In an hour and a half we were at the foot of the Great Pyramid, leaving the Sphynx to our left; but no feeling of awe, not even of wonder, much less of admiration, saluted us: there is nothing to compare the Pyramid with; you remain from first to last insensible of its great size, which, as it is its only quality, is unfortunate. As it was now calm, and the wind might rise, we immediately began to go up. As to the difficulty, people exaggerate it tremendously; — there is none, the Arabs are so strong, so quick, and I will say so gentlemanly; they drag you in step, giving the signal, so that you are not pulled up piecemeal. The only part of the plan I did not savour was the stopping every time you are warm for a chill on a cold stone, so that I came to the top long before the others. Arrived here, I walked about, trying to call up a sentiment: the stones certainly were remarkably large — the view was remarkably large — the European names cut there were remarkably large. Here are *three* sentiments; which will you have?

I do not know why the desert of Gizeh is so much less striking than that of Sakhara. One can, in Egypt, seldom render an account to oneself of any impression. Perhaps it is that Sakhara lookes like the burial-place of the world, it is so grand and desolate and lone, and so riddled with graves. Gizeh looks like what it is, the burial-place of a family of kings and their courtiers; the remains of buildings, too, about the place, give it the look of habitation, make one think of porters and sextons, and men and women; the *utter* loneliness of Sakhara, away from all that one is accustomed to see under the sun, makes one think of souls, not men, — of another planet set apart to be the churchyard of this which is the dwelling place.

It was not at all cold or windy at the top, and we did not hurry ourselves; then we came down again, but no spirit of Rameses or of Moses helped me down the steps; only the spirit of Cheops gave me his arm, and very bad company I found him. About half way is a grotto, formed by a very few stones having been taken out; and this does give one some idea of size. You stop a few courses short of the bottom, under the wonderful pointed doorway, which makes the entrance to the inside; everybody knows it by picture. It is made of four huge blocks. Here, clad in brown holland and flannel (one comfort is that the Arabs look upon this last with very different eyes from the English, as it is a festive or state garment, and two of our crew, to whom I gave flannel waistcoats, always wore them *outside* their mantles or zaaboots), having taken off your shoes, you are dragged by two Arabs (before you had three) down one granite drain, up another limestone one, hoisted up a place, where they broke a passage (how they ever found the real one is a miracle); you creep along a ledge, and at last find yourself in the lofty groove, I can call it nothing else, up which you ascend to the king's chamber. This is the most striking part of the whole; you look up to what seems an immeasurable height, for your light does not *approach* the roof; only the

A sandstorm by the Sphynx by Johann Jakob Frey (Owen Edgar)

overlappings in the sides, which gradually approach one another as they come nearer the top, give you any measure, and you see nothing but black stone blocks; blocks you should not call them, but surface, for you can barely perceive the joints. Except this, I think the imagination can

The Pyramids at Gizeh

very well supply your place in the Pyramid. After you have crawled, ramped, and scrambled for two hours in black granite sheaths, without an inscription, without a picture of any kind, but the Arabs fighting for the candle, "the mind", I assure you, "is satisfied". As to the difficulty, here again, there is none: people talk of heat, the Theban tombs are much hotter; of suffocation, I did not even feel the thirst, which in Egypt is no joke; of the slipperiness, it is impossible to fall with those Arabs. The only danger you can possibly run is that of catching an awful cold in your bones; this is unavoidable.

But I suppose, as we have got so far, I must go through with you, though very unwillingly. When I was a rat then, not in Pythagoras' time, but on March 29, 1850, which I can but too well remember, I arrived, after running in my usual manner down one drain and up two others — large airy drains they were for me — to a sort of black thing like a tank with a flat roof, and a lesser granite tank in it without a cover, where they say a very bad rat indeed, and the grandson of a worse, Shafra Chabryes, laid his bones; and he made the rats work so hard to heap up this mound which the Big Rat, his grandfather, had begun, that they would have no more kings of that family. There is a very curious way of getting out of the grandson rat's chamber; it seems the architect thought to stop it up for ever by granite portcullises, which you can still see with their grooves on the four sides of the entrance drain, and to climb out themselves either over the portcullis, or by a passage which, some say, came out under the chin of the great Sphynx, shutting up the drain as they came along. But the portcullises are broken through, and I, for my part, got under very well; some of the native rats with me spitting continually to moisten the stone for our pats. In the great granite tank are outlets to the outside of the rat hill, such as ants practise in *their* anthills, to let in air. I was very curious about these portcullises, which I thought surprising to have been made by my forefather rats 5000 years ago, and went over them again and again, but could not make out how they were managed; then I ran through a very easy drain without a fall in it, to a room with a gabled roof, just under the middle of the mound. After this, we wanted to run down the lowest drain which burrows almost to the centre of the earth, in the living rock underneath; but the rubbish has filled it up so entirely that even we rats are worsted, and it requires a mole; so we were obliged to give it up, as you know we abhor the infidel race of moles. The drains are so much like one another, that a travelled rat like me, who has seen one, has seen all. The other rats were very good-natured in hauling me down the broken drain, and then we ran out above the ground; I, for my part, thinking that the rat who made all this might as well never have lived at all.

As I was leisurely crawling up the last passage, my two Arabs having been left fighting for an end of candle, Abool Ali ran down from the outside, seized my hand, and dragged me up triumphantly to the top with the usual Hel-e-hel, with which they haul up the yard or pole the boat off a sand-bank. With this appropriate introduction, I ·emerged (oh, could anyone but have seen that scene!) to find a hareem from Constantinople; about fifty women, all looking like feather beds in their huge "habarahs", veiled up to the eyes, and three grave Turks, their happy possessors, all sitting *over* the door of the Pyramid, like a semicircle of vultures, waiting to see me come out (and drinking coffee in that happy prospect), bonnetless, shoeless, in my flannel and brown holland. If I had had "an umbrella in case of fire, it would have been something": but Σ was my good angel; she had not been in, and, though she could not speak for laughing, she pounced upon me, wrapped me in a shawl, and stuck on my bonnet. The Turks *never moved a muscle;* they probably thought me some description of sheytan, which are very common, as well as efreets, in Egypt.

Well, my dears, I expect you will murder me; I could almost murder myself: all I can say for myself is, that I have faithfully rendered in blue ink what impressions the Pyramid makes.

And now, what will become of me? That I can never revisit my native country, an outcast from my hearth and home, is certain; and — the smallest evil resulting from an ill-timed sincerity — a victim to truth I must remain. In England, where Egypt is considered as a tray for pyramids and little else, where not to have prostrated oneself at the foot of the Pyramid is not to have admired Egypt, where Egypt=Pyr. and Pyr.=Egy., because things which are = the same thing, are = one another, which is out of Euclid; it is mathematically proved that either I have not been in Egypt, or I am no fit inhabitant of the land of England: Q.E.D. Goodbye. You will never see me more. One thing is a comfort, neither will the Pyramids.

But before I sink, a victim to persecution, I will endeavour to atone for my errors by riding round the other Pyramids. The second, built by the first Cheops, 3229 B.C. (abominable man!), is the most perfect in its exterior casing; but we did not go in. The great one is built by the second Cheops, and finished by his grandson, the last of the fourth dynasty. It is no doubt a marvel of mathematical accuracy — the four sides lying to the four points of the compass — no easy matter with that size of building; height : base :: 5 : 8; ½ base : perpend. height :: inclined height : base, &c., &c. All that is very fine, but does not make an impression.

Next we rode round the third and small pyramid, where Mycerinus the Holy, who still lives in songs and hymns, was laid by a grateful people: he was the third of that unlucky dynasty. We have his body and the cover of his sarcophagus in England: there is a beautiful prayer on our lid. Beyond this are three little pyramids, half ruined, where the second Mycerinus and his wife and daughter were laid. Nitocris, the heroine of all the romance of Egypt, finished the third pyramid, in which she lies. She is the original of "Cin-derella", of Herodotus' story of "Rhodopis", the "rosy-cheeked", of Strabo's fable of "Naucratis", — her name means Neith the Victorious. She is still seen by the Arabs, a beautiful shade, wandering round her Pyramid. She main-tained the throne six years in the name of her murdered husband (2973 B.C. sixth dynasty), finished her Pyramid, invited the murderers to the consecration, when she avenged her husband and then perished by her own hand. But her sarcophagus has disappeared.

Here you can see plainly the two causeways which led from the Pyramids to the river, a rounded head of rock forming one side of something like a great entrance, and

The Great Sphynx and the Pyramids at Gizeh

near it the Sphynx. People ought to have some conscience; as to the expression of the Sphynx, you might as well talk about the expression of our High Tor. You can make out much more perfect faces there. Well, some people have imaginations, and some have not. Go to. I hope when my portrait is exposed in the same condition as this of Thothmosis IV of blessed memory, people will discover as many marks of profound intellect, great sweetness and

propriety of conduct, united with perfection of feature. A wonderful gift is "Einbildungskraft" certainly. May a "portion for seven, and also for eight" thereof be mine before I visit the Sphynx again. It is the more abominable, because Thothmosis IV, being so late as 1509 B.C. has no right to be so defaced. I cannot help it. He is said to be inside; but some may say the Sphynx only contained the outlet for the workmen, who closed the entrance to the great Pyramid. Well, let them all rest in peace, and let me rest too.

As we rode away we saw the tombs hewn in the rock, and another causeway, leading to the Libyan hills. We found our boat, stretching out its motherly arms to us, off the Nilometer at Roda, and dropped down directly to the lower end of the island (where we lay the *first* night we went on board). There we found Mr. ——, who came on board directly with his charming daughter, a black, and a great friend of mine; and the only pretty picture I had had in my mind all day, she gave me. Years ago she used to sit with her father and his gun in the moonlight on the side of the Pyramid, a few courses up, watching the jackals and wolves run by. Fancy the old white-headed man, the little black dab of a child (the ugliness of the scene softened by the moonlight), watching the troop of jackals whistling by like a rushing wind in the deep shadow.

OVERLOOKING THE EZBEKEEYEH

Palm Sunday 1850.

I am afraid to think of what I've done: look on it again, I dare not. What? Disparaged the Great Pyramid? But, after all, would any Christian lady or gentleman of my acquaintance feel much interested by crawling in drains, of which the only observable trait is "granite"? or "limestone"? "limestone"? or "granite"? for more than twelve or fourteen hours, the time varying according to the taste and pursuits of the crawler. That cannot be so *very* interesting which nobody but an explorer wants to go to twice. Egypt is like a vast library, the finest, the Alexandrian library of the world. You read, and look, and study; and read, and look, and study again; and if it is so interesting to me, you say, who can only read one word in a page, what must it be to him who can read two? At last you come to a huge folio, which, the librarian tells you, is the oldest and biggest book in the world. You run up the ladder, and turn over one blank page after another: you soon get tired of that work, and you will never run up those steps to look at that book again. And I do not call any book worth reading which is not worth returning to many times.

Mr. Harris discovered some names of the Shepherd Kings in the tombs about the Pyramids, which may lead to something.

On the twentieth we rode up into Cairo to find some rooms, where I am sitting at this moment with open windows, six o'clock in the morning, three minarets and a palm visible above the trees of the Ezbekeeyeh; the beloved Nubian, old friend of a sakia, going under the windows, and all kinds of Eastern groups under the trees. We have returned to what we call civilised habits — but how much less really savage was the dinner of our poor Arabs, which took ten minutes preparing, ten minutes eating, when they all jumped up, and thought no more about it, than the mortal hour and a half we spend every day here, out of the twenty-four God has given us, at a *table-d'hôte* of Indians, one chef and two assistants at the least to prepare it, that is thirty-six hours of time to get it ready, and if we are thirty at dinner, that is forty-five hours to eat it.

After taking our rooms, we returned to the boat, to pack up in a khamsin; and between our feelings and the khamsin, a camel would have pitied us. Towards sunset we took our last walk on Roda; but the sun went down, that khamsin day, in a glare of red sand, and we came back, without waiting for sunset. This was our last night in the *Parthenope;* the next morning we dropped down at sunrise to Boulak, intending to go to Shoobra, but the north wind was so high we could get no further, so we were dug out of the boat, as it were, joint by joint, and forced into the little sandal, where six of our men rowed us down in a nor-wester to Shoobra, mounted us on asses, had a great hand-kissing, and launched us on the wide world again. I had had my head out of the window all night to enjoy my last night on board the quiet boat, the sweet *Parthenope*. She has done us good service; and now she is looking dirty and desolate, no one to clean her out and make her look pretty; I dare say by this time she is full of fleas and hareems, and not *my Parthenope* any more: and she was so sorry to part with us. *I have another Parthenope, but she will never have anyone to value her as we did.*

We left the dear old boat wringing her hands, while we irrigated the ground with our tears all the way to Heliopolis; but we had a glorious day there, to let us down easy at parting; we could not have adjourned to the noisy, dusty, bustling inn and Indian *table-d'hôte* at once. I had always made a sort of saint's day to myself of the day I should spend at Heliopolis, where Plato walked and Moses prayed, where Pythagoras, and Solon, and Thales learnt all their wisdom; the nurse of Athens, the Alma Mater of Egypt, and, through her, of the world; that small city which had so great an influence, where the priests of the Sun dwelt, who were celebrated all over the world "for learning and meditation". It shall be my Sunday, I thought; not even Thebes is so sacred as this — and oh, how Nature has respected it.

We reached it through rich fields of corn. The mounds are small. A gateway of Thothmosis III, the king of the Exodus, has just been dug up by the Arabs, proving that there were two temples here, one beside the famous Temple of the Sun, to which the obelisk belongs. The hieroglyphs on these prostrate door-jambs are just as fresh as ever. In them, Atmoo, who was a form of Ra, and peculiarly the Lord of the Obelisk, promises the king purity, life, &c., and calls him the friend of truth. From here we rode into a garden of citron, orange, and almond trees, and there among them stood the famous obelisk, with the cartouche of Osirtasen I upon it, fresh as the day it was cut — the oldest existing "sunbeam" (its companion is gone) — yet equal in beauty to those of the best times. Now the wild bees have settled all over the obelisk, and each has made himself a house to live in — an uncomfortable place, I must say, to stick upon; but they seemed to like it, and their pleasant hum filled the citron trees and cactuses, and the sweet smells floated on the air. How pleasant it was, how lovely. This obelisk stood

before the temple where all the learning of the world was cherished! — here Moses sat, and Plato, the pair of truest gentlemen that ever breathed. But Moses was the greater man; for whereas Plato only formed a school, which formed the world, Moses went straight to work upon the world ("as

The Obelisk at Heliopolis

if a God had been abroad and left his impress on the world"), the chisel as it were to the block, his delicate perceptions acting upon those miserable savages. He was not only the sculptor, but the workman of the statue, the scholar, the gentleman, and the hard-working man, all in one.

Tell A——M—— I ran all over Roda desperately to find her a bulrush, without success; I could only bring her some rose leaves; but I gathered her a citron branch from Heliopolis, which is to me more sacred; as much more sacred as the grown-up man is than the child — and I dare say he was a very naughty one. He must have been a dreadful child at three months old to make such a noise that they could not keep him. Here was the place where he learnt, and felt, and thought, and I could have walked in that garden for days; but we were obliged to go. Here Plato lived for thirteen years; he did not think three enough to finish his education. The Grecian and the Hebrew philosophers, how they twine themselves round one's heart here! I feel as if I should know them again, better than many people I have lived with all my life — should know Plato's child-like simplicity and humility, who was "meek and lowly in heart", and gave all the glory to Socrates, his friend, and Moses' dauntless soul but sensitive mind: he *was* a man — I cannot approve St. Paul's sentiment, and say of whom "the world was not worthy", but a man worthy to do his work in the world. Oh, Moses! come again; how much are you wanted!

I did not walk so much with Pythagoras there; I believe he was mostly at Thebes, when he came over with an introduction from Polycrates to Amasis (XXVI, dynasty). Amasis gave him letters to the priests of Heliopolis, who referred him to those of Memphis, who referred him to Thebes, where they were very much surprised that he was willing to undergo the ordeal and the severe preparation necessary to be initiated. At Dendera there are some maxims on the wall about the Unity of God, signed with the name of Unnofre, the teacher of Pythagoras.

I am glad that doorway of Thothmosis has been found, because, if he was the king of the Exodus, it was built at the very time Moses was here. Some think that a fortified wall extended all the way from Heliopolis to Avaris, and that Migdol was upon it, and that Thothmosis III, brother of the Third, drove the Hyksos all along this wall to Avaris, near Pelusium, whence the Third expelled them, and raised this temple on his way back.

We were loath to leave the garden; we rode about it and found a broken stone of my friend Rameses, and the well where Mary rested — for Heliopolis has recollections from Moses and Pythagoras and Plato down to Mary — a man with an ass was coming out at the time just like old Joseph. Then we rode home through long avenues to Cairo, the very way Mary and the baby must have come on their road to Fostat; and I thought of her all the way, how tired she must have been.

The next day we sat at home, we were weary, and the H——s came to wish us goodbye, and to see my sacred Ibis, and compare it with the ancient sculptures — they had never seen one, it has become so rare. Mr. Harris is now the best antiquarian in Egypt, and his daughter is very learned too; I was very sorry to part; she is almost the only person I can talk to about Egypt — we "understand each other".

I ran about all the next morning after bird-men for S.; in the evening we rode up through those never-ending pictures of streets to the citadel. Mr. L——, who has been everywhere, says there is no Moorish architecture to be compared with that of Cairo for the best style; no Arabian city that he knows comes near it; Constantinople is a degenerate mixture of the worst Italian. As to Mehemet Ali's mosque on the citadel, how such a building could ever have entered the imagination of men to conceive passes belief: two minarets, like Mordan's patent pencil-cases, set on end — a mass of white ugliness, and you see it from everywhere. We were allured into the old lion's den, where our drawing-room sofa first met my eye, then two of our chairs. We made out the corner where he sat, with the Pyramids seen through a window, with splendid French curtains, to his right! Then we went down Joseph's well, that incredible

The Carpet Bazaar, Cairo by William James Muller (Bristol Museum and Art Gallery)

work, a square shaft hewn through the living rock from the top of the citadel to a sakia, which pumps up the waters from the Nile. Some call it the work of Saladin, but there is no doubt that he only cleared it out, and that it is a work of the old Egyptians. No others would have done it; it may have been ordered by Joseph. They show a something at the bottom which they call his tomb.

Sunday we went to church: but how could a man preach such a sermon in the land of Moses! Oh, go out, good people, to Heliopolis, and see what your race can do; you will not learn it in that church at all events. Σ and I stayed at home the rest of Palm Sunday: it is very interesting to see in the old Egyptian sculptures the custom of strewing palms in the way.

Cairo is overflowing with Franks; but we have hitherto refused all invitations, we were too tired.

Today we have been to the bazaar; but you have no idea how difficult it is to find anything in Cairo you like unless you buy the house and window — that *would* be a present. I never saw such a picture as the end of the silk bazaar, with a Moorish arch at the farthest corner, and two others on either side, where it is fastened up by a chain, and you can look about without danger of being borne down by a string of camels. And then the groups you see! I did buy a scribe's ink-horn, such as they wear stuck in their girdles in the sculptures, like Ezekiel's man, "which had the writer's ink-horn by his side". They sell all goldsmith's things by weight, and, as government manages everything, we had to go to the government scales to have it weighed, for which we had to pay. In the little goldsmith's shop, which is nothing but a square box or shed open upon the street, sat, on the front, a woman wrapped in her black silk habarah, all but one eye, which was a very pretty one, who had brought all her diamonds and pretty things, and even her silver goolleh tops for sale — she was probably separated from her husband. She asked no questions, showed no interest, but sat, the picture of meekness, and despair, and resignation, while her things were offered to us by the goldsmith. But the bazaars are so queer; there is no choice, no stock, but people walk up and down the shady street, roofed in at the top, with their bracelets and things in their hands, which, if you catch a sight of, you may buy, if not, not.

Alas! we have now done with Egypt — Cairo is not Egyptian, it is Arabian. The day we sailed into Cairo we were at the place, a little south of Old Cairo, where Moses, after going to the Pharaoh at Rameses, and returning to the people several times, led them away at last. The Arabs have a tradition marking the spot where he sat and counted them passing by. "Goshen" took in Old Cairo and Heliopolis, and extended northward along all the right (eastern) bank of the Nile.

The only thing which now remains to us of Egypt is the Pyramids, which stand there, looking as if they would wear out the air, boring holes in it all day long.

I am sure that no European can at all imagine the entirely different feeling with which one lives in Egypt compared to anywhere else, nor describe it. It is perfectly distinct from that in any of our living countries. It is like going into the Sun, and finding there not one living being left; but strewed about, as if they had been just used, all the work, books, furniture, all the learning, poetry, religion of the race, all the marks fitted to give one an idea of their mind, heart, soul and imagination, to make one feel perfectly acquainted with their thoughts, feelings and ideas, much more so than with those of many of one's own kin. You open the journal left lying on the table, and feel almost ashamed of prying into its secrets; you see the place where they have been praying; you walk about, expecting every moment the people to come in, but not a living being — all, all are gone, and not one "escaped alone to tell thee". But it is not necessary for anyone to tell the tale, you read it written everywhere. But still, the star is a deserted one; it had a race, of which not one remains, for besides that Egypt to an European is all but uninhabited. The present race no more disturbs this impression than would a race of lizards, scrambling over the broken monuments of such a star. You would not call *them* inhabitants, no more do you these.

So farewell, dear, beautiful, noble, dead Egypt, the country which brought forth a race of giants — giants in war, art, science and philosophy. Farewell, without regret, without pain (except a merely personal sorrow), for there is nothing mournful in the remains of a country which, like its own old Nile, has overflowed and fertilised the world, and to which you can so plainly hear its Maker saying "Well done".

Goodbye, dear people: I am afraid you are tired of Egypt; but I have mercy now upon people for writing such stupid things upon her, it is impossible to write anything else.

AT CAIRO

March 1850.

I knew so little about the Mahometan religion, and it interested me so little, that I felt quite strange in the mosques of Cairo. In Karnak I felt that their God was my God. In Ipsamboul I felt more *at home,* perhaps, than in any place of worship I ever was in. But Egyptian Mahometanism I never could understand, never could feel any interest in, never could look upon as a religion at all. However, I must say that Arabian Mahometanism is very different, and that the mosques of Cairo are quite as wonderful, quite as poetic an incarnation of the intercourse of man with God as anything in Thebes or Nubia itself. When one goes into any church, be it the temple of Karnak, be it St. Peter's, be it the Mosque El Azhar, be it St. James's, one always feels, Here is the foot of Jacob's ladder, and angels are ascending and descending upon it — this is the gate of heaven. But in London, the room that they can spare to plant the foot of Jacob's ladder is so small; twenty-six inches to each person, is it not? They fulfil so literally the word that *strait* is the gate, that sometimes the "angels of God" have not room to spread their wings, and decline coming; and, at best, we cannot call it the poetic incarnation, i.e. the incarnation of the *spirit* of the thing, but the matter of business incarnation, i.e. a man must go to church, therefore take as little room, and get as much for your money as possible. What does man want room to think for? — thinking does not pay.

In Karnak it is, above all, the philosophical incarnation. In Cairo — what shall I call it? If you would look for a contrast, striking and glaring in every respect, small and great, it is between the Arabian and the Egyptian. In Thebes you never see two lines parallel, two sides alike, two columns the same size. In the Moorish architecture every pattern grows out of a mathematical figure — give the key note, and you can finish the air for yourself. But there are deeper differences than these.

The mosques of Cairo are the most beautiful, the most gorgeous, the fairest in the world — those of Constantinople are barns in comparison, they say. Even the Moorish art of Spain cannot vie with the Moorish part of Cairo, which is one great Alhambra. But it is impossible to describe, and the great drawback is that, as you must have a firman and a Pacha's janissary, and pistols, and whips, and I don't know what besides, to visit them, you must not loiter, you cannot go again, and they remain in one's mind, quite ineffaceable, but still one great dream of confused magnificence. It is more like a dream than anything else to me, now that I have been in Cairo, though I must say it surpasses everything that the names of Bagdad, and Damascus, and Haroun El Rascheed ever did conjure up in those childhood days of dreams.

We spent many days among the tombs of the Mameluke Sultans in the desert, and I wish we had spent as many weeks. So wild, so dreary, so beautiful, so deadly fair, as they raise their spirit-like heads in the desert, you become an efreet yourself wandering among them; yet there is nothing in them hideous, like the Pyramids, which become more utterly repulsive the longer you look back upon them; for here the mosque and the "Foundation" are always the principal feature, the tomb is merely supplemental — the place for fellow-creatures to worship God, the school for them to learn God, is the main thought; the human element is always the uppermost, while in the Pyramids it is only the selfish.

Still, though it is against all truth to feel melancholy among images of decay or change, I must confess that those Mameluke tombs are the most profoundly melancholy places I ever was in.

There sit the Pyramids on the other side the river (I knew they were there, though I did not choose to look), utterly repulsive, but defying time, though they have been the quarry for half Cairo, — here lie the most beautiful creations of man's hand, crumbling away; in a very few centuries they will be quite gone — and one asks, are beauty and decay the same thing? Can ugliness and selfishness only be compatible with duration? If it is God's thought, there can be nothing melancholy in it. But what *is* God's thought about it? It cannot be a law that only perishable forms have beauty.

I wish I could describe these mosques and tombs. There were three to which we always managed to go — El Berkook, El Ashraf, and Kait Bey. You know the general plan or plans of them; there are but two; one after the original pattern of Asur (the first built after the Hegira), viz., a square hypæthral court, with the tank in the middle, and porticoes all round; the portico opposite the entrance being the deepest, five to seven ranges of columns, and out of this, under its little dome, the tomb of the founder. Under this portico is the pulpit, and the niche towards Mecca. Turn thy face to Mecca, I soon found myself saying; but these wonderful places of worship, what idea do they incarnate? I cannot call it anything but sensual Unitarianism. I do not feel that I understand it in the least, and I doubt whether it is possible for an European really to seize the mixture of sensuous enthusiasm and severe unity and purity of idea in these extraordinary places — thrice extraordinary to those coming out of old Egypt. Where is the Holy Place? you say. Where is the Secret Sanctuary? You walk round an open court, you look up to a cloudless sky, down into a pure cistern, nothing but air, earth, and water is here. Where shall I hide myself? was my first feeling — are there no mysteries, no initiations, no ceremonies in this religion for the poor human mind, striving after images, to lay hold of? None. But here is silence, here is space, here is room for thought in these vast colonnades; turn in here, walk up and down among those columns, no one will disturb you but those prostrate men, with their faces to the ground, as silent as yourself. Are you tired of your daily work and the busy city? Here are places where everyone may have rest and thought. And so it is. Oh! if the poor women had but been there, I could have said, this is the very thing I have so often sighed for in London, where there are tens of thousands who never, from their first to their seventieth year, *never* have one moment alone, one place in which to pray, to think. And here, in this noisy and infidel Cairo, they have spared these magnificent spaces, always open, and open to all.

But what am I to think about? is the next question. Are there no images, no deeds of God or of God's saints to speak to my eye, to excite my thought? None; there is not a single image. A sentence of the Koran is the frieze, the ornament. The most rigid Unitarianism is the first thing which strikes you, and the last. Nothing is to alter the purity of the idea of the one God.

Even the very domes catch the sentiment. At St. Peter's I observed the bridge of rays was three, which entered through the windows at the rising sun, to remind us of the Father, the Son, and the Holy Ghost. At Sultan Hassan, the dome which after St. Peter's has struck me the most, two rays bridged the vast mysterious solitary space; for there is but one God, and Mahomet his prophet.

But it is not the Western Unitarian who has built this; though here is severity in doctrine, there must be enthusiasm

in practice. And I cannot tell you how touching it is to see (among these "infidel dogs") man giving *all* his best to God, the fairest that he has, the most precious, the most costly, instead of keeping it for himself — it is literally lavishing his best. Ceiling, wall and floor are inlaid with the most delicate mathematical patterns; those of the ceiling made of mother-o'-pearl and different coloured woods; those of the walls of mother-o'-pearl, lapis lazuli, and precious marbles; those of the floor of *pietra dura*, more beautiful than anything I have seen in Rome. Here there is nothing held back: God was to have *all, all*, the best. It was not, How can I choose that which will make most show, at least cost? but, What is most beautiful, most costly? — that must be for the house of God. And yet there is nothing of the pomp of wealth here. On the contrary, upon the first coming in, nothing strikes your eye, you are only pleased by the perfect harmony of the whole, by the wonderful and subdued richness. After a time you discover that you are in the midst of gold, and precious stones, and mother-o'-pearl. Certainly, as Jacob said, "this is none other but the house of God".

Then they could find no other frieze worthy of it but what they believed to be the word of God; in all, round the springing of the dome, runs, in gigantic gold letters, upon a sober blue ground or yellow, a sentence from the Koran, sometimes outside as well as in. And, certainly, no more poetic frieze could have been invented; perhaps it is this that kept the Arabic character so beautiful, while all others have become so prosaic. In the Mecca niche the name of God, no image of Him, no glory round it, generally holds its solitary place.

You never go into a mosque and find it empty.

But what go ye out for to see? What are the worshippers of this most dreamy, yet most sensuous Unitarianism assembled for there every day and every hour of the day? Is it for a daily sacrifice, either actual or commemorative? For a sacrament, like the Jewish, the Roman Catholic, and the

Mosque Interior, Cairo by Rudolph Swoboda (Mathaf Gallery)

Protestant? For a mysterious charm, which wins the Divine presence down upon earth, like the S.S. Sacramento? The God of the Muslims has no sacrifices, no mysteries, no charms; the only incantation by which the Muslim invokes his presence, is his own devout spirit; the only place where he seeks and hopes to find Him is in himself. This is, after all, the most enthusiastic faith, which, disregarding the help of ceremonies, disdaining the use of images, sets itself to finding God in the *heart*, in its own solitary heart, unaided by communion with others, by the infection of enthusiasm (except occasionally, as in the dervish dance). It is impossible not to be touched with admiration and sympathy at the sight of a Mahometan at his prayers, of his perfect abstraction and his entire simplicity.

I think a Cairo mosque gives you a better insight into the Oriental mind than anything else can. It is the religion of the Arabian Nights, of Solomon's Song, of Genii. It is the most dreamy, the most fantastic, the most airy, and yet sensuous religion. It is the religion of Undine before she had a soul. But it is not the religion of men — not of rugged, crooked, hard-necked man, but of spirits. It will never lead a man to morality, to inflexible unswerving duty, to the spirit of sacrifice, excepting in as far as with his sense of beauty and his dreamy enthusiasm, he loves to give all to God. The Egyptian is to me the philosophical view of religion, the Protestant is the moral (nothing else), the Roman Catholic the spiritual, which makes self-sacrifice an enthusiastic pleasure, and goes merrily to its martyrdom; the Moorish is the imaginative, I had almost thought the fanciful view of religion.

I am afraid I can give you no idea of these mosques and tombs, the purest of Moorish architecture. I confess, to me the lines are far more beautiful than the Gothic. In the Gothic arch, diminishing and diminishing and diminishing, like within line, and again within line, I am troubled and provoked; and it seems to me to be the hand of man

diminishing the thought of God, and adding precept within precept, till he has twaddled it all away with his nineteenth-ly and his twentiethly. But in those airy caves, which fill the top of the Moorish arch, in those delicate stalactites overhead, I seem to look up into an ocean cave, to see the

The Tombs of the Mamelukes

hand of man simply applying the thought of God, to see almost a work of God himself. In beauty, nothing surely can come near the Moorish architecture.

In the Mameluke tombs, we always went first to that of Sultan Berkook (E' Zaher Berkook). You know his history — how he was first a Circassian slave — then regent for the last of the Bahree Mameluke Sultans, and deposing him, in 1382, how he founded the dynasty of the Circassian

Mameluke Sultans, to whom Egypt and Syria remained subject for a century and a half. Berkook twice repulsed the Tartars under Tamerlane. Round that solitary mosque are evident traces of a learned Foundation, and of "riwaks" or apartments, for the students, where now the jackals dwell — I mean the Egyptians. I like those first words of the Creed, "I believe in God", so much, I want no others. I have so often said them to myself in Egypt. Those four words run in one's head perpetually here. I believe in God — Him who knows all, who can all, who loves all, and *therefore* no one can ever be lost — and therefore Egypt *will* be saved – and therefore one can believe, even of *these* creatures, that "it is good for them to be here" — I believe in God, and therefore Egypt is not hell, as one would otherwise believe.

But I have left El Berkook and his two minarets, which I think are the most beautiful in Cairo; not rising in steps, one story above the other, nor yet like a Chinese cap, but each exquisite little balcony bowing down to meet the one below it.

After El Berkook we go to the tomb of El Ashraf, a Sultan of the same Circassian dynasty, and perhaps the gem of them all. It is on the other plan — no hypæthral court — an oblong mosque, with coloured glass windows, and roof inlaid, and leading out of it the tomb, a double cube, including the dome, with dado, niche and floor, all rich with marbles and mother-o'-pearl. A new pattern you discover every time you go, or a new figure, forming itself out of an old one; and yet — though the longer you look the more you see, a cross here, another figure there — there is no confusion, the eye is not displeased by the intricacy. The colours are very few, generally red, black and white, with a little blue. Here a little girl, who I believe was a mother, held my paper with one hand and her baby with the other, while I was tracing, and did not ask for baksheesh — a fact which I record. Our third tomb was El Kait Bey (near the end of the same dynasty), during whose reign Grenada was lost by the Moors, 1492. This is the most magnificent of them all;

you have the square mosque, with the horse-shoe arch on the four sides, opening on every side to a raised divan or recess, the floors of which were strewed with palms, and the ceilings rich with the sober colouring of the most beautiful and precious inlaying — the Koran frieze — the tomb within, double cube, with the beautiful woodwork screen round the grave. Mahomet left his sacred foot-print here — one of the few fanatics I never could feel any respect for — it was easy to manage men in his way. The beautiful entrance to the mosque has a little school opening out of one side, where the master, with his little establishment of a few beads, a few leaves of the Koran, and a few bits of tin for the boys to write upon, welcomed us rather unusually.

After our second day at the tombs we rode back, past Kaït Bey and the citadel wall, and stopped at the spot where Mary, on her way back to old Cairo, must have looked down. From this point six cities of the dead and one city of the living lay before us — all the vast southern cemetery, which we had not yet visited — all the plain, through which Moses once led out the Israelites, on the morning of the Exodus, and beyond, on the other side of the river, the whole line of the Pyramids, Dashoor, Sakhara, Aboush, and Gizeh — I never saw a more extraordinary view. We rode on though the tombs, and in at another gate, Bab el Karafeh, within which lies the great square of the Rumeyleh, surrounded by its splendid mosques, and overtopped by the citadel. From the Rumeyleh you pass down a narrow street, with a beautiful black wooden house with meshrebeeyehs on one side, and on the other, high, high above your heads, the gorgeous arch of the porch of the mosque of Sultan Hassan — to my mind, the most beautiful thing in Cairo. This gentleman belongs to the dynasty of the Bahree Mamelukes, the one preceding the Circassians, and his mosque was built about 1356, two years after his death. (I have such difficulty in not putting the B.C. to my dates). When Saladin and his successors ruled over Egypt, they strengthened themselves by buying Turcoman Mamelukes, or white slaves, and bringing them up as military slaves on the island of Roda, wherefore they were called the *Bahree* Mamelukes or Mamelukes of the river — Bahr is river. One of these white female slaves, the "tree of pearls", Sheger-ed-

The Mosque of Sultan Hassan

Durr, was married by one of the Sultans descended of Saladin, and she began the dynasty of the Bahree Mamelukes, putting to death her step-son for this purpose. This was in the time of St. Louis, at Damietta. Sultan Hassan was later by a century.

Oh, the glory of that mosque! You enter from the top of a flight of steps by this towering arch, with its little caves at the top, into a dark porch, surrounded by four arches, and with an inlaid wall in the front, and turn to the left, where

men bring you straw *canoes*, and fit them on over your shoes. Then you cross the sacred threshold, and find yourself in such a court! — hypæthral, as large as any of the mosques; instead of being enclosed on each side by rows of colonnades, vast arches span the whole space (like the Temple of Peace). The eastern, the largest and loftiest of them all, seemed to me like one of those dreams which one has when one is a child, when the bed seems to rise and rise over your head, and to expand at last into something unknown in magnitude. I felt as if I had seen Sultan Hassan before. His eastern arched vault is like Westminister Hall in grandeur; it rises free and clear to its summit; only a gigantic sentence of the Koran on an arabesque ground runs round it. Behind is the mysterious vastness of the tomb, as you look into it from this arch, with, perhaps, one solitary figure, in his flowing scarlet robes, entering it — the dome rising to one knows not where, and the corners for the dome filled with those woodwork caves! How I should have liked to have gone there alone, and again and again!

The next day we went to the mosque of Sultan Teyloon, which is very curious as a "monument of architectural history"; its pointed arches prove that they existed in Saracenic architecture three centuries before they are found in ours; and that we borrowed them from the Saracens. Ibri Teyloon lived in 883, and was the man who first, like Mehemet Ali, declined allegiance to the Caliphs of Bagdad, saying, "I will reign in your stead, not only in Egypt but in Syria". But as he was a Turkish slave, he could not be Caliph, or descendant of the Prophet, therefore the Caliph, as head of the church, was still prayed for — there were farces then as well as now. The Arab name for the place, "Kalat el Kebsh", recording the tradition that this was the place where Abraham sacrificed the ram, interested me more. We went along the ruined roof and up the minaret; the decay of the mosque, which is crumbling away, arches and all, is cruel, and it is dangerous walking there. In the large ruinous court grow trees about the tank, and while the party walked round, Σ and I sat and meditated.

From Sultan Teyloon we came out by another gate into a narrow little street, so rich with woodwork, meshrebeeyehs, and carved doorways, that this must have been the place of

Interior of the Mosque of Sultan Hassan

the Arabian nobility. Then we rode through the town, and stopping at the small city-gate, got off and went into a little street, where we could not ride — such a picture of oriental life. In the tiniest meshrebeeyehs we saw blue bundles, showing that the women had got in, body and all — I wonder they did not break down. We peeped into shady courts, and then we rode out across the southern country of tombs, which we had seen yesterday, to a mosque in the

side of the Mokattàm. Even the Mokattàm is riddled with old Egyptian tombs, like Lycopolis, and in its yellow rock this modern mosque, the tomb of a Sultan, nestles itself: we wound up the cliff to it — such a view! — and in a gay little dressing-room, laid out upon a tray, and with an open window, through which he is looking out at that wonderful view, lies his Vizier — such a nice way to be buried!

I crawled into some curious little cells; I do not know what they were. Then we came down into a modern Turkish family tomb, so clean and dressed with flowers, such a nice *homey* place. But I did not stay in it, for there was a mysterious, gloomy, lurid sunset behind the Pyramids — the first and only time I have ever seen them look well — like the fall of Babylon; they looked immensely large and spectral. The ground descended, from where we stood, in a series of vast sweeps, all deserts, to the river. It was like the Last Day — that sunset among the tombs — as we rode home through them in the gathering darkness, for it was already twilight. The tombs all looked wan and spectral as we passed them — there was still that lurid glare in the West, and the graves of nations seemed to lie about us. We rode in through the great Place of the Rumeyleh, and passed Sultan Hassan with his towering arch in the twilight — he, too, looked like a spectre, but a friendly one.

Aimé, how little I can tell about our field-day among the mosques! We enjoyed at last the privilege of going out like princes, and, furnished with a firman, we set forth. First rode the Pacha's janissary, armed, and carrying besides a whip; then the Consul's cawass, entirely arrayed in white, and also armed, then our janissary, and finally we. But oh, if you knew how difficult it is to bring away a single impression, hurried through them with a party! — The Consul calling to us, and very properly, to keep close, and not to loiter, the Pacha's cawass driving back the people — as well you might try to see Rome in a day. We went first to El Hakim, a ruined mosque, of enormous size, through which a thoroughfare now runs. It is close to Bab el Mur, and was founded in 1012 by that man — I don't know whether he was a true man or an impostor — who founded the Druses — the El Hakim, of that race of Fatimeh which, at first, ruled only over Northern Africa (over the real Moorish race), having made themselves independent of Harouh El Rascheed in 800. They then thought proper to possess themselves of Egypt, and founded El Kahirch, and called themselves Caliphs. After it we went to the mosque of Sultan Kalaoon. He was the founder of that dynasty of Bahree Mamelukes to which Sultan Hassan belonged, and this mosque was built in 1284. In Kalaoon's tomb, a little quiet place, we found a man praying; he moved when we disturbed him, and began again, so intently, so intensely, yet so quietly, you would hardly have thought he was yet in the body. But the mosques are all mixed up in my head, and miserable has been my account to you of them. However, it could not be helped, so I will just say that Sultan Kalaoon stands by the Morostàn, the madhouse, which he founded, in the most beautiful of all the streets in Cairo. We were so hustled at the corner, where we got off our asses, by the angry people, that we could not stop a moment; but we would not submit to drive in a carriage, as some of our party did. We made a vow, and kept it "strong", that we would not get into a carriage all the while we were in Cairo. You can see nothing of the best streets, if you do, it is brutal, and it is unsafe.

I bethink me I have not told you about El Jama el Azhar, "the splendid mosque", certainly the most curious mosque in Cairo. After passing the usual winding porch and passage,

you find yourself in the large square hypæthral court, crowded with people, sitting, standing, praying, talking, and making, so unlike the silence of the other mosques, a most tremendous noise. The whole court is surrounded with buildings, and at the farther end is the deep, deep

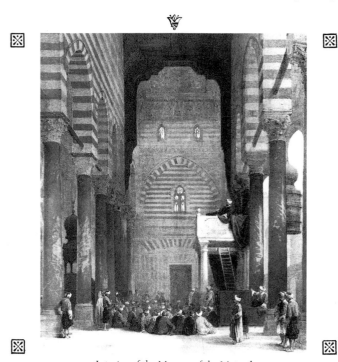

Interior of the Mosque of the Metwalys

portico, eight columns deep, divided in this case from the court by partitions between the front row. It was all matted or carpeted, the walls and ceiling quite plain; and here there was the most profound silence; only, leaning against a pillar, here and there stood a sheikh or imàm, and at his feet sat a circle of men, either intently listening, or writing, or learning by heart — grown-up men — none of them boys — and the Muslims put us to shame by the care with which they learn their religion, with which they study the Koran, and listen to commentaries. It is said that in Cairo the Muslims are generally much better instructed in their religion than the average of Christians ever are in theirs — how these grown-up men can find the time is the wonder.

That was the most oriental sight I ever saw — those lecturing ulama, those silent circles sitting on the ground: no need of desks or benches; each had his little plate to write on upon his knee, his ink-horn, like Ezekiel, in his girdle, each sat cross-legged on the mat. It carried one back into the Temple of Jerusalem, where the boy Christ sat down in like manner among a similar circle — into the days of Arabic learning, when Bagdad and Damascus were the Universities of the world. You cannot conceive what a picture it was — the robed and turbaned professor — the Oriental dignity of the listeners. We went into a side chapel, called the Chapel of the Blind, where 300 blind students are maintained upon a foundation. One was sitting with his back to the wall, chuckling at having got his lesson well.

We could not stay, for the people were getting irritated at the presence of the Christian female dogs in this sacred mosque, and the cawass was obliged to protect our departure, not with his sword, but with his whip, which he carried on purpose, beating back the people. Our departure was very like the way in which one backs out of a field where there are angry cows. As to the Mahometan horror of us, I never could feel anything but the deepest sympathy for it, the deepest humiliation at exciting it. When you think that a woman who goes with her face uncovered is, with them, more indecent than a woman who should go without clothes among us— that it is here the stamp of a disgraced character — it is exactly as if a dancer were to come, in her disgraceful dress, into Salisbury Cathedral, during the time

of service. Would not the vergers put her out? I only wonder at the tolerance with which we are treated here, not at the contrary — but it makes an European woman's life in the East a misery.

The Azhar is the university of the East, for it is the

Gate of the Metwalys

university of Cairo, and Cairo is the only city which keeps up its reputation as a school of Arabic literature. The riwaks or apartments for the students still surround three sides of the court, each country or province having its foundation. All the instruction is gratis, and formerly the students, who

The Street and the Mosque of the Ghoreeyah, Cairo by John Frederick Lewis (Forbes Magazine Collection)

are mostly poor men, were fed; but that man, Mehemet Ali, that great prince, who has such a reputation for advancing civilisation, took possession of all the lands of the Azhar (among the other mosques), and consequently of all the salaries of the ulama, or learned men, so that they now receive nothing, but are obliged to maintain themselves by private lessons, &c. There is some credit in being a professor in the Azhar now, and giving away learning gratis. To do so, permission must be obtained from the sheikh of the mosque — I should like to see our Cambridge men asking permission to teach gratis. The poor students must also get their living as they can, and the imàms of mosques are generally chosen from among them; but since this great confiscation, their number has, of course, diminished; and what between Mehemet Ali and the French invasion, the learning of the Azhar has altogether deteriorated, which, no doubt, that good and wise man was glad to see.

From the Azhar, we went to the Hasaneyn, the most sacred of all the mosques. The sheikh at the door read our firman over twice before he would believe that we were to come in, and then an imàm ran to shut the silver doors of the place where the head of the martyr El Hoseyn is buried, the grandson of Mahomet, the son of his daughter. I had got off from my ass first, and might have run forward too, but I was ashamed to give them pain in a place where we were only upon sufferance at all. In the Hasaneyn there is nothing to see any more than in El Azhar. There is no hypæthral court; it is simply a portico, carpeted and supported by many columns. But the silence and twilight of the place are very striking. One solitary professor leaned against a column, with a circle of, I suppose, eighty men at his feet.

We rode home past my favourite sebeel, one of those public fountains which there are in almost every street in Cairo — the most beautiful specimens of Moorish architecture and Moorish hospitality. It has a semicircular front, jutting out into the street, with three grated windows;

behind each window a trough of water and a chained mug — you put your hand through the grating and drink. A deep wooden coping, carved and coloured, overhangs the windows, generally with all the beauty of Moorish fretwork; and above, or beside, is a school-room, open (except by pillars), to the street. But Mehemet Ali seized upon the funds of all the sebeels, which were generally the gift of private individuals, and they are fast going to decay. When there is not a sebeel, there is a hod at every corner of the streets — a trough under a little arched recess. But the commonest thing is to see a sakia, or one of the old water-carriers, with a goatskin of water at his back, giving to drink out of his spout to everyone who passes by, having been paid to do so by somebody, either for the sake of a dead friend or of some welee, whose festival is being kept — or if the person has been simply making a visit to a tomb. The sakias chant while they are doing this, offering a charity in the name of God. It is very pretty; and you are supposed to implore a blessing, if you drink, for the person who is gone.

Riding through the streets of Cairo is endless in its delight, though how you ever get through you know not; the ass manages it. It is true your ass-driver keeps up an incessant "shemâlak, shelmâlak", thy left, thy left; "riglak, riglak", thy foot, thy foot; "hôy, hôt", attention, attention: though whether this is addressed to the ass or the passengers, I never could make out, for, in spite of hôt, shemâlak, and riglak, nobody stirs; and the 20,000 asses which are said to "perambulate the district" every day — for in Cairo no one but the slave and the beggar walks — tread on to the tune of squashed babbies.

OFF ALEXANDRIA

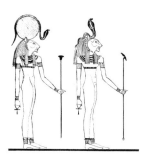

April 1850.

WELL, DEAREST PEOPLE,

I suppose you are waiting for a description of Cairo, but you will not get it, I am sorry to say. You might as well try to record a dream: and I do not know whether the waking dream of the living city within, or the silent vision of the dead city without, is the most unreal. I am sorry we have not seen the dervishes dance, to which I had looked forward much; but it so happened that Good Friday and Easter Sunday were their only days; and we did not like to go galloping off the instant after that service was over. Did you think of me on Easter Sunday at the Sacrament? And on the full moon of Holy Thursday, as I looked out upon that vast city, which did not know its right hand from its left — which did not know, perhaps not fifty of them, perhaps not five, what they were put into this world for, as the night-cry from the minarets fell on the still air, and told how they were really seeking God — I thought how Christ, if he had been there, would have felt; how he would have yearned over Cairo, and how he would have been straitened till his task was accomplished. Behold that great city — how would he have set about her deliverance?

I never told you about our day to the Petrified Forest. It had been a long settled thing that we should have a day in the desert — that Mr. Murray should send out a tent for us to spend the heat of the day in, &c. This party swelled to inordinate dimensions — Lord Lincoln and the North-amptons, &c., made part of it. We were all to go out separately at whatever hour we pleased. We set out late, as we do not mind the heat, and had a great deal to do that morning.

It was not till noon that we issued forth, Mr. B. and the German professor on dromedaries and we on asses.

So we rode through the desert — Sheikh Bisharee with us. We rode a long way, and could see no traces of the tent, till we met one of the Bedouins, who offered to show us the way, and we found it at last in a little valley, under the ridge of Gebel Attaka, the Valley of the Deliverance, believed to be the line by which Moses led the Israelites. The Petrified Forest is a very curious deposit of immense palms, bamboos, and many trees not belonging to Egypt; evidently left by the subsiding of some mighty stream. The desert for miles is strewed by them, and we measured some of vast size. I believe the thing is quite unique in geology. From the top of a ridge, we saw a wonderful view of the Pyramids, which look larger and larger the farther you get from them. The encampment looked very pretty as we rode up, with all the white Arabian horses and dromedaries picquetted about, and the Arab servants. But the hills and valleys of that wild desert, which Moses, so strong of purpose, actually persuaded the infirm of will to pass through, when within the very sight of the flesh-pots of Egypt, are not places for the flesh-pots of picnicking.

We left Cairo a week earlier than we intended, which is the reason why we have seen so little of the Arabian city; we idled at first, being tired, and then afterwards found no place for repentance.

Easter Monday was our last day. We went before

breakfast to Dr. Abbott's museum, to look at his funeral papyrus, which we could now understand a little about. The different transformations of the dead, different trials, and subduings of successive vices under the form of beasts, like the labours of Hercules, are all there. Then we went to

The principal Mosque at Boulak

Schranz's, to get you some photographs; and long we stood in his little narrow street, in the Copt quarter, where the meshrebeeyehs not only met, but folded in overhead, fitting in and dovetailing into one another; and friendly walls, tottering to one another, supported each other by a

horizontal prop between them. Every story projects a little farther than the lower one, till the top all but meets. A solitary old water-carrier, a blue-veiled woman, sauntered occasionally along. On a sunny day the effect is too spotty for beauty; the streaks of light and the deep shadows are too zebra like, too chequered; but on a cloudy day, the light and shade is beautiful — in a glaring sun, you would not believe it (in an accurate drawing), nor admire it, if you did.

Easter Tuesday we left Cairo — the Transit driving us down to Boulak in thorough English style, to our great disgust, with an English coachman, and an omnibus and four. On board the boat for Atfeh we found my dear Madame Rosetti, the Tuscan Consul's wife, all the Zizinias, Count Benczik the Hungarian, a sick French woman, and the reverend Mother of the Good Shepherdesses at Cairo, — all her sisters clinging round her as she was bidding them adieu to return to France upon a mission.

We were a day and night on our way to Alexandria — and what a curious day and night it was! There was the mother of the Zizinias, an old Smyrniote, her beautiful hair, at sixty years of age, dressed round a red tarboosh, with a blue gauze cockade — a sort of cross between an Indian Begum and Lady Holland — putting everybody to rights who sat where it did not please her, and looking like the head wife of a pacha. What curious contrasts there were that night, between this fierce, undisciplined, clever old Smyrniote, with her fine beetling brow and brutal mouth, and the severely disciplined and repressed and chastened white nun, with every passion in order, and every feeling checked, except that which belonged to her vocation. She was a German of high family (and gave me a letter to her sister, at Munster), had gone through the cholera and every disease at Cairo, where she had had her sisterhood *thrice* renewed from Europe during her five years' superiority, for the sake of establishing the first sisterhood that ever has been there; and having utterly failed, and, as she said herself, wasted life for nothing (alas! she ought to have all Cairo in her Refuge), was undertaking this journey to the Maison Mère, at Angers, for the sake of having the Refuge re-organised upon a different system. So suffer those who pioneer a new road — so fall those who throw their bodies in the breach; but they bridge the way for others to tread upon them. Yet the woman was as serene, and simple, and cheerful as if she were a child gathering daisies, instead of a prophet gathering souls. Another contrast was between the weak, wicked, gambling, dying Frenchwoman, who dragged herself in the middle of the night into the gentlemen's cabin to play cards, though dying of a hideous complaint, and the devoted, genial, fervent Madame Rosetti, who sat wherever no one else would sit, slept where no one else would lie, subdued even the fierce old Smyrniote to help her in making poor people's clothes, nursed the sick woman, and melted all these different raw ores under her sunshine; not disciplined, like the white nun, but denying herself out of the very fervour of her benevolence, and as anxious to get us into a hareem as she was to perform her Easter *retraite*, and to read a good book to the boat with an inflammation of the windpipe, working the whole time at her poor's clothes.

It was a curious night. A third contrast was between a languid, spoilt, pretty Indian we had under our charge, and a little ugly tiger of a Zizinia, who, under cover of being a fiancée, ran about giving her lap-dog to hold to any gentleman she met, but as free with her coffee and her bonbons, with which she kept all the company alive. We did not get to Atfeh till ten o'clock, too late to bid adieu to our solemn Nile; who, indeed, had been all that day as ugly and as contrary as it was possible to be. It was pitch dark. We had heaps of luggage. Nobody helpful but Σ. There was the wretched sick woman to be carried. Mrs. ——'s spoilt child would not part with its wax doll. What was to be done? A good-natured man took charge of the doll and the

child, and I took charge of his baggage, as being the least helpless thing of the two, and of Mrs. ——. At last we arrived at the Mahmoudieh Canal — you have to walk across to the boat, as they do not open the locks at night. If anybody could have drawn that scene, how good it would have been. The imperious old Smyrniote, with her blue cockade in the foreground; the miserable Benczik, with the Zizinia dog in his arms, which it became a *tour de force* to be able to hold; behind, helpless females not daring to step across the plank. At last Mrs. —— and I were left alone on the shore. Paolo came. "Take Mrs. ——," I heroically cried: "I will not stir from the hat-box of the man who has taken charge of the doll."

At last we were all lodged on board the Mahmoudieh boat, where you sit bolt upright all night on the benches round the cabin, with a large company of biting animals of every description. The moon shone, the horses, each mounted by a wild Arab, galloped — for you are towed by horses — and we went along very merrily, only occasionally going aground, owing to the lowness of the water. At breakfast, the old Smyrniote ate enough for ten men's dinners. It was too cold and too ugly to go on deck. We reached Alexandria about twelve, and spent the rest of the day in making ourselves clean, and seeing after that wretched Frenchwoman.

The news from Greece was bad; and all thought it best and shortest to go to Corfu by the Trieste boat — do our quarantine there, instead of perhaps two quarantines at Smyrna and Syra — and get the latest news of Athens.

I was sorry to leave Alexandria, where I had troops of friends: all the Sisters of St. Vincent de Paul, Mme. Rosetti, Miss H——, and the white reverend Mother.

On Thursday we had a knocking-up day: we had to wash up and pack up in a great hurry for a final farewell to Egypt, and we paid a visit to Miss H——. Abbas Pacha is said to be very ill with the *fêtes* which he gave on the

Camel Train at Twilight by Charles Theodore Frere (Mathaf Gallery)

marriage of his eldest son. It is hoped that he will die, in which case Said Pacha, who is an excellent man, an educated man, and a gentleman, will succeed. The viceroyship goes to the oldest male heir of Mehemet Ali.

On Friday I was up early, and spent the morning in the St. Vincent Schools. At Alexandria, Abraham would have found the thirty righteous men — women, I mean. I never saw so charming a woman as the schoolmistress nun, and when I observed her careful knowledge of the disposition of *every child* (300), and thought of the patent improved-man-making principle at home — the machine warranted to turn out children wholesale, like pins, with patent heads, — I did not wonder at the small success of our education. Except in the Ragged Schools in Edinburgh, and one in Westminster, I have never seen anything so perfect as this. The horrid system of classes was entirely done away with, by which *we* reverse the system of Providence, who does not make children come into the world like rabbits in a litter, but gives (to the majority) that finest of all educations, the having a younger to take care of, an older to look up to: beginning in early life the discipline we all have afterwards. In my nun's school, each of the elder children was the *bon ange* of a little one. Those in whom she had most confidence had two or three "daughters"; this was the highest privilege she could give. And when you consider that her scholars were taken out of the most degraded population in the world, the Arab, Smyrniot and Maltese, you can hardly overrate the importance of the principle she thus set in motion in their hearts. The carelessness for infant life here, the horrible neglect and filth in which the children live, or rather die, is what no Mungo-Park-description of the misery of an African village can give the least idea of. The mortality among infants in consequence is something you would hardly believe; you cannot blame the people for it, when you know that the best service a mother can do her own child, and the one she most frequently performs, is to put

— *A street scene* —

out its right eye, or cut off its forefinger, to save its being enlisted for the Pacha's army. Here was the indefatigable nun writing another law in her scholars' hearts, for the time when they should become mothers. She said she found that the necessity of setting a good example to the protégées was everything as an influence with the protectors. It saved her, too, the necessity of many a scold. When the little one came late, the *ange* scolded for her, and if the *ange* scolded too zealously, which often happened, she said, "You must scold like a guardian angel, always keeping that idea as your model." In class a big girl and a little one stood alternately.

In their hospital the noise had been at first inconceivable. The Arab knew neither how to sit nor to be silent; the sisters could not make their voice heard. But they began with raising their hands before they could raise their voices, as the signal for silence, and now the most perfect discipline is observed.

I have seen the idea of the "*ange*" system in the Ragged Schools, where the dirtiest boy is made to look after the cleanliness of the others, and a large thief to superintend the morals of a smaller, and where it acts excellently too, but never so well carried out as here. We muddled away all the rest of the day in our preparations, packed up the boxes for England, and so forth.

Saturday was our day for leaving Egypt — our last day in the East; and really I think my most curious day — perhaps the most curious day of my life. The things were to be on board by eight o'clock, so I was up early; and by seven, I had plenty of time to go and wish the sisters goodbye. As I was like a tame cat there, I went in without ringing, and straight to the dispensary, where I generally found two or three hundred Arabs waiting. I found one of the sisters digging in the garden, and, coming in with her, was just sitting down for a chat among the bottles, when the reverend Mother of the Good Shepherd, my white Cairene friend, came in, hearing I was there, and wanting to talk to me about her

sister at Munster. We were all very merry together, when a message came that there were some English sisters in the Parlatorio, and "would I go in, as there was no one in the Convent who could understand them?" So we all adjourned; there we found the Superior of the Sisters of Mercy in Australia, who had been founding an establishment there, with one of the sisters and a little "Bush" child. She had undertaken this immense voyage home for the sake of getting help and more sisters from the mother establishment; had been up three nights, and was going off that very afternoon. She was to leave the little "Bush", who was quite tame, in Europe, to be educated. There is a freemasonry, instead of a jealousy, among the Orders; they all go to one another's houses for hospitality; and whether they can speak one another's language or not, they are always sure to find help and sympathy. And here were three superiors, none of them old women, meeting from different quarters of the world, all on their way home (for the Alexandrian mother was going too), one to Angers, one to Paris, one to Dublin; not on ther own business or their own pleasures, but on objects of their mission to their Maison Mères, for purposes of re-organising, enlarging, &c.; and all so simple, quiet, and merry about it. You would have thought it a very cheerful morning visit if you had made such a one in London.

The superior of Australia would not allow she was glad to be going home; she said she longed to be back, there were so few sisters to do the work; and they had nine little Bushes in the house, besides their day-schools, a refuge for servants of *good* character out of place, and the sick to visit. She said the work of the Egyptian sister was harder than theirs, for the "Bushes" had no religion, — absolutely none; and therefore there was nothing to undo: it was all doing. The little child she had with her was an orphan, and had been bought for a shilling (a hundred miles up the country from Perth) from her tribe, who were going to eat her. Others had been rescued in like manner, but they had now some

The Hareem by John Frederick Lewis (Victoria and Albert Museum)

scholars whom the mothers themselves had brought — a great encouragement. The establishment is at Perth, has been founded four years. Tired as they were, they wanted to see the house, the Arabs in the dispensary, the schools. I took them round. The little Bush was taken to the little Arabs, who cried out, "Here is a sister!" She behaved very well. Then we went into the dispensary, where the patients asked if that was the head Hakim, pointing to the Australian sister, who was a very tall and beautiful woman, and whom in her black robes, different from the dress of *their* sisters, they took for the first physician.

They wanted a priest to confess, but there was none who could speak English. They were eager to learn all they could about the Arabs; pitied the Egyptian sisters, who are decimated by the climate, thought themselves "so well off". The St. Vincent sisters take no vows, and are not engaged for more than a year, when they may marry, or do anything else, *sans blesser leur conscience*. They support the establishment by taking *pensionnaires,* and reckon that, for every *pensionnaire,* they can take two *orphelines*. So that these labourers not only bring in the harvest, but work for their bread; — not only work without hire, but pay for their own work. I think St. Paul would have been pleased.

Alas, I was obliged to go, to my great distress, for I was afrid of being too late; and so we parted, all four, they to their work, never to meet again.

Madame Rosetti had made, unknown to us, an appointment with Engeli Hanum, the wife of Said Pacha, for us, which she could not break, so off we set on asses, in our travelling coats, to the hareem. Two successive curtains (two successive gardens between) were lifted up to let us pass. Troops of beautiful white Circassians came to receive us; a black showed the way. Through marble halls, with fountains in the middle, we passed, till we reached the room where Engeli Hanum rose to receive us. Tall, and with a beautiful figure, unlike these Turkish women, she seemed to

Egyptian lady waited upon by a Galla slave

us the most lovely woman we had ever seen, with that soft melancholy eye, that exquisite mouth and complexion. Everyone says that she is unique among the Turks. Such manners: so sweet, so humble, so benevolent to the poor.

I am glad our hareem specimen did not send us away in disgust. I felt that I could have died a martyr to give her one hour of such feelings as those Sisters have; but I was nearer the consummation of my kind wishes than you can have any idea of, for certainly a little more of such a place would have killed us. Luckily, we were obliged to hurry away for the boat, though the first time we got up, she would not let us go, having no idea that there could be such a thing as necessity. Oh, the *ennui* of that magnificent palace, it will stand in my memory as a circle of hell! Not one thing was there lying about, to be done or to be looked at. We almost longed to send her a cup and ball. She was dressed in a green pelisse, lined with fur, over yellow trousers and train, and was sitting in an immense marble hall, with no article of furniture but the divan, embroidered with the moon and star. She was too much of a born gentlewoman to examine our dress, and there we sat, without even the weather to talk of; coffee came, of course, and pipes covered with diamonds; and the Circassians, the most graceful, and the most sensual-looking creatures I ever saw (like dancers) stood in a semicircle, or knelt round us. The very windows into the garden were wood-worked, so that you could not see out. The cold, the melancholy of that place! I felt inclined to cry. Presently she got up, and took us into another hall, to see the family pictures; the tears filled those soft melancholy eyes, when she looked at that of Mehemet Ali. She was the only thing the old Lion loved, and he would have given her his kingdom. I don't wonder at it. I would have died for her, but I could not have lived with her. She was herself a Circassian slave, adopted by Nezleh Hanum, Mehemet Ali's eldest daughter, which is done by the process of passing the child through the dress; this gives all the legitimate rights of a daughter. She is the only wife of Said Pacha, the youngest son of Mehemet Ali, and the future viceroy.

A little adopted daughter of her own was brought in for us to see, dressed in yellow satin, and a shawl round its waist, with a turban and a little train — a sweet little child; but I felt how much I would rather be that little Bush; how much better chance *she* had than this. After this penance was over, we went away, she as gracious as real kindliness could make her, sending her compliments to our husbands, and begging us to come back. There was nothing sensual in *her* countenance as in that of the slaves — she looked sighing for better things. I had rather have felt less interested in her, though that is wrong. But, if heaven and hell exist on this earth, it is in the two worlds I saw on that one morning — the Dispensary and the Hareem.

The princess did something for Madame Rosetti's poor while we were there, and I was pleased to see how Madame R. was welcomed by everybody in the hareem.

That afternoon we sailed.

APPENDIX I
GODS OF ANCIENT EGYPT

(Names in brackets represent present-day usual spelling)

AMUN (Amon) the god of Thebes, who adopted the attributes of other gods. His name meant "hidden" and he was represented as a bearded man wearing twinfeathers on his head. After the defeat of the Hyksos, which was thought to be due to his influence, he adopted the attributes of the god Ra and was called AMUN-RA, the "King of Gods" and was the principal god in the great triad of Thebes.

ANOUKE (Anqet) goddess of the Cataracts and wife or daughter of Khnum, the god who was supposed to have created man on his potter's wheel. Together with Sati, they formed the great triad of Elephantine and the first Cataract. She was represented as a woman with a tall feather headdress.

ANUBIS the divine physician and god of the Dead, who embalmed the body of the murdered Osiris and was guardian of mummies. He was represented as a jackal or as a man with a jackal's head.

ATHOR (Hathor) the cow or cow-headed goddess, known as "the Golden One". She was goddess of love, beauty and fertility and was often associated with the Greek goddess Aphrodite. She was the nurse of the child Horus.

ATMOO (Atum) was always represented as a man. An ancient solar god, he was adopted by the priests of Heliopolis as their chief god and, as such, wore the double crown of Upper and Lower Egypt.

EILETHYIA (Nekhbet) the oldest mother-goddess of Upper Egypt and protectress of pregnant women, she was represented as a woman wearing the white crown of Upper Egypt or as a vulture, which was her sacred bird.

HORPIRE (Harpocrates) Horus the Son, the third god of the triad of Hermonthis, proceeding from Mandoo and Raettawy.

HORUS the falcon god who came to be seen as the son of Isis and Osiris and who is therefore represented either as the falcon, the solar god, or as Horus the child – both have various representations.

ISIS sister and wife of Osiris and mother of Horus, whom she delivered in the lotus swamps of the Delta. She wore the hieroglyph of her name on her head and was often represented suckling Horus. She was the ideal of mother and wife.

MANDOO (Montu) the leading god of the triad of Hermonthis, he had the head of a hawk and wore the feathers of Amun with the globe of Ra.

NEPH (Khnum) represented as a man with a ram's head and sometimes wearing an asp, which was sacred to him.

OSIRIS god and judge of the Dead, husband of Isis. He was murdered by Set and was represented as a bearded man in mummiform: His hands were crossed over his chest and held a crook and a whip. He was the greatest of all the gods of Upper Egypt and humans assumed his form when they died in the hope of resurrection.

PHTHAH (Ptah) the great god of Memphis, who appeared as a mummified man. He assisted Khnum in the creation of the world and was the patron of the arts and crafts.

RA (Re) the sun god of Heliopolis who assumed the attributes of the old solar gods and became the head of the "Company of Gods". He was often represented as a falcon-headed man who wore a solar disc and the sacred asp on his head. He was compounded with other gods, including Amun as Amun-Ra.

SET (Seth) the god of evil and destruction, brother and murderer of Osiris and perpetual adversary of Horus and the sun gods. He was also the god of tempests and was represented as an unidentified animal, similar to an okapi or zebra.

THMEI (Ma'at) the goddess of truth and justice, she was shown as a woman with an ostrich feather (the symbol of truth) on her head. Wilkinson explains that Thmei is the Coptic word for truth.

THOTH represented as an ibis-headed man, or as an ibis, he was the scribe of the gods and the lord of wisdom and magic, who invented writing and mathematics. He was represented as the heart and mind of the creator of the world.

APPENDIX II
KINGS AND PHARAOHS OF ANCIENT EGYPT

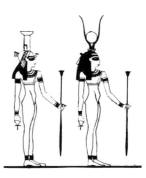

(Names in brackets represent present-day usual spelling)

ALEXANDER III (THE GREAT) the first of the Macedonian kings of Egypt, who defeated the Persian Darius III at Issus and arrived in Egypt in 332 B.C. Received with enthusiasm at Memphis, he was crowned pharaoh, but left Egypt in 331 B.C. to pursue Darius and never returned. He founded Alexandria, where he was buried in 323 B.C.

AMUNOPH (Amenhotep) III 1417-1379 B.C., 9th king of the XVIII Dynasty, called Memnon by the Greeks.

AMOSIS (Ahmose) II 570-526 B.C., 6th king of the XXVI Dynasty.

CHEOPS (Khufu) 2nd king of the IV Dynasty, c.2613-2494 B.C., builder of the first (the Great) Pyramid at Gizeh.

CLEOPATRA VII PHILOPATOR 51-30 B.C., joint sovereign with her brother, Ptolemy XIV, who drowned, and with Ptolemy XV, who was poisoned. Through her marriage to

Julius Caesar, she bore Ptolemy XVI, called Caesarion, with whom she ruled. He was killed by Octavian and she committed suicide in 30 B.C.

HYKSOS c.1674-1567 B.C., XV and XVI Dynasties. During the weakened reigns of the XIII and XIV Dynasty kings at Thebes, a number of Semitic tribes settled in the Nile Delta, which led to the establishment of an independent kingdom in the north. The settlers, who were called the Hyksos, or Shepherd Kings, established their captial at Avaris and worshipped the god Set.

MENES I (Aha) 1st king of the I Dynasty c.3100-2890 B.C., who unified Upper and Lower Egypt and established the capital at Memphis.

MYCERINUS (Menkaure) 5th king of the IV Dynasty, c.2613-2494 B.C., builder of the third pyramid at Gizeh.

NITOCRIS first woman recorded as an independent sovereign in Egypt. Manetho called her "the noblest and most beautiful woman of her time". The last ruler of the VI Dynasty, who completed, enlarged and was buried in the Third Pyramid at Gizeh.

OSIRTASEN (Osorkon) I 924-889 B.C., 2nd king of the XXII Dynasty.

PTOLEMIES 323-30 B.C. Ptolemy I, Soter I, was one of Alexander's generals who took control of the country and founded his own dynasty on the death of the Macedonian. He reigned from Alexandria where he founded the famous Alexandrian Library. The Ptolemaic Dynasty ended with the death of Cleopatra VII, when Egypt became a Roman province.

RAMESES (Ramesses) II (THE GREAT) 1304-1237 B.C., 3rd king of the XIX Dynasty, a great builder and successful general.

RAMESES (Ramesses) III 1198-1166 B.C., 2nd king of the XX Dynasty, developed the Egyptian navy.

RAMESES (Ramesses) IV 1166-1160 B.C., 3rd king of the XX Dynasty.

RAMESES (Ramesses) V 1160-1156 B.C., 4th king of the XX Dynasty.

RAMESES (Ramesses) VIII 1147-1140 B.C., 7th king of the XX Dynasty.

SABACO (Shabaka) 716-702 B.C., 2nd king of the XXV Dynasty, whom Budge suggests can be identified as So, of 2 Kings xvii,4, and who had his rival, the lawgiver Bocchoris, burnt alive.

SESORCHRIS (Zozer) I 2nd king of the III Dynasty c.2686-2613 B.C., who built the Step Pyramid at Sakhara, the first large stone construction.

SETHOS (Seti) I 1318-1304 B.C., 2nd king of the XIX Dynasty.

SHISHAK (Sheshonq) name of four kings of the XXII Dynasty, c.945-730 B.C. Sheshonq I was the Shishak of I Kings xiv,25, and 2 Chronicles xii, 5, 7, 9, who conquered Palestine and sacked Jerusalem.

THOTHMOSIS (Tuthmosis) I 1525-1512 B.C., 3rd king of XVIII Dynasty who set up two obelisks at Karnak and was the first king to be buried in the Valley of the Kings.

THOTHMOSIS (Tuthmosis) III 1504-1450 B.C., 5th king of the XVIII Dynasty.

THOTHMOSIS (Tuthmosis) IV 1425-1417 B.C., 7th king of the XVIII Dynasty.

APPENDIX III
19th CENTURY CHARACTERS MENTIONED IN THE LETTERS

ABBOTT, Dr. Henry joined the Royal Navy as a youth and trained as a ship's surgeon. Left his ship at Alexandria and was physician to the Egyptian fleet until 1830, when he set up his own practice in Cairo. He had an important collection of Egyptian antiquities, which was recorded by Bonomi in 1846 and which Abbott tried unsuccessfully to sell in New York in 1853. He did eventually sell it to the New York Historical Society, although it was transferred to the Brooklyn Museum in 1948. Dr. Abbott died in Cairo in 1859.

BRACEBRIDGE, Charles a well-known traveller and ardent Hellenist, whom Florence met in Paris through Mary Clarke. He and his wife took Florence with them to Italy in 1847 and it was on their suggestion that she accompanied them to Egypt. Both he and his wife went with Florence to the Crimea in 1854. When he died in 1872, Florence wrote that he was "the best and noblest of men. All his life he was fighting battles against cruelty and oppression."

BRACEBRIDGE, Selina the wife of Charles Bracebridge and Florence's confidante. The Nightingales referred to her as Σ, the Greek letter *sigma*, in recognition of her love of Greece. Mary Clarke described her as "a tall, stately, irresistable, line of battle ship" and Florence called her "more than a mother to me". Two of her watercolours of Egypt are included in the introduction to this book.

HARRIS, Anthony Charles a merchant and commissariat official at Alexandria, he built an important and valuable collection of Egyptian antiquities which he bequeathed to his daughter on his death, in Alexandria, in 1869. He was President of the Egyptian Society in Cairo.

HARRIS, Selima adopted negress daughter of Anthony Harris, who sent her to England for her education. On her return to Egypt, she was his constant companion. She inherited his collection on his death and eventually sold it to the British Museum. She died in Alexandria in 1895.

LEIDER, Rev. Rudolph Theophilus a German missionary born in Prussia in 1797, who worked in Cairo for many years for the Church Missionary Society. He became a priest of the Church of England in 1842 and translated or revised a number of texts in Arabic. He built a collection of 186 items of antiquities which Lord Amherst bought for £200. He died of cholera in Cairo in 1865.

MAI, Aunt Mrs. Samuel Smith, Florence's paternal aunt who was in sympathy with her desire to work and who went to join her in Scutari during the Crimean War.

MURRAY, Charles Augustus an Eton and Oxford educated lawyer, who was appointed secretary to the British Legation in Naples in 1844 and Consul-General in Egypt in 1846, a post which he held until 1863, after which he served in a number of other foreign missions. A funerary papyrus, which was bought for the British Museum in 1861, was named after him. He was knighted in 1866.

PARTHENOPE Florence's elder sister who was given the Greek name for Naples, where she was born. She collected and edited Florence's letters from Egypt in their first edition of 1854. She married Sir Harry Verney in 1858, after Florence had rejected his proposal of marriage. Parthenope later gained a considerable reputation as a hostess in society and wrote several novels, one of which, *Cornhill*, was published in 1865.

ROSETTI, **Madame** wife of the Consul for Tuscany in Egypt, who had received Champollion on his visit to Egypt in 1828. Her father-in-law had been the Consul-General for Austria and other countries and had been employed by Napoleon during the French occupation.

GLOSSARY

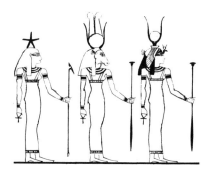

ADYTUM the innermost part of a temple, a sanctuary.

ALTO RILIEVO a relief or sculpture in which the figures project more than half their thickness from the base or background.

BASTINADO to beat or whip, a common occurrence in Egypt, as Florence noticed. It usually meant a whipping of the soles of the feet.

BAKSHEESH a tip, or a gift of money, as it was often demanded for no reason. The cry of "Baksheesh" was a familiar one in Egypt.

BAYADERE a dancing girl, usually unveiled, often confused with an almeh (a public singer). Public female dancing was prohibited by law – along with prostitution – in 1834. The punishment for a first infringement of the new law was a whipping of fifty lashes. A second offence was punished with a year or more of hard labour.

BEDOUINS Arabs of the desert. They were originally nomadic tribesmen who, as the crew of the *Parthenope* were aware, were often beyond the law.

BEY a (Turkish) title of rank, usually that of governor.

BOOZA an intoxicating liquor made from fermented barley-bread. It was especially popular with the Nile boatmen. It was not, however, the origin of the English word "booze".

CALIPH the Muslim title for a civil and religious leader, a successor to Mohammed. The Caliphs were the ruling power in Egypt from Omar's invasion of 638 A.D. to the death of Mohammed El Motawukkel al Allah in 1543, when the Sultans of Constantinople assumed the title of Caliph.

CAROUBA a carob tree.

DAHABIEH/DAHABEEYAH a large sailing boat on the Nile, usually with two or more inside cabins. They could be rowed or pulled up river if there was no wind. Travelling by dahabieh was considered the most stylish way to see the Nile, although, with the introduction of steamers, it also became one of the slower means of travel.

DAYR/DEIR a walled monastery, of which there were several along the banks of the Nile.

DERVISH a devout Muslim of no specific nationality or religious order. The most famous were the dancing, or whirling dervishes, who performed as part of their religious devotions.

DOURA a millet or maize which was usually sown on land too high to be irrigated by the inundation of the Nile.

DROMOS a pathway or avenue, lined with rows of sphinxes, leading to a temple. The most famous dromos was the one connecting the temples of Karnak and Luxor.

EFFENDI a (Turkish) title of respect, often used as a greeting.

EFREET a powerful demon, often applied to an evil genie, but also to the spirits of the dead. Florence often uses it in a figurative sense to suggest her attendant or guard.

FELLAH a peasant or country person, usually a farmer (plural, FELLAHIN).

FELUCCA a small, open, single-sailed boat on the Nile.

FIRMAN an edict or licence. It was necessary for Europeans to obtain firmans in order to visit some mosques, shrines and other sites away from the usual touristic route. The firman would guarantee their safety.

FLAGELLUM a whip, held by Osiris, god of the Afterworld, in his left hand. It was a symbol of royal authority.

GUBBEH a long cloth coat of any colour which had loose sleeves which stopped before the wrist.

HABARAH an enormous outer robe, usually of silk, worn by Egyptian women when leaving the house.

HAKIM a physician in Muslim countries.

HOD a drinking trough for cattle.

JANISSARY a (Turkish) soldier or escort, especially for travellers from Europe and America.

JINN/JINNEE or genie, a class of beings between angels and humans and created from fire. They were believed to be capable of assuming any form or of becoming invisible at will.

KHAN a caravanserai, a large rectangular building enclosing a large court which was used to accommodate merchants and travellers.

LEVINGE a mosquito net, hung from the ceiling or from a hook, which was attached to the top of a pair of sown sheets. Named after its inventor, who received his inspiration while travelling in the East, it was recommended by Sir John Gardner Wilkinson in his 1843 guide to Egypt. Florence considered it invaluable against draughts as well as mosquitoes.

MESHREBEEYEH windows which often projected several feet from the wall of a house and which were covered in lattice-worked wooden screens. They were often used by women who were able to look out into the street while remaining hidden from view.

MODEER the governor of a province.

MUFTI a chief doctor of religious law, a lawyer.

NAOS the inner sanctuary of a temple, where the images of the gods were kept. The PRONAOS was the antechamber to the naos.

PACHA/PASHA a title, originally Turkish, denoting high rank.

PARA an Egyptian coin, the fortieth part of a piastre.

PROPYLÆUM the entrance to a temple or sacred building.

PROPYLON a gate standing in front of the PYLON, or temple entrance.

REIS the captain of a boat.

SAKIA a water pump consisting of a vertical wheel with earthen pots attached to it.

SANTON a Muslim hermit.

SARCOPHAGUS a stone coffin, often richly embellished, which held the mummy as well as inner coffins of wood.

SCARABÆUS a beetle, eaten by ancient Egyptian women as a fertility rite and worshipped as a god, associated with the rising sun and, therefore, with resurrection. Images of the scarab beetle, usually from carved stone, were found in tombs in great numbers and were also incorporated into jewellery worn by the living.

SMYRNIA a port in western Turkey and hence a SMYRNIOT, a native of that region.

STELA a slab of stone or wood decorated with paintings or reliefs.

TARBOOSH a close-fitting cloth cap with a tassel hanging from its crown. The cap was most commonly red, with a blue silk tassel.

TEMENOS a sacred enclosure, such as a temple precinct, often surrounded by a high wall.

TOB a large, loose silk gown which was worn over house clothes by Egyptian women when they went out.

WALDENSES a Christian sect founded in the twelfth century by Peter Waldo, a merchant from Lyons. Adherents lived in voluntary poverty, refused to take oaths or to fight.

WELEE a Muslim saint, although sometimes used for a simpleton.

YELEK a long, loose vest, similar to a kaftan.

ZAABOOT a long, full gown of brown wool, open from the neck to the waist and with loose sleeves.

BIBLIOGRAPHY

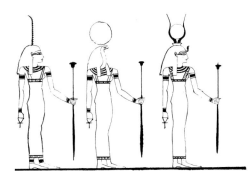

(Works cited in the letters)

BELZONI, Giovanni Battista *Narrative of the Operations and Recent Discoveries within the Pyramids, Temples, Tombs, and Excavations, in Egypt and Nubia; and of a Journey to the Coast of the Red Sea, in search of the Ancient Berenice; and another to the Oasis of Jupiter Ammon.* (Mrs. Belzoni's Trifling Account of the Women of Egypt, Nubia and Syria – Appendix.) London, 1820.
—— *Forty-four Plates illustrative of the Researches and Operations of Belzoni in Egypt and Nubia*, London, 1822.
—— *Six new plates*, London, 1822.

BRUCE, James *Travels to Discover the Source of the Nile in the Years 1768, 1769, 1770, 1771, 1772 and 1773*, London, 1790.

BUNSEN, Christian Carl Josias, Baron von *Egypt's Place in Universal History*, London, 1848-59.

CHAMPOLLION, Jean Francois *Lettre à M. Dacier . . . relative à l'alphabet des hiéroglyphes phonétiques employés par les Égyptiens pour inscrire sur leurs monuments les titres, les noms et les surnoms des souverains grecs et romains*, Paris, 1822.
—— *Lettres écrits d'Égypte et de Nubie, en 1828 et 1829*, Paris, 1833.
—— *Les Monuments de l'Égypte et de la Nubie*, Paris, 1844.

LANE, Edward William *An Account of the Manners and Customs of the Modern Egyptians*, London, 1836.
—— *The Thousand and One Nights (a new translation)*, London, 1839.

LEPSIUS, Carl Richard *Denkmäler aus Aegypten und Aethiopien*, Berlin 1849–58.
—— *Letters from Egypt, Ethiopia, and the Peninsula of Sinai*, London, 1847.

MARTINEAU, Harriet *Eastern Life, past and present*, London, 1848.

PARK, Mungo *Travels in the interior districts of Africa: performed under the direction and patronage of the African Association, in the years 1795, 1796, and 1797*, London, 1799.

ROBERTS, David *The Holy Land, Syria, Egypt and Nubia*, London, 1842–49.

TRISMEGISTUS Hermes the author of a number of Neoplatonic writings which have survived.

WILKINSON, Sir John Gardner *Manners and Customs of the Ancient Egyptians*, London, 1837–41.
—— *Modern Egypt and Thebes*, London, 1843.

INDEX

ACKNOWLEDGEMENTS

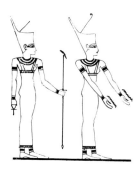

Acknowledgement is due to the following sources for permission to reproduce colour and black and white illustrations: *Ashmolean Museum*: Thomas Seddon (1821–56) 70; *BBC Hulton Picture Library*: 3, 31, 197; *Birmingham Museum and Art Gallery*: Selina Bracebridge 16, 19; *Bridgeman Art Library*: H.D.S. Corrodi (1844–1905) 43, Edward Lear (1812–88) 18, 94, John Frederick Lewis (1805–76) 206, Prosper Marilhat (1811–47) 143, William James Muller (1812–45) 186; *Courtauld Institute of Art/Searight Collection*: John Absolon (1815–95) 22, Carl Haag (1820–1916) 56, Hippolyte d'Orschwiller (1810–68) 51, Emile Prisse d'Avennes (1807–79) 128, Elijah Walton (1832–80) 72; *Owen Edgar Gallery, London*: Johann Jakob Frey (1813–65) 179, J.F. Lewis 10; *Mary Evans Picture Library*: 21, 29, 172; *The Fine Art Society*: Frederick Goodall (1822–1904) 107, J.F. Lewis 198, Thomas Seddon 171; *Fotomas*: David Roberts (1796–1864) 102, 118, 130; *Mathaf Gallery, London*: Leon Belly (1827–77) 59, Benjamin Constant (1845–1902) 122, Narcisse Berchere (1819–91) 30, Edward William Cooke (1811–80) cover, Jean Discart 110, Charles Theodore Frere (1814–88) 38, 46, 127, 166, 203, Eugene Fromentin (1820–76) 138, Alexius Geyer (1816–83) 35, Frederick Goodall 27, Augustus Osborne Lamplough (1877–1930) 135, 163, David Roberts 115, Rudolph Swoboda (1859–1914) 191, John Varley Jnr. (fl. 1870–99) 174, Carl Werner (1808–94) 15; *Private Collections*: David Roberts 2, 83; *Schuster Gallery, London*: John Harrison Allan (fl.1840s) 96, 126, George Belton Moore (1805–75) 134, Henry Pilleau (1813–99) 42, 139, E. Prisse 68, 88, 92, 93, 112, 116, 155, 164, 167, 177, 204, 207; *Spink & Son Ltd., London*: William James Muller 158; *Wallace Collection*: Prosper Marilhat 62; *Weinreb Architectural Gallery, London*: David Roberts (lithographed by Louis Haghe) 25, 32, 33, 36, 37, 41, 53, 61, 66, 77, 78, 79, 82, 84, 87, 89, 90, 97, 98, 100, 103, 105, 108, 109, 113, 117, 119, 121, 124, 129, 132, 141, 144, 146, 148, 149, 153, 159, 160, 180, 182, 184, 192, 194, 195, 196, 201.

The illustrations of the gods of ancient Egypt which appear at the head of each letter have been taken from the supplement to Sir John Gardner Wilkinson's *Manners and Customs of the Ancient Egyptians*, London, 1841.

The map of Egypt and the plans of Cairo and Thebes have been drawn by Caroline Simpson, after Wilkinson and Murray.